Old Wine in
New Wineskins

Stuart Briscoe, Senior Pastor, Elmbrook Church: "Many preachers who were taught to 'preach the word' are in a bind because they are now being told that people don't like preaching and they can't abide doctrine. So what should preachers do? Find an alternative to preaching or avoid doctrine like the plague? Neither! They should read this book which will encourage them to believe that preaching is still God's method and that doctrine is still food for the soul. But it will also give them practical help in understanding the problems, avoiding the pitfalls, and developing preaching that is God honoring, truth telling, and life changing."

Duane Litfin, President, Wheaton College: "'For those wrestling with the task of how to communicate God's truth to a self-centered, sound-bite generation that has lost confidence in the very notion of truth, *Old Wine in New Wineskins* may be just the book to turn to. Erickson and Heflin have done an excellent job of understanding the challenge and offering usable instruction on how to meet it. This book is recommended reading for preachers of the Bible as we launch out into a new millennium."

David L. Larsen, Professor Emeritus of Preaching, Trinity Evangelical Divinity School: "If, as one evangelical savant has well argued, 'Theological ideas rest inconsequentially upon the evangelical world,' Millard Erickson and James Heflin's *Old Wine in New Wineskins* is a bold and direct antidote. This is a substantive and an insightful inquiry which faces into the questions we must confront in doing doctrinal preaching today. The treatment of how doctrine is derived from the various literary genres is particularly strong."

David S. Dockery, President, Union University: "The church has lost its understanding of the importance of doctrine. The need for doctrinal preaching is great and the need for guidance in this area for preachers is greater! Erickson and Heflin have produced a well-informed volume that will positively shape and influence the life of the church in the 21st century. The reader will here find engaging, challenging, and helpful material. I heartily recommend this book."

Paul Scott Wilson, Professor of Homiletics, Emmanuel College, University of Toronto: "This is a thoughtful, well-researched, up-to-date book on doctrinal preaching written from an evangelical perspective. It is the best such book available and will benefit readers from various backgrounds."

J. I. Packer, Sangwoo Youtong Chee Professor of Theology, Regent College: "Any seminary student who wants to become a disciplined and accurate preacher, and any pastor who wants to keep clear of bad pulpit habits, will find help in these pages."

Bill Hogan, Professor of Preaching, Reformed Theological Seminary: "In this day when preaching, and especially doctrinal preaching, is being minimized in some quarters, this book provides a well-reasoned and nicely balanced remedy. This book deserves to be read, and used, by every preacher."

Old Wine in
New Wineskins

Doctrinal Preaching in a Changing World

Millard J. Erickson
and
James L. Heflin

Published by Baker Books
a division of Baker Book House Company
P.O. Box 6287, Grand Rapids, MI 49516-6287

Printed in the United States of America

Library of Congress Cataloging-in-Publication Data

Erickson, Millard J.
    Old wine in new wineskins / Millard J. Erickson and James L. Heflin.
       p.   cm.
    Includes bibliographical references and index.
    ISBN 0-8010-2113-8 (paper)
    1. Doctrinal preaching. I. Heflin, James L., 1943– . II. Title.
BV4235.D63E75   1997
251—dc21   96-53603

For information about academic books, resources for Christian leaders, and all new releases available from Baker Book House, visit our web site:
http://www.bakerbooks.com

To

Dr. Russell H. Dilday

Distinguished Professor of Homiletics and Special Assistant to the President
George W. Truett Theological Seminary, Baylor University

President, Southwestern Baptist Theological Seminary, 1978–94

Without whose vision and commitment to theological scholarship
this book would not have been written

Contents

Preface

There have been few times in the history of the church when solid doctrinal preaching and teaching have been more needed. Yet seldom has such preaching been more difficult and problematic. That pair of convictions, held by the authors, lies behind the writing of this book. There are voices being heard today that decry the lack of biblical and theological teaching from our pulpits. Yet those who preach on a regular basis know how difficult it is to communicate doctrinal truths in the contemporary environment. This book is an attempt to find ways to preach the crucial doctrines in ways that may be more effective than some of the past practices.

This book represents the fruit of discussions over many years of friendship between the authors. Those discussions go back to a time when one of us was a seminary professor of preaching and the other was a seminary dean seeking a preaching professor. When we subsequently became colleagues at a third seminary, they were continued over numerous lunches, leading to planning and team teaching a course on doctrinal preaching. Although now separated by several thousand miles, we have continued to probe the question of how best to accomplish this important task of communicating timeless doctrinal truths in a timely fashion.

This book is a genuinely co-authored work. Professor Erickson had primary responsibility for the writing of chapters 2, 3, 6, 7, 8, and 9. Professor Heflin is the primary author of chapters 4, 5, 10, 11, 12, and 13. Chapters 1 and 14 were joint efforts. Each author read each of several drafts of the other's work and offered comments and suggestions.

We wish to acknowledge several persons who have made this volume possible. Dr. Russell Dilday, former president of Southwestern Baptist Theological Seminary, made the faculty appointments which brought the two authors together. Dr. Bruce Corley, former dean of the School of Theology at Southwestern, encouraged us to offer an experimental team taught course in doctrinal preaching under somewhat unusual circumstances. The students in that course during the fall semesters of 1993 and 1994 provided helpful feedback on the ideas presented here and helped translate them into practice. Mr. Endel Lee, Ph.D. student and teaching assistant in preaching at Southwestern, assisted with checking bibliographical references during the 1995–96 year when Professor Heflin was on sabbatical leave in Berlin, Germany. Mrs. Sarah Boyles, Mrs. Joy Valdez, and Mrs. Connie Cox provided secretarial assistance. Dr. Jim B. Gilbert, Director of Computer Services at Southwestern, provided computer equipment and arranged on-line services during that year. This proved invaluable, since, except for one visit in Berlin in March, 1996, and exchange of a couple of computer disks, all correspondence and file transfer between the two authors from July, 1995, to July, 1996, was done by electronic mail on the Internet. Dr. Dennis Phelps, Associate Professor of Preaching at Bethel Theological Seminary, made available to us some needed technological assistance and equipment at a crucial juncture in the assembly of the manuscript. Mr. Jim Weaver, Academic Books Editor at Baker Book House, encouraged the development and publication of the book. Maria denBoer's editorial skill has done much to improve the manuscript.

This volume is sent forth with the hope and the prayer that it will prove helpful to all who seek to communicate the eternal truths of the Gospel.

Millard J. Erickson
James L. Heflin

Part 1

Understanding the Issues

1

We've Heard It All Before

Scene: A seminary classroom. It is the first class session of the semester. The two professors who are team teaching a course in doctrinal preaching have presented the course syllabus and have alternated turns explaining the objectives, requirements, schedule, and grading criteria.[1]

Professor Heflin: So that is what the course will be. We think this can be a very exciting and profitable course if we all resolve to do our part. Do you have anything further to add, Dr. Erickson?

Professor Erickson: Well, Dr. Helfin, I have been sitting here doing some thinking. I think in fairness to the students, I ought to express those thoughts at this time.

Heflin: Yes, please do so.

Erickson: Well, I have been having grave doubts about the possibility of teaching a course like this. I confess that this has been a growing matter of concern with me, but it has really come to a climax as I have envisioned what we expect these students to do during the semester.

Heflin: I see. Would you like to explain?

Erickson: Thank you. My difficulty really results from the problematic status of preaching today. I wonder if perhaps preaching is now obsolete.

---

1. This chapter is a transcript of a tongue-in-cheek portion of a class session the authors conducted on August 30, 1994. The chapters that follow constitute their attempt to answer the questions raised in this brief skit.

Heflin: Go on.

Erickson: Well, I hate to say this, but the way people listen and learn
                these days seems almost antithetical to the way preaching
                has usually been done.

Heflin: In what way?

Erickson: Well, for one thing, preaching is not sufficiently visual.
                People today are more oriented to what comes in through
                the eye than through the ear. Television has supplanted
                radio. Videorecordings are the thing now, not audio.
                Preaching assumes that we learn by listening, but that
                isn't really true since we have developed a generation
                raised on television.

Heflin: Well, your objection seems to be a bit overstated. After all,
                the audience can see, as well as hear, the preacher.

Erickson: That is true, but what we are discussing here seems to be
                a talking head type of thing. When we watch the evening
                news, the anchors don't just tell us about what has hap-
                pened; they show us pictures. That simply is not possible
                for the preacher. How do you show a video of God, for
                example?

Heflin: You're right.

Erickson: There's more to the problem, however. The attention span
                of persons today is much shorter than it used to be. No
                longer can we engage in a thirty-minute discourse, in
                which a lengthy and complex argument is presented. Peo-
                ple just can't follow that anymore. That's why political
                speeches rely on "sound-bites"—pithy statements that last
                only a few seconds. We have been expecting them to swal-
                low a whole hog, but they can only take a few small bits.

Heflin: Again, you've hit the nail on the head. But is that all?

Erickson: No, colleague, I'm afraid not. I hate to say this about a dis-
                cipline that you've given your life to studying, practicing,
                and teaching, but preaching calls for passivity in a day
                when people expect to participate. Preaching is too much
                like the old definition of a lecture, where information is
                transferred from the notes of the teacher to the notes of
                the student, without passing through the mind of either
                one. The only difference is that members of our congrega-

tions don't usually take notes, because they know they will never be tested on the material. So they just don't learn. They're bored, and some of them even literally sleep through the sermon.

What we need is some sort of active participation. Studies show that people retain much more of what they learn when they participate in the communication process. That's why we have these interactive learning devices these days. Don't forget that the younger members of our audiences have become quite enamored of video games. What can preaching offer that can match that?

Heflin: Oh, how right you are. But these are just communication problems, aren't they? We should be able to solve them.

Erickson: I am afraid it goes deeper than that. Preaching is perceived as authoritarian, and that's not good. I guess that is part of why the very word, "preaching," has such a negative connotation. To say that something is preachy is to say that it is dogmatic, judgmental, and so on. That goes contrary to the more relativistic and subjective orientation of contemporary society. It once was the case that we could stand in the pulpit and say, "Thus says the Lord," and people would accept it. Now, if they give any reaction at all, it will probably be, "So what?" It used to be that we could say, "Jesus said . . ." Now we have to say, "Jesus said . . . What do you think about that?"

Heflin: Well, you've drawn a rather bleak picture of the situation. Class, do you agree with the assessment Dr. Erickson has given?

Student # 1: I'm afraid he has described the way a lot of my people seem to respond to my sermons.

Student # 2: Yes, and it's not just the people out there in the pews. Look what happens to chapel attendance the days that the seminary drama group makes the presentation. The place is packed, standing room only. The next day, with a regular preaching service, the chapel has fewer people than the coffee shop.

(Other students nod their heads in agreement.)

Heflin: It's interesting, Dr. Erickson, that you have said what you have about preaching, because I must confess I have had similar questions about your discipline of theology. I don't want you to think I am just giving you some of your own medicine, but I am afraid theology, as it has usually been done and taught, is passé.

Erickson: Indeed! Tell me more.

Heflin: Well, doctrine does not really fit the contemporary milieu of our society. It appeals to the mind, to rational thought, but most of our contemporaries are much more feeling-oriented. The Clinical Pastoral Education people have grasped this. They say, "Don't tell us what you think; tell us what you feel." It really does not fit the biblical idea of faith, either. Jesus did not say to Nicodemus, "Repeat after me, 'You must be born again,'" nor did Paul tell the Philippian jailor who asked what he must do to be saved, "Memorize this so that you can pass a test on it, 'Believe on the Lord Jesus Christ and you shall be saved.'"

Erickson: I'm sorry to say you are right.

Heflin: More than that, doctrine is terribly abstract, whereas most people think much more concretely. Presenting doctrine is like trying to sell insurance as opposed to pots and pans. Doctrine, unfortunately, does not deal with things that people can see and handle.

Erickson: That is the very nature of doctrine. You can't take a congregation on a field trip to heaven, at least not a round trip.

Heflin: And then there's that dreaded word, "irrelevant." People are hurting these days. They don't come to church to hear a discussion about forensic justification or the virgin birth. They want a word of encouragement, of hope. They want to leave church feeling good, rather than having their heads filled with information that has no bearing on their marital and family problems, for example.

Erickson: You're correct in everything you've said.

Heflin: But further . . .

Erickson: There's more?

Heflin: I'm afraid so. Doctrine, by its very nature, works against the aim of building churches. Doctrine, especially the hair-splitting variety, splits more than hairs; it also splits churches. In a day in which all Christians need to stick together as much as possible, doctrine divides. Look at the Reformation. Luther and Zwingli met in Marburg to discuss doctrine, with the aim of bringing their two branches of the Reformation together. They had 15 items of doctrine to discuss, and they agreed on 14 1/2 of them; but the question of the nature of the presence of Christ in the elements of the Lord's Supper kept them divided. The church growth specialists tell us these days that you need to avoid discussing these doctrinal differences if you are going to grow a church. Much doctrine was the distinctive of specific denominations, and as is well known nowadays, denominationalism is not popular. People are more interested in the availability of parking and the quality of the church nursery than they are in whether the church is Calvinistic or Arminian. They are turned off by doctrinal discussions. Doctrine does not contribute to church growth, but to church shrinkage.

Erickson: What would you have me do—go around and hold "Church Ensmallment" seminars?

Heflin: And you'll never make a living that way.

Erickson: Speaking of making a living, what are you going to do now? In light of what we have concluded about preaching, there certainly won't be a teaching position available to you any longer. You're still a comparatively young man. What do you plan to do after you leave the seminary?

Heflin: You really don't mince any words, do you?

Erickson: No, but you are my friend, and I don't think you would want me to beat around the bush.

Heflin: I appreciate that. If your friends won't tell you, who will? And what about you? Have you done any thinking about vocation?

Erickson: What do you mean?

Heflin: I thought it was obvious. Theology will undoubtedly be dropped from the curriculum, along with preaching. I hate to tell you this, but unemployment will probably be as large a problem for seminary theology professors as for homileticians.

Erickson: That's right. Well, I've had quite an interest in the stock market of late. I think it might be fun to be a broker.

Heflin: I hear you, but personally, I think I would prefer to try my hand at real estate. It's that matter of tangibility we were talking about, you know.

Erickson: Great! I think this might really be enjoyable, much better than teaching seminary. (Pause) But what about our students here? I think we sort of forgot about them.

Heflin: True. (Turning to class). My colleague and I want to thank you for your interest, shown in registering for this course. As you can see, however, the course as we originally conceived it is neither feasible nor justifiable. It would not be ethical of us to let you continue in a course such as this. If you hurry, you can get to the registrar's office before it closes and register for another class without any sort of penalty. We wish you well.

Students in unison: No, No!

Student #1:   What you have said just isn't so. The Lord has called us to proclaim the Good News. That is the church's only reason for existing.

Student #2:   That involves preaching. Paul said, "Woe is me, if I preach not the gospel."

Student #3:   And the message in the Bible is a very doctrinal one. It involves God's love and judgment, the fact of human sin, the deity, sacrificial death, and resurrection of the Lord, the reality of new birth. If we don't have that, we don't have anything.

Student #4:   Yes, Paul said of the resurrection, "If only in this life we have hope, we are of all persons most to be pitied."

Student #5:   If the church doesn't preach the Word, it really isn't the church anymore.

Student #6:   With all due respect, Dr. Heflin and Dr. Erickson, what you are proposing seems to be accommodation to the world. We have to challenge it.

Student #7:   Not preaching the great truths of the message is just not an option. It may be difficult to do today, but there has to be a way. We acknowledge the problems you have been talking about, but we want you to help us find a way to do doctrinal preaching in our time.

Students in unison: Amen!

The two professors look at each other and say simultaneously, "What do you think?"

And you, reader, what do you think?

2

The Value and Benefit of Doctrine

Why, with all the things busy pastors must be concerned with, should they bother about the detailed and tedious questions of doctrine? And with the many types of preaching they can engage in, and the many topics that could be potential subjects of that preaching, why bother to do doctrinal preaching? These are the questions being raised in our time, not always outwardly and overtly, but nonetheless in the minds (sometimes, in the *back* of the minds) of contemporary pastors. It is the topic that must be engaged first, for if doctrine is not really important to Christianity and to the life of the church, then it really does not matter how we communicate it. In other words, the question of doctrine precedes the question of preaching. There was a time when such a question did not really need to be discussed. It was taken for granted that doctrine was vital. Now, however, it cannot be taken for granted.

The value of doctrine is being called into question even by some whom one would expect to see its benefit. I think of two experiences I had recently. One was a rare occasion when I sat in an adult Sunday school class. It was the last day of the quarter, and the president of the class was announcing the topic that would be studied during the coming quarter, a survey of doctrine. Then the teacher of that quarter's study on interpreting the Bible got up to begin her final lesson. Before she did so, however, she commented on the immediately preceding announcement by saying, "Doctrine is boring." What she failed to realize and acknowledge, however, was that she had been assertively promoting some of her own doctrinal beliefs during the course of the lessons she had taught.

The second was a conversation I had with the dean of an evangelical seminary. He was explaining the new curricular developments at his school, in which the academic subjects comprised one-third of the program, which clearly favored the practical and personal/professional development areas of the curriculum. His comment was, "We have found that very few pastors fail not because they do not know their theology, but because of lack of personal and professional skills." He was right, of course, in terms of the explicit reasons that pastors are terminated by their churches. He was less correct about the reason pastors "burn out" or become obsolete by age forty-five or fifty. And in the course of the conversation he revealed a rather vague uneasiness about developments in the life of the church in general, failing to realize that these stem from very ideological issues, such as the nature of the church, the nature of Christian discipleship, the relativity or absoluteness of Christian truth, and the like.

Are doctrine and the teaching of it really important to the church in the late twentieth and early twenty-first centuries? Our answer to that is a resounding yes! Doctrine has always been important to the life of the church, and especially so in our time.

Doctrine as Definitional or Constitutive of Christian Religion

One major set of reasons why we understand doctrine to be important is because of the evidences that it is an inseparable component of the Christian religion.

Prominence in the Bible

Doctrine is important first of all because of its prominence in the Bible. The very first words of the Old Testament are, "In the beginning, God created the heavens and the earth" (Gen. 1:1). Note that two major doctrines are the very introduction to what is to follow: the doctrine of the existence of God and the doctrine of creation. What could be more fundamental to our thinking than the question of ultimate reality and the question of origins? Within the first three chapters of that first book other crucial doctrines are introduced: the doctrine of humanity, created in the image of God (1:26); the doctrine of sin and of its consequences (chap. 3); even an illusion to the doctrines of incarnation, atonement, and salvation (3:15). Some even believe that there are at least hints of the doctrine of the Trinity (or part of it) in the statement in Genesis 1:26: "And God said [singular], 'Let us make [plural] man in the image of us [plural].'" It is apparent that the story that the Bible intends to tell us is very much wrapped up with the crucial topics of belief that we term doctrine.

This sort of emphasis continues throughout the Bible. The prophets repeatedly spoke of God's nature and will. They identified their message as something God had revealed to them. They spoke of his past acts of providence and predicted his future judgment as well as his future provision of salvation. The psalmists especially dwelt on the attributes of the mighty God. When John the Baptist came declaring his message, it was of the necessity of repentance and of the redeeming work that the "Lamb of God" would perform. Jesus spoke much of the Father and the way in which he loved, watched over, protected, and provided for his earthly human children. He spoke of the necessity of regeneration. He pointed forward to the last things: his second coming, the resurrection, the judgment, the life to come. The Gospel writers were clear about the importance of correct belief: John, for example, tied eternal life and adoption as children of the Heavenly Father to "belief in the name" of Jesus (John 1:12). Paul was clear regarding what must be done to be saved: "Believe on the Lord Jesus Christ, and you shall be saved" (Acts 16:31). And lest there be any question about the doctrinal dimension of this belief, we may bear in mind his words in Galatians: "If any one is preaching a different kind of gospel, let him be eternally condemned" (Gal. 1:8–9).

Prominence in Church History

This same importance has been attached to doctrine by the church throughout its history. This can be seen by examining the issues that the church distinguished as important by arguing over them. It was over questions of fundamental belief that the great councils of the church were convened.

Several of those early councils dealt with the question of who Jesus really was, whether he was God, in the same sense and to the same degree as was the Father, or whether he was a created being. They believed that the answer to the question was crucially important, for it affected whether Jesus could effectively do that which was necessary to save human beings from their predicament. One group, known as the semi-Arians, proposed that Jesus was not of the same substance (*homoousious*) with the Father, but rather that he was of a similar substance (*homoiousious*). This particular issue has been referred to by some as a battle over a diphthong.[1] Yet it was not, as the expression would seem to indicate, a trivial matter. It was a literally a matter of life and death, *spiritual* life and death.

Another dispute that arose during the early centuries of church history was the Augustinian-Pelagian dispute over the condition of the human being apart from Christ, and the necessity of any sort of supernatural transformation. Pelagius maintained that people were basi-

---

1. Edward Gibbon, *The History of the Decline and Fall of the Roman Empire* (New York: Peter Fenelon Collier), vol. 2, p. 322.

cally good, and that all they needed was some proper instruction, a correct motivation, and a good example. The role of Jesus in such a scheme was not to pay a penalty for sin, but to give an example of the way one is to live. This, of course, meant a very different approach to the gospel.

A third major dispute in the church took place between Martin Luther and the Roman Catholic Church. The Catholic understanding of salvation was that it was granted only on the basis of true repentance. That required genuine sorrow for one's sin, or contrition. This was more than mere attrition, which meant simply that the sinner regretted having committed the sin, perhaps because of its unfortunate results. Contrition meant sorrow for one's sin because it was an offense against God. In practice, of course, true repentance, accompanied by contrition, was difficult to achieve. Thus, there arose the system of doing penance, which was some act assigned by the priest at the point of absolution of sins, to be done by the sinner as a demonstration of sincerity. Then from this there developed the system known as indulgences, by which penance could be done in advance of the sin—for example, by paying a fine or penalty. This virtually became a license to sin. Forgiveness could be earned by doing a certain work, which led to the conception that salvation was by works.

In each of these cases, the church was very concerned about its conclusion, because it was sensed that very crucial questions about its nature, message, and mission were at stake. If it came out on the wrong side of one of these issues, its very essence and existence might be imperiled. And the dispute in each case involved a doctrinal matter, a question of what was to be believed. At least historically, the church has judged doctrine to be very important.

Essential to the Relationship with God

Further, doctrine is important because it is essential to the relationship with God. The writer of the Letter to the Hebrews says, "Without faith it is impossible to please him. For everyone who comes to him must believe that he is, and that he is the rewarder of those who diligently seek him" (Heb. 11:6). Jesus asked his disciples who people believed him to be, and then asked them who they thought he was. Peter replied, "You are the Christ, the son of the living God," an answer that obviously pleased Jesus (Matt. 16:16–17). This, he said, had not been revealed to Peter by flesh and blood, but by the Father. It was only when he understood that the disciples really believed in him as he really was, not as they imagined him to be, that Jesus entrusted them with the authority to carry on the ministry of his kingdom.

But is this so? It appears that the very nature of the Christian experience depends on belief, on holding correct doctrine. The great discovery, or more correctly, rediscovery, of the Reformation was Martin Luther's "the just shall live by faith." Justification by faith is the most prominent expression of the truth that the Christian is someone who has faith in Jesus Christ. But we must ask further what this faith involves.

Faith, as represented by the Greek verb πιστεύω, and the noun πίστις, is not merely a matter of correct opinion about a subject; it is trust or commitment to a person. In the middle third of the twentieth century it became quite popular to hold that faith was therefore this personal trust, or a relational matter, rather than an intellectual matter of belief. This conception built on the assertion that biblical faith is not merely correct understanding and belief. James, after all, indicated that the demons believe—and tremble—but they are not thereby saved (James 2:19). From this, however, there was a subtle transition to saying that what you believed about Jesus was not important, but simply the commitment to him.

This position, identified in general with neo-orthodoxy, was incomplete and therefore inaccurate. It neglected the fact that in ordinary human life and relationships, our trust in another person is not separate from the beliefs we hold about that person's identity and qualities. If I am to meet my wife outside a certain store, I do not simply take the first woman who comes out the door at the appointed time and say, "Let's go home, dear." I will make some preliminary judgments to determine that this is indeed she. We do not commit ourselves to another person as we would to our spouse without ascertaining, in a very simple and nonanalytical fashion, that this is the right person. We do not trust ourselves or our possessions to another person in a business dealing without some sort of judgment about the honesty and reliability of that person. This is particularly important in matters of religion, where we do not have empirical perception of the object of our trust. To be related to the God of Abraham, Isaac, and Jacob, or to Jesus of Nazareth, requires some belief about the identity of that person in whom we place our faith.[2]

The importance of doctrine is also seen in the specific content of the gospel. It is notable that when the early church presented its message to those who were not part of their group, the appeal was not primarily social or organizational. They did, of course, welcome nonmembers, and at least in the case of the Jews and Gentiles, the breakdown of the

---

2. Edward John Carnell, *The Case for Orthodox Theology* (Philadelphia: Westminster, 1959), pp. 29–30.

wall of opposition was one manifestation of the Spirit's work. The appeal was not to the hearer to become related to them, but to their god. It was to believe certain great truths, not simply to live and behave in a different way or even to feel something especially strongly. There were several great facts on which the salvation of the hearer would depend. Yet salvation did not simply result from what was true. Rather, it was essential to understand and believe those truths.

What, then, were these great truths of the gospel that formed the central content of the preaching of the apostles? The first is the existence of a God who has created everything simply by his own free will, without using any preexisting materials. He has brought human beings to life, each with a unique personality and set of characteristics. He has a plan and is working it out throughout history and into eternity. He has a certain character, and must act consistently with that character.

A second basic background truth is that humans are divinely created beings. They, among all the creatures, are described as being made in "the image and likeness of God" (Gen. 1:26–27). This expression is a way of conveying the unusual truth that humans alone were intended to be able to relate consciously to God. They are only completely human and most fulfilled when this is true.

The Bible also teaches, however, that something happened to spoil this intended fellowship between humans and God, and thus to embody the image of God in the human. In the biblical account of the first sin, this involved direct disobedience against God; sin is failure to obey and love God fully. This fact is not simply an isolated truth about the first man and woman. In the New Testament, Paul makes very clear that this is true of all humans: "For all have sinned and come short of the glory of God" (Rom. 3:23). Sin, which constitutes being or doing something other than or less than what God intends for us, separates us from God and his love. It means that we come under the judgment of God, that is, become guilty or liable to punishment. Because God is the all-powerful ruler of the universe, each of us owes him complete obedience to his commands. This means, however, that there really is no way to win God's favor, since even if we perfectly fulfilled his law, that would only be what is expected of us. It would not qualify us for any special standing. There is only one way to satisfy God's demand, and that is to suffer the penalty for our sin. It is as if one had broken a law and must either pay a fine or experience the penalty. If, however, one has nothing to offer God in payment of the fine, then there is no alternative but to experience the penalty or the punishment.

A further basic truth is the reality of the incarnation in Jesus Christ. The Bible teaches that God is one, but also that there are three who are God. The second of these three persons, referred to in Scripture as God the Son, without ceasing to be God, left heaven and came to earth, being born as a human. He added humanity to his deity. As such he led a life of perfect obedience to the will of the Father. He was crucified and buried. On the third day, he was raised from the dead, overcoming death. Because he had perfectly fulfilled the divine requirements for a human being, he did not need to die as a payment for his own sin, for he had no such sin of his own. Thus, his death could have a value and a benefit above and beyond the law's requirements. Because he was both God and man, his death had infinite value. Thus, the Father accepted his death in place of humans' death as a substitute for the penalty for our sins.

The primary effect of Christ's death is on God the Father. He could not simply ignore sin, which as the very antithesis of his holy nature was repulsive and abhorrent to him. He could only forgive it if it were atoned for, that is, if someone bore its consequences. If this was not done by individual humans, it must be done by Christ on their behalf. Now, however, everything had been made right, and humans could be restored to God's favor.

The benefit of Christ's death as depicted in Scripture, however, is not automatic. It is only as a person believes in Christ that it becomes effectual in his or her life. This belief involves two major components. There has to be assent to the truth of certain basic realities, those we have just been describing. Beyond that, however, there has to be trust or commitment of oneself to the person of Christ. This positive movement of faith toward Christ is genuine, however, only when accompanied by the negative movement known as repentance, a godly sorrow for one's sin and a desire to abandon it completely. This combination of factors, as the initiation of the Christian life, is known as conversion.

Conversion leads to a number of changes in a person. One of these is in the relationship to God. God now no longer sees the person as guilty of his or her own sins. Rather, God sees the spiritual condition of the person in combination with Christ. Thus, the liabilities (sin) of the person and the assets (righteousness) of Christ are seen together. These in combination are such that God considers or calculates the person as holy and righteous in his sight. Beyond that, however, the person is actually changed. This change, referred to as regeneration or new birth, involves the implantation of a new principle of life, a new source of vitality. It means a new sensitivity to spiritual things, and a positive inclination toward the right things along with an ability to do them. There also is growth in this actual holiness, so that the person becomes increasingly what God considers him or her to be. This growth is termed sanctification. There is an expectation that the Christian will live in obedience to Christ, and will seek to emulate his example. The eternal consequences of this conversion are that at death the person goes into the presence of the Lord, there to spend eternity. The person who does not believe, on the other hand, spends eternity apart from God in endless suffering. The Bible presents these truths not as interesting ideas, but as ultimate or eternal truths, which must be believed and acted on.

Relationship of Christian Living to Belief

Doctrine is also important because so much of our Christian living is based on, or at least related to, our belief. Frequently, the appeals to Christian behavior are motivated by doctrine. So, for example, Paul, in urging his readers to be more concerned about others than about their own welfare, expounds the doctrine of Christ's incarnation (Phil. 2:1–11). He urges them to have the same mind in them that was in Christ. Similarly, having declared the doctrine of salvation by grace through faith (Eph. 2:8–9), he goes on to make this the appeal to a certain kind of works: "For we are his workmanship, created in Christ Jesus for good works, which God prepared beforehand, that we should walk in them" (v. 10). Elsewhere, he three times calls on his readers to "walk worthy" of their calling, or of the Lord (Eph. 4:1; Col. 1:10; 1 Thess. 2:12). Twice he exhorts the Corinthians to a certain kind of life because they have been "bought with a price" (1 Cor. 6:20; 7:23). Paul is not the only one to make such appeals. Peter urges his readers to be holy, as God is holy (1 Peter 1:14–16). He goes on to point out that they were ransomed from their futile ways by the precious blood of Christ (vv. 17–19). Peter's quotation is from Leviticus 11:44–45. Even the call to obedience to the Old Testament law was based on the motivation of belief in God's holiness. This same theme could be repeated over and over.

Effect of Doctrine on Emotions

Doctrine is also important because even Christian feelings or emotions are a result of what we believe. In our time, a great deal of emphasis is placed on feelings, and efforts are made to stir those in a rather direct fashion. In the Bible, however, the believer's feelings are expected to result from what he or she believes. So, for example, the psalmists call on their people to rejoice, in light of what God is and does. Two examples are: "I will rejoice and be glad for thy steadfast love, because thou hast seen my affliction, thou hast taken heed of my adversities" (Ps. 31:7); and "But may all who seek thee rejoice and be glad in thee; may those who love thy salvation say continually, 'Great is the LORD!'" (Ps. 40:16). A similar thought is expressed in Isaiah 61:10: "I will greatly rejoice in the LORD, my soul shall exult in my God; for he has clothed me with the garments of salvation, he has covered me with the robe of righteousness, as a bridegroom decks himself with a garland, and as a bride adorns herself with her jewels." A somewhat different emphasis is Paul's statement to the sorrowing Thessalonians about Jesus' second coming (1 Thess. 4:13–18), which ends with an exhortation: "Therefore comfort one another with these words" (v. 18). Innumerable additional examples could be given to demonstrate that the biblical conception is that our Christian sentiments follow from our doctrinal understanding, rather than the reverse.

There has been a tendency in recent years to separate emotions from the intellect. The idea that our emotions follow from our thinking is believed to be a form of intellectualism, or more frequently, the rather loosely used expression, "rationalism." In some rather extreme forms, one's emotional state is thought to be quite independent of the facts. Reflection on the experiences of life show that this is not the case, however. One may be in emotional denial of the death of a loved one, for example, but sooner or later, reality sets in, and the emotions must follow the belief. The old story of the person who falls from an upper floor of a tall building and calls out as he passes each floor on the way down, "I'm still doing fine!" nonetheless reminds us that sooner or later reality will make an impact on experience.

Priority of Being over Doing

Doctrine is important because being ultimately precedes doing. There is a popular tendency to think of one's identity in terms of what one does. This may especially be true in terms of occupation. Beyond that, however, personal traits and qualities are equated with certain actions. For example, persons are thought of as persons of integrity because they habitually tell the truth. In actuality, however, persons who tell the truth do so because they are persons of integrity. What they are is the cause of what they do. Lest this be thought of as simply a debatable point, think of some of Jesus' statements. He said that good trees bear good fruit and evil trees bear evil fruit and then said, "The good man out of the good treasure of his heart produces good, and the evil man out of his evil treasure produces evil; for out of the abundance of the heart his mouth speaks" (Luke 6:45). He condemned hypocrisy because it involved superimposing a false external appearance on an evil interior (e.g., Matt. 23:27). He told the Pharisees to first cleanse the interior of the cup and the plate, and the interior would also be clean (v. 26). His emphasis that not merely the external act but also the inward desire was sin fit the same conception (Matt. 5:21–28).

But what is the inward, the being? It includes many things—attitudes, values, beliefs. Certainly the things that make us what we are include the most basic beliefs, the things that we consider real and important. Being does precede doing. As the comic strip character Ziggy put it, "That's why we are called human beings, rather than human doings."

Ideological Factors of Society and the Church

A further group of considerations bearing on the importance of doctrine today can be seen in the challenges and opportunities presented by the current state of ideology, within both the church and the broader culture.

Doctrinal Import of Issues Being Debated within Society

Another reason for the importance of doctrine is that many of the issues being debated in society today are fundamentally doctrinal in nature. Not that the public is debating issues of Christian doctrine, but the arguments are about the kinds of issues that Christian doctrine also concerns itself with, and are in some cases the same issues. Many political debates today hinge on issues such as what humanity really is, what the good for the human being is, what brings fulfillment, what is wrong with humans, and what the solution to the problem is. Questions involving freedom, responsibility, and fairness are at the root of the debates about practical matters, and are fundamentally issues about ideas. Consequently, it is important that we understand what we believe about these matters, so that our political activity is informed by our Christian belief. It is also because of such considerations that Christianity has some real pertinence in the larger discussions.

Doctrine as a Basis for Contemporizing Biblical Truth

Doctrine is of special importance because it is a very significant basis for applying Scripture to the present time. This is particularly true of narrative passages, but also of the more practical passages. In the former case, we have instances of the way in which God acted in the past. The question, then, becomes whether we can expect him to act in a similar way in the present, or to require of us in the present that which he required of others in the past. The situation in which God worked in the past may be different from the present situation, and we cannot expect that he will do precisely the same thing that he did on that earlier occasion. Nonetheless, what he did is really a revelation and a proof of what he is. That has not changed, so that we can expect that he will act in the present in a way consistent with who and what he is. The same is true of his expectations of us. Because the situations have changed, his expectations may not require exactly the same actions. Nonetheless, his qualities that called for those actions, such as his love, justice, and holiness, which he expects us to emulate, have not changed.

As we shall see in a later chapter, we are sometimes urged to move from "what it meant" to "what it means." That, however, requires, as the transitional element "what it always means," or the doctrinal factor. The key to making the biblical message relevant, contemporary, and applicable is knowing and understanding the underlying doctrinal factors.

Wide Variety of Options in Our Contemporary World

A further need for correctly defining and enunciating doctrine is the wide variety of views to which Christians are now being exposed. In some cases, these do not sound very different from Christianity to those who are not thoroughly grounded in the Christian faith. There are cults, some of which present teachings that sound good, until investigated in greater depth. In fact, they sound like improvements on orthodox Christian doctrine, or at least, they are designed to sound that way. In many cases, they especially target as prospects for their proselytization evangelical Christians, especially those who have a poor understanding of their beliefs.

I think of two cases from my first pastorate where constituents of my congregation were exposed to and attracted to the teachings of cults. One of the men began subscribing to a correspondence course. He said, "It sounded quite good until the lessons came to the doctrine of the Trinity. Then I realized I was dealing with something quite different from biblical Christianity." The other case did not turn out quite so happily. This was a man whom, together with his wife, I had led to faith in Jesus Christ. They began attending our services quite regularly, then began to miss one Sunday out of two and then two out of three. I visited their home, and the man explained that he had always had difficulty understanding the Trinity, a difficulty that I also conceded. He told me that he had recently begun attending a storefront church to which a fellow worker had invited him. He brought out a pamphlet that he said had been of great help to him, because it explained the Trinity perfectly. As I read through the pamphlet, it quickly became apparent that it was an example of modalism, a doctrine condemned by the church almost sixteen centuries earlier, a fact that I did not have the heart to tell him. After attempting unsuccessfully to persuade the man of the difficulties with the view, I left sadly. He and his wife never returned to a worship service at my church.

Tendency toward Redefinition of Terms

One phenomenon that characterized the modernist–fundamentalist debate of the early twentieth century was that the modernists or liberals continued to use traditional theological terms that had been employed in earlier theological discussions, but gave them slightly different meanings. Some of these persons, such as Harry Emerson Fosdick, were quite clear about what they were doing. In some cases, however, this was not done. The change in meaning had to be discovered inductively. This had the effect of playing on the tendency described earlier, of reacting to the connotation of the term without really asking about or grasping its denotation. This led the humanist John Herman Randall to comment as follows:

> In these contentions the Fundamentalists are correct: it is precisely the abandonment of such doctrines which the Modernists desire to effect in the Protestant churches; and to an impartial observer there does seem in the liberal positions, much confusion and lack of precise thinking, as well as the appearance at least of a lack of frankness and a fondness for esoteric 'reinterpretation' that may approach in its effects actual hypocrisy. The cleavage, however seems to be more basic: the Fundamentalists do not, and the Modernists do, accept present-day philosophies, and without agreement upon these basic assumptions of thinking, it seems difficult to see how the two parties can even hope to understand each other.[3]

Such redefinition is not necessarily intentional. It does, however, occur, if for no other reason than that the meanings of words change with the passage of time. We must therefore continue to teach explicitly the meaning of doctrines.

Superficial Grasp of the Meaning of Doctrines

Many Christians today have either mistaken understandings or insufficiently profound grasps of the doctrines to which they subscribe. One explanation for this is the tendency to respond to theological terms traditionally or emotionally. Words sometimes become signals, evoking certain emotional responses rather than understanding of their meaning. This may have adverse effects, whether it involves a positive response to something that actually should be thought of as negative, or a negative response to something that should be regarded as positive. For example, my doctoral mentor told of a conversation that he had in

---

3. John Herman Randall Jr., *The Making of the Modern Mind: A Survey of the Intellectual Background of the Present Age* (Boston: Houghton Mifflin, 1940), p. 542.

the 1950s with a fellow doctoral student at Union Seminary in New York. The student, who was quite liberal in his theology, was preaching Harry Emerson Fosdick's sermons in a very conservative church in up-state New York. When asked how he could do this successfully, he re-plied, "Oh, I simply throw in an expression like 'washed in the blood of the Lamb,' every ten minutes or so and they love it." I once served as in-terim pastor of a rather large and growing church where the expression, "Let Christ work in and through you," was the key formula for the Christian life. This was how the church members had been taught by the previous pastor to use this formula, and anything that smacked of human effort on their part was suspect. I inquired of one of the leaders of the church whether they did not believe in the indwelling of the Holy Spirit, and whether this was not the same thing as what they were talk-ing about. "No," he said. "It's close, but it isn't right." Complementary truths were excluded if they did not fit the formula.

These responses to verbal signals were positive; there are also nega-tive reactions. In my first year of teaching undergraduates, I found that when we came to one specific doctrine, there were widespread and vi-olent emotional reactions. Hands went up all over the classroom and strong objections were registered. It was apparent I had struck a theo-logical landmine. The next time I taught the course, I took a somewhat different approach. I deliberately avoided the use of the traditional term for that doctrine, both in the course syllabus and in my teaching. While I made the same affirmations I had a year earlier, I used a variety of synonyms. The students, who I am sure were not much different from my previous year's students, really liked and agreed with what they were hearing. Then, when I finished the unit, the old sinful nature overcame me for a moment, and I said, "Now that we have finished the topic of the [the traditional term], let us move on to the next topic." All over the room, heads snapped up with surprised, even startled, and in some cases, angry expressions. They had been tricked! They had lis-tened to, understood, and agreed with something to which they should have been violently opposed.

Sometimes what seems to be agreement is really not. I recall a man with whom I was sharing the gospel. I talked at some length about the nature of salvation by grace, and how that was the only way of salvation available to persons, and my conversation partner seemed to be in total agreement. Then, almost by way of summing up the discussion, he said, "That's what I always say: we just have to do the best we can, and God will take care of us."

A certain term may carry connotations or associations for some peo-ple that it should not. That may mean that we need to use different terms, or at least help people understand more correctly the definitions of terms they use. I once spoke to a group of denominational leaders. One pastor who gave an official response to the presentation said, "If I had met a person who holds this view this way, I would have been a believer in that doctrine long ago." We need to help people, whether leaders or laypersons, get past the emotional associations or blockages that may be preventing them from hearing correctly what these doctrines mean.

Tendencies to Pluralism and Relativism

There is evidence that the widespread pluralism and relativism that characterize the beliefs of society in general are also affecting Christians. The Barna organization has for several years been surveying representative samples of persons in the United States. This has revealed some interesting points of confusion. Their polling data published in 1992 indicated a rather high degree of correct understanding of the basis of salvation. When asked to describe their belief about life after death, 62 percent of the general sample responded, "When you die, you will go to heaven because you have confessed your sins and have accepted Jesus Christ as your Savior." Only 6 percent said, "When you die you will go to heaven because you have tried to obey the Ten Commandments"; 9 percent said, "because you are basically a good person"; and 6 percent said, "because God loves all people and will not let them perish."[4] When asked to respond to the statement, "All good people, whether they consider Jesus Christ to be their Savior or not, will live in heaven after they die on earth," somewhat different results occurred. Of those who said they had made a personal commitment to Jesus Christ (which, in turn, constituted 65 percent of the total adult sample), 25 percent agreed strongly and 15 percent agreed moderately; 16 percent disagreed moderately and 33 percent disagreed strongly; 11 percent did not know. Thus, of the persons who would hazard an opinion, those who disagreed outnumbered those who agreed by less than a 5 to 4 ratio! Even 29 percent of the born again agreed, either strongly or somewhat. For various reasons, there was a conflict between their statement of their understanding of the basis of their own salvation, and their understanding of the basis of salvation for others.

Of further interest is the view of truth that this polling revealed. One statement posed was: "There is no such thing as absolute truth; different people can define truth in conflicting ways and still be correct." Of the total sample, which was carefully balanced to match the actual de-

4. George Barna, *The Barna Report 1992–93: America Renews Its Search for God* (Ventura, Calif.:Regal, 1992), pp. 76–78, 294–95.

mographics of the national population, 28 percent agreed strongly; 39 percent agreed somewhat; 13 percent disagreed somewhat; and 16 percent disagreed strongly. Among church attenders, the figures were 23, 36, 14, and 21 percent, respectively. Even evangelicals showed 23, 30, 17, and 25 percent, and the born again answered with 23, 29, 15, and 27 percent.[5] Thus, even among those usually considered most conservative and most committed, more than half agreed with the idea of the relativity of truth. The wording of the question may be too ambiguous to ferret out the difference between belief in relativity of truth and limitation and consequent relativity of understanding. Even so, this indicates a considerably greater degree of relativity in the thinking of Christian people than one might have anticipated. This problem of confusion and even of absence of belief in things objective is more serious and becoming more so with the coming generation.[6]

This might seem to create a particular problem for Christianity. When taken at face value, it appears to be very universal and absolute in its teachings. It seems to claim that it is the only true religion. Thus, for example, the people of Israel did not ordinarily reject Jehovah, or even relegate him to less than first place in their loyalties. The problem was that they did not worship him exclusively. Hence we get God's statement, "You shall have no other gods before [or besides] me" (Exod. 20:2). Similarly, the apostles proclaimed, "Neither is there salvation in any other; for there is no other name under heaven given among men, whereby we must be saved" (Acts 4:12). It would seem that Christian proclamation that claims the absoluteness of the Christian message has its work cut out for it.

There is an opportunity here, however. One characteristic of the postmodern period in which we now find ourselves is a belief in relativity of truth. Yet in the long run, this stance really cannot be maintained. One may believe in relativity when it comes to one's responsibilities, but few persons do when it comes to their rights. Sooner or later, however, such claims and appeals have to settle on something objective, or they are simple exercises in comparative power. The difficulty is that as long as truth is judged by human opinion, there is dispute. What is needed is something beyond the limited and relative opinions and understandings of humans, something that transcends these. It is here that Christianity has a real opportunity to offer such an objective standard and basis for truth and for right and good. While the absoluteness of Christianity has to be presented carefully and with much preparation in

5. Ibid., pp. 83–85.
6. James Davison Hunter, *Evangelicalism: The Coming Generation* (Chicago: University of Chicago Press, 1987), pp. 183–84.

many cases, persons have a real need for some sort of objective truth, some measure of all things.

Practical Effects of Doctrine

The final group of reasons why doctrine is important involves its practical effects and benefits.

Influence on the Style and Content of Ministry

Doctrine informs and influences not only our own Christian living, but the nature of our ministry, whether we are laypersons or clergy. Technique in practice is not enough. It must also be informed by an understanding of the issues. We may develop great skill in persuading others. This can be either positive, neutral, or negative, however. If we are able to convince people to respond to our invitation to make some sort of religious or even Christian commitment, what we attempt to direct them to do will depend on our understanding of humanity, the human predicament, the nature and basis of salvation, and so on.

In this respect, the Christian might compare the practice of ministry to the practice of medicine. A surgeon must have some basic manual skills (cutting, suturing, etc.). If that is all she has, however, she may simply be a specialized type of carpenter or seamstress. It is important that the surgeon knows what she is cutting, and why.

On one occasion, a seminary faculty curriculum committee was discussing possible modifications in the curriculum for preparing pastors. As is usual in such discussions, there was some disagreement about the relative place of classical or theoretical disciplines (Bible, theology, church history, etc.), and of applied or practical disciplines (preaching, counseling, church management, etc.). One of the committee members from one of the classical disciplines was emphasizing the importance of the pastor knowing the biblical content on which the sermon was based, or the counselor having a good doctrinal understanding of human nature, sin, and grace. He told the committee what a medical student friend of his had told him. In teaching surgery in a hospital, the instructor placed his scalpel on a piece of skin on the patient's abdomen and asked, "If I cut through the first layer, what will I hit then?" and repeated the question after each answer. "Now," said the professor, "I am concerned that our preachers not simply know how to communicate, but also what they should communicate." At this point, another professor from one of the applied fields spoke up: "That's not analogous. The patient could die if the doctor doesn't know anatomy." "You're right," said the first professor, "but it's only physical death, not eternal death."

Effect on Success of Ministry

Doctrine is also important because correct doctrine affects the success of ministry. This may be seen on a large scale. Measuring truth pragmatically is a questionable practice. There are ways in which the gospel could be "improved on," by appealing to natural tendencies of humans rather than calling for transformation. Short-range, these methods may prove very effective, statistically. One church in New York City attracted huge crowds by featuring topless dancers. There was no carryover, however, to attendance at its other services. What had happened was that the church had succeeded, but not at being the church. It had succeeded at being something other than what it was supposed to be. Yet if the church is preaching a gospel that is in accord with what its Lord gave it to proclaim, then there will be some indications of this, and some of them may be measurable statistically and on an ongoing basis.

Throughout the history of the church, there have been numerous departures from the apostolic faith, the faith "once for all delivered to the saints." Some of these have been quite bizarre, and some have persisted for a long time. It is interesting, however, to ask what has become of some of those movements. A striking observation has been made by the great twentieth-century church historian, Kenneth Scott Latourette. Near the end of his massive *History of the Expansion of Christianity*, he looks back over those centuries of the church's history and writes,

> Those forms [of the church] which conformed so much to the environment that they sacrificed this timeless and placeless identity died out with the passing of the age, the society, and the climate of opinion to which they had adjusted themselves. The central core of the uniqueness of Jesus, of fidelity to his birth, life, teachings, death, and resurrection as events in history, and of belief in God's working through him for the revelation of Himself and the redemption of man proved essential to continuing life.[7]

The evidence of this truth is not confined to the early centuries of church history. In the twentieth century, a struggle took place within American Protestantism. One party insisted on adherence to a set of basic doctrines of the Christian faith, which it termed "Fundamentals," insisting that doctrinal beliefs are part of the essence of Christianity. The other party modified these considerably, in part because they did not think doctrinal beliefs were that important. Focus was placed on experience, more than on beliefs. The liberals, or "modernists" were called

---

7. Kenneth Scott Latourette, *A History of the Expansion of Christianity* (New York: Harper and Brothers, 1945), vol. 7, p. 492.

that because they were attempting to modernize the Christian message, to make it more acceptable to contemporary persons. Eventually, these two parties separated in many if not most denominations. While the two types of churches coexisted within major denominations side by side, it was difficult to assess the relative success of their ministries. When, however, the conservative churches withdrew from or were forced out of the major denominations, it became possible to compare the two groups. While the popular expectation within society and within the major denominations was that the fundamentalist movement would drift off into obscurity and irrelevance, it soon became apparent that the momentum was actually with them. They vastly outstripped their more liberal counterparts in numerical growth, in both membership and attendance. Their missionary programs continued to grow, while those of the more liberal churches declined, in some cases rather radically. And, although their membership was drawn from lower-income classes, their per capita giving far exceeded that of the higher-income liberal church members. In part, this was a result of the conservative churches' higher percentage of active members, but the results went beyond that.[8]

More recent statistics confirm the continuation of this trend. Statistics regarding the missions programs of various types of churches reveal a sharp decline in the number of missionaries under appointment in the "mainline" denominations.[9] Indeed, the Episcopal Church recently decided to terminate its official missions program.[10] In many cases, these mainline denominations have developed their theology in such a fashion that it is not really essential to take the Christian message to non-Christians, because either they are not considered to be really lost or other routes to salvation are believed to exist. This has led to failure to reproduce themselves in any number. There really is no alternative given to the non-Christian, no real reason to become a Christian.

This trend has been documented by Dean Kelley in *Why Conservative Churches Are Growing*. Kelley shows that those groups that demand much of their adherents, which generally stems from a very conservative theology, have prospered and grown whereas others have faded and lost ground.[11]

---

8. William Hordern, *New Directions in Theology Today:* vol. 1, *Introduction* (Philadelphia: Westminster, 1966), pp. 75–76. Cf. *Yearbook of American Churches*, ed. Herman C. Weber (New York: Round Table), 1933 ed., pp. 300–305; 1939 ed., pp. 6–17; 1941 ed., pp. 129–38.

9. Dean M. Kelley, *Why Conservative Churches Are Growing* (San Francisco: Harper and Row, 1977), p. 10.

10. Doug LeBlanc, "New Budget Cuts Missions," *Christianity Today* 38, no. 5 (April 25, 1994): 47.

11. Kelley, *Why Conservative Churches Are Growing*, pp. 20–32.

This effect of theology is not limited to any one variety of theology or any one position on the theological scale, however. Thus, certain very strongly Calvinistic Christians, such as the "Hard-shell Baptists," did not really engage in evangelism, thinking this unnecessary, in light of their theology. They have diminished to negligible sized groups.

Doctrine is important, perhaps more in our time than at almost any other period in the history of the church. We must continue to sharpen our own understanding and find creative ways of teaching others.

3

The Difficulty of Doctrine Today

In the first chapter we noted the importance of doctrine. This importance is not diminished in our day. In fact, in many ways the need today is greater than previously. Not only are the perpetual reasons for the importance of doctrine still with us, but they are heightened; some facets of our current situation especially call for it. Yet, at the same time, it is in some ways more difficult to do doctrine, especially correct biblical doctrine, than at some times in the past. There are unique obstacles to thinking doctrinally and emphasizing the doctrinal dimensions of Christianity. While some of these are continuations and even amplifications of trends, others are of relatively recent origin.

The factors currently militating against the formulation and the proclamation of doctrine can be classified into four major groups, in terms of the nature of the challenge they present. The first group stems from general cultural factors. The second collection is religious, but represents non-Christian religious alternatives, such as one of the other world religions or a popular cultural phenomenon such as New Age. Third, there are those objections or hindrances from within the practicing Christian community itself. These contend that doctrine, at least as conventionally conceived, is a problem or a hindrance or at least unnecessary to the work of the church. This might be termed the antidoctrinal Christian objections. Finally, there are obstacles unique to the preacher, which we might term clergy factors.

General Cultural Factors

1. One major movement of our time that works against Christian doctrine is naturalism, the view that reality is basically composed of nature, or of the observable universe. Consequently, everything that occurs within our experience is caused by natural forces within that

closed arena. While this may be either highly sophisticated or very simple in its construction, it is the operating philosophy for large numbers of persons in the world, especially in the West. It is an implicit assumption underlying much of science, which studies the observable. It carries with it the powerful argument that we know what we can perceive exists (barring the views of some idealists). Religion, especially theology, can offer little to match this. The problems raised regarding observable phenomena can be settled in relatively simple fashion as well. One has only to look at something (with however sophisticated a viewing device) to see whether it is one way or the other. By contrast, conflicting opinions in matters theological seem insusceptible to any sort of easy mediation.

The very difficulty of doing doctrine stems in large part from the fact that it deals with intangibles, and these are notoriously difficult to describe or induce others to believe in. Persons who have sold tangible items (pots and pans, automobiles, etc.) and then begin selling intangibles such as insurance can attest to this difficulty. While an insurance salesperson can place a policy in the hands of the prospective purchaser, the paper is not really what is being sold; rather, what is being sold is protection against certain unfortunate possibilities. In a sense the salesperson is selling money, money that will be received by the policyholder or the beneficiary if one of those possibilities becomes actual, but that means that the money is hypothetical money, money one will receive *if*. Doctrine similarly deals with matters like forgiveness, eternal life, the nature of God—all of which fall outside verification by sensory perception. Attempting to make doctrine intelligible and relevant to people who live in this natural world and who are concerned with the here and now is a difficult task.

2. A further obstacle to doing and expressing doctrine is the set of issues in our culture that together form what we might best term relativism. This general term denotes the idea that there is no truth that is true for everyone, a truth that simply is how things are. One facet of this is intense individualism. This may take the form of opposition to authority in any form. It may be a reflection of an epistemology in which truth is apprehended through intuition, rather than through discursive objective thought and argument. In any event, the conclusion is that I alone am the judge of what is right for me.

This is also related more specifically to relativism proper, the idea that there may be several true positions on a given issue. Traditionally, it was believed that if view A was true, then its contradictory, not-A, must be false. In the contemporary environment, however, there is a tendency to regard both A and not-A as capable of being true simultaneously. This may be based on the idea that there is no objective standard of reality, of what is true or right. One cannot evaluate two ideas by measuring them against some absolute standard of truth. One can only compare them against one another. This, of course, generally appeals, perhaps tacitly, to some other form of understanding about the nature of truth, frequently a pragmatic view.

That this general sort of relativism or even pluralism is gaining strength in our society has been well documented. What is surprising and disturbing is research indicating that such ideas have made serious inroads into conservative Christian thinking. Thus, research done by the Barna organization reveals that even a majority of persons who claimed to be born again agree with the statement, "There is no absolute truth; different people can define truth in conflicting ways and still be correct."[1] While the way the question is framed may have caused some who simply did not want to be dogmatic to agree, it nonetheless appears that a substantial number of persons indeed think that there are various truths for different persons.

Part of this may simply be what James Davison Hunter has termed "the ethic of civility."[2] This refers to the tendency not to want to tell anyone they are wrong. Thus, truth becomes secondary to etiquette. I am right and you are also right becomes the easy way to avoid conflict between two persons whose views are actually diametrically opposed.

A more extreme form of relativism, and one still largely at the level of intellectuals but beginning to trickle down to the person in the street is deconstruction. This way of thinking, which arose as a school of literary criticism, may well represent a paradigm change from the modern to the postmodern period of our culture. In the traditional view of language, words ultimately referred to something other than words, to objects or states of affairs existing independently of personal beliefs about them. In this newer understanding, words refer only to other words. There is no bedrock of extralinguistic material on which they rest.[3] In such a situation, the value of language is in expressing the feelings of the speaker or writer and in evoking feelings in the hearer or reader. As this view of language is translated into the idiom of the people, its relativizing effects can be expected to continue.

In this atmosphere, anything that claims to be "the" way things are encounters resistance. Doctrine, however, makes such claims. It affirms that certain teachings are true, and therefore are to be believed.

---

1. George Barna, *What Americans Believe: An Annual Survey of Values and Religious Views in the United States* (Ventura, Calif.: Regal, 1991), pp. 84–85.

2. James Davison Hunter, *Evangelicalism* (Chicago: University of Chicago Press, 1987), pp. 183–84.

3. Richard Rorty, *Consequences of Pragmatism: Essays 1972–1980* (Minneapolis: University of Minnesota Press, 1982), p. xxxv.

The claim is that all persons should believe this, since it is an expression of something existing independently of how persons feel about it.

Part of the difficulty experienced by the purveyors of doctrine is the dispute over who establishes or determines what is true and right. In an earlier period, truth was thought of as originating from God. Then, as belief in the supernatural declined, there was a shift to seeing nature as the source and guarantor of truth and right. More recently, humans are seeing themselves as making truth. One of the most interesting revelations of this phenomenon occurred during the confirmation hearings for Clarence Thomas for the United States Supreme Court in the fall of 1991. While most of the attention was directed to the attempt to determine whether Thomas or Anita Hill was telling the truth regarding his alleged sexual harassment of her, this other issue was also being played out, largely unnoticed. Some of the more liberal members of the Senate judiciary committee conducting the hearings were concerned that because Thomas had been educated in Catholic schools, he might believe in natural law, the idea that certain values are objectively present in the nature of things. The climax of the discussion came when the committee chairman, Senator Joseph Biden of Rhode Island, declared, "Right and wrong are what Congress decides they are!" A more overt declaration of the philosophy that truth and morality are human constructs could hardly be found.

Actually, of course, persons do not really hold to this relativism in practice. They cannot, if they are to function and contend for their ideas over against those of others. There is a belief that these ideas are not merely preferences, but reflect the way things really are, making these beliefs superior to those of others. During the Viet Nam War, the protesters were often college and university students who ostensibly were relativists in their official beliefs in many areas. Yet they steadfastly insisted that "The war is immoral!" They did not merely mean that they disliked the war, although they surely did, but they seemed to hold that somehow this was contrary to the way things are, or the ways things should be.

3. One reason doctrine is more difficult today is because of trends in the nature of communication. We hear continually that our age is a visually, rather than verbally, oriented generation. The old adage that "a picture is worth a thousand words" is becoming more emphatic. Consequently, Christian ministries are adopting other forms of communication than the traditional verbally oriented preaching and teaching. The use of drama and multimedia presentations comes to mind. Some of these types of communication, however, are inherently not as capable of doctrinal refinement as are verbal presentations. The analysis, elaboration, and interpretation done in a spoken sermon are difficult to

present in a drama. Greater ambiguity exists. Several years ago one of the authors attended a Kabuki theater in Tokyo with a Japanese pastor who had been his student several years earlier. Because he did not understand Japanese, the American was given a small radio receiver with an earphone, over which he could hear an English summary of what was being said. At the intermission, the two men discovered to their surprise that the American visitor understood more about the play than did his Japanese host. The narrative he was hearing included explanation and interpretation of the words and actions of the actors, which could not be conveyed in the script being followed by the actors.

4. Another difficulty for the formulator and purveyor of doctrine comes from the passage of time, with its concomitant apparent obsolescence of ideas. The doctrines Christianity holds as tenets and commands for belief are based on centuries-old documents, which claim to be a revelation from God. They have been articulated in their basic form almost that long ago. Since that time, great cultural change has taken place in our world. How, then, are people today to understand these doctrines, and how can they be expected to believe them? Virtually no one in a developed society believes today that the sun revolves around the earth or that bloodletting is a good way to cure certain diseases. How, then, can people be expected to believe Christian doctrines that apparently partake of the same cultural ethos? In some cases, the difficulty is not simply whether one can believe the doctrine, but rather whether one can even understand what one is being asked to believe. The upshot of this is that doctrine must be constantly redone. It will not suffice simply to continue to repeat the expressions of a given doctrine that were delineated several centuries ago. Yet this becomes an exceedingly delicate undertaking, something like performing brain surgery. One might successfully remove a tumor, but destroy the brain in the process. In the endeavor to give a fresh, intelligible, relevant statement of an ancient doctrine, how does one ensure that the doctrine is really preserved? In other words, how can one be certain that it really is the Christian doctrine of divine love, or immanence, or atonement?

5. A further factor is atomism. By this we mean the tendency to think only in small pieces, rather than in a great synoptic whole. Doctrine, to the extent that it is systematic theology, is concerned with a full synthesis or integration of the various elements of Christian belief into a coherent whole, within which everything has meaning. This kind of "worldview-ish" approach is becoming ever scarcer in our society.

In part, this is a result of the tremendous information explosion. The time of the greater metaphysicians, the spinners of grand synoptic systems, was a simpler one; one person, if a true genius and intellectually versatile, could know, at least on some level, enough about all areas of learning to be able to look over all of truth and see its interconnections. That time is past. Information is growing at an incredible rate. It is very difficult for anyone to keep abreast of the growing body of knowledge in one field, let alone know what is happening in others. The resultant usual method of coping is to become more and more specialized. There was a time when a person had one doctor, who basically knew what there was to know about medicine. It may have been possible then to say, "An apple a day keeps the doctor away," but if that slogan were to be used today, it would have to be doctors, in the plural. One's primary care physician is frequently someone who has specialized in internal medicine, and who knows enough about the various fields of medicine to know where to refer a patient.

The same phenomenon occurs in theology. A church historian cannot ordinarily also be conversant with all the latest trends in Old Testament studies. Thus, the very idea of doctrine as a summation of the entire Bible's teaching on a subject appears to be an impossibility, or at least, an endeavor of great difficulty. Doctrine must give way to much more modest treatments of Christianity's teachings.

On a popular level, some persons simply are detail-oriented, and have difficulty fitting these details together into a whole. They can see all the trees, but cannot see the forest. They have difficulty with the "big picture."

6. A final general cultural problem is the fact that some biblical and theological concepts and terminology have been displaced by secular thought. In some cases the concepts have been replaced by alternative concepts; in others, the terminology has been retained but has been so redefined as to become virtually meaningless. We have an example of the former in the substitution of "psychological wholeness" for "personal holiness," a matter of psychology usurping theology's usual function. Another example is seen in the idea of "fate," according to which events occur because they were destined to happen, but without any real question being raised regarding who or what does the destining. Here a blind force of some kind serves the function that an intelligent god was previously thought to serve. The idea is retained that some force greater than the individual human is responsible for influencing what occurs, but without any real specification of what that may be.

The other type of factor is seen in the redefinition of terminology in our language and culture. Much of this is simply popular jargon or slang. As much as theologians, doctors, and others are regaled for the use of specialized terminology, the same problem pertains in more popular circles as well. Any adult who has ever attempted, without previous language study of some kind, to understand adolescent conversation, especially that of certain cultural subgroups, knows that there is a language there just as impenetrable as any technical vocabulary and much more difficult because of its instability. This has a detrimental effect on the ability to communicate theologically. We have in mind, for example, something such as generalized use of the word "awesome." That has been a perfectly good and expressive adjective to use of God. Now, however, a substitute must be found for that adjective, since it has been so trivialized.

In some cases, this breakdown in the traditional meaning of language occurs without the awareness of the persons using it in the traditional fashion, thus exacerbating the misunderstanding. As one evangelism teacher observed, "We say, 'God loves you,' and the person seems to indicate recognition, so we assume communication, where it has not really occurred. The hearer thinks, 'God means the force, and loves means lusts after.' Thus, the speaker says, 'God loves you,' and the hearer hears, 'The force lusts after me.'" This development is not only a difficulty for doctrine; it is a reason for the importance of such doctrine.

Religious Factors

Not all of doctrine's opposition comes from the outright rejection of religion or doctrinal concepts. It stems from the fact that, like the Athenians whom Paul addressed in Acts 17, people are religious—in fact, too religious.

1. There is competition from other world religions. The time is past when even for North Americans the alternatives are either Christianity or nothing. Formerly people believed that the choice between Christianity and Islam, Hinduism, or one of the other religions faced only previous devotees of the non-Christian religion. Now, however, Christians, nominal and genuine alike, are faced with this choice. Other major religions, especially Islam, are targeting the West for their evangelistic endeavor. Islam, in particular, is growing rapidly and is coming to be considered in the West as a viable alternative to Christianity and Judaism.[4] This means that people have more options. It is not Christianity or nothing. There are other variations of belief in the supernatural that will become increasingly appealing. Thus, with the presence of a variety of religious ideas within our culture, some of the tenets of these other religions will begin to creep into our thinking and even modify or dilute our Christian beliefs. The apparent novelty of these ideas will make them especially appealing to some.

---

4. Harold A. Netland, *Dissonant Voices: Religious Pluralism and the Question of Truth* (Grand Rapids: Eerdmans, 1991), p. 72.

2. There are also pseudo- or quasi-religions in our society. The pantheistic philosophy/religion known as New Age is becoming quite widespread. In some cases, this is not substituted for the Christian faith so much as attached to and blended with it, with a diluting and corrupting effect on those Christian beliefs. Beyond that, however, there are numerous psychological and sociological ways of life, some of them of the self-help variety. They will prove to be difficult competitors for Christianity.

3. A growing factor within the understanding of religions is the idea that they really are not that distinctive. On the intellectual level, and to a growing extent also on the popular level, there is a tendency to regard all religions as basically the same. They are all saying pretty much the same thing, but in different conceptual "languages." Hinduism is the way Indians attempt to understand the universe and their place in it, and it serves them well in their endeavor to live happily and successfully. Islam does the same thing for Arabs.[5] In such a setting, the attempt to discuss specific teachings of Christianity as if they were *the* correct understanding of things seems quaintly naive.

4. Finally, there is a sort of unofficial pluralism growing out of the tensions of our divided world. It is no longer possible to live in one's own corner of the world and ignore the way others in it believe and act. We must learn to understand each other and live with one another. Globalization and cultural shrinkage require that. Rejection or disdain for other cultural practices must be supplanted by learning to appreciate. So, says much modern thought, we must also accept as equally valid the religious views of others. To fail to do so is as intolerant as to reject their dress, language, form of family organization, or other mores.[6]

Christian Factors

In addition to the factors that in one way or another are hostile to the whole of Christianity, or to certain of its doctrines, there are also problematic factors at work within Christian circles themselves. We are referring here to elements or varieties of the Christian faith that object to the use or legitimacy of doctrine within Christianity. These may not be overt forces of opposition. They may in some cases be simply characteristics of the church and of doctrine that make the task of the theologian difficult to carry out.

1. The first of these is the growing pragmatism in ministry. For some time, there has been a decline of the Christian faith in Europe. Only sin-

---

5. Peter Berger, "The Pluralistic Situation and the Coming Dialogue between the World Religions," *Buddhist-Christian Studies* 1 (1981): 33.

6. Netland, *Dissonant Voices*, pp. 32–33.

gle-digit percentages of the general population attend Sunday worship in virtually any of the countries of Western Europe. Throughout much of this period of decline, Christianity's popularity has continued unabated in North America, especially in the United States. Periodic resurgences of religious interest have brought things back, just when it appeared a slide was beginning.

Now, however, that trend may be overtaking the churches of the United States as well. Secularism seems to be affecting the religious practice of many Americans. One facet of this is decline in worship attendance. One denominational group in Ohio and Pennsylvania that studied the attendance patterns in its churches over a ten-year period discovered that 51 percent showed a moderate to severe decline, 33 percent showed a moderate to large increase, and 15 percent showed little change (an increase or decrease of 5 percent or less).[7] In even such a conservative and aggressively evangelistic denomination as the Southern Baptist Convention 49.5 percent of all churches are plateaued (membership change of less than 10 percent increase or decrease in the past five years), and 20.2 percent have declined by more than 10 percent.[8] This decline is not atypical of evangelical churches, and it is accentuated when one turns to more liberal churches (often labeled "mainline," for some inexplicable reason, presumably because these were the large groups, but perhaps for more "politically correct" reasons).[9]

Such a situation places great psychological pressure on pastors. They, after all, want to succeed for a variety of reasons, and beyond that, in many cases their church members also want to see results, frequently defined in terms of numerical increase. Some of these laypersons, involved in management, sales, or marketing positions, are accustomed to being held responsible for the results in their department, and expect no less from their pastor. It is a difficult situation for a pastor, who works with volunteer workers, not simply employees, and who possesses no rights of tenure in office. Some studies of the present predicament of the church, while basically on target, display a lack of empathy for the difficulties facing the local church pastor, often betraying a lack of experiential familiarity with the pastorate.[10]

7. Dan Peterson, *Middle East Baptist Conference District Assessment* (Youngstown, Ohio: Middle East Baptist Conference, 1994), p. 6.

8. Terri Lackey, "Plateaued, Declining Church Growth Is Pervasive, Pesky, Sneaky Illness," *Baptist Press*, April 2, 1996.

9. Dean M. Kelley, *Why Conservative Churches Are Growing* (New York: Harper and Row, 1972), pp. 20–35.

10. E.g., David Wells, *No Place for Truth: Or, Whatever Happened to Evangelical Theology* (Grand Rapids: Eerdmans, 1993); *No God But God: Breaking with the Idols of Our Age*, ed. Os Guinness and John Seel (Chicago: Moody, 1992).

In such situations, where there is pressure to succeed and such success is measured by statistics, there is a strong tendency to make decisions regarding programming and emphases on the basis of pragmatism rather than ideology. Examples abound. In 1993 one of the authors lectured at a Seventh-day Adventist College. At a faculty luncheon he was asked how he felt about the practice of Seventh-day Adventists of worshiping on Saturday rather than on Sunday. He replied that while differing with their practice and belief on this matter, he respected them because this practice was based on a genuine conviction that this is what the Bible teaches, a practice he assumed may have impeded somewhat their growth in a culture in which, if they are going to worship at all, most people will likely do so on Sunday. Quite different, he said, is the establishment of a worship service on Saturday evening to reach persons who would prefer to worship then in order to keep Sunday free.

Denominational distinctives are being blurred today. Originally, these distinctives were matters of deep conviction. Those who held to believers' baptism by immersion could not be part of a church that practiced infant baptism, because the command to be baptized as a public testimony to one's faith was considered a matter of obedience to an important command given by the Lord Jesus Christ himself and the mode of that baptism was considered essential to the practice. Today, however, some Baptist churches are opening their membership to those who have not undergone such baptism. In some cases, the decision may be made on the basis of having deeply studied the matter and concluding that the Scriptures are not sufficiently clear to justify such a practice. In other cases, however, the decision is being made on pragmatic grounds: It will make it easier to attract more people.

This has not always been so, however. Among the pioneers of a Baptist group now allowing open membership were two nineteenth-century Swedish immigrants, John and Brita Sundstrom. They had come from Sweden in large part for religious freedom. When they settled in rural Minnesota they found that the nearest Baptist church was eleven miles away. Rather than attending a nearby Lutheran church, they walked that distance to the Baptist church each Sunday, carrying their infant daughters, Ida and Christine, on their backs. After several years of this practice, they founded a Baptist church in their home, John serving as the lay pastor of the church for the first five years of its existence.[11] Twenty miles away another Baptist church was formed by a group that had emigrated from a town in Sweden where the persecu-

11. P. Ryden, *Svenska Baptisternas i Minnesota Historia; Från 1850 -Talet till 1918* (Minneapolis: Minnesota Statskonferens, 1918), p. 122.

tion of the Baptists had been the most severe. One leader of the group had been imprisoned for twenty-three days on a diet of bread and water, a punishment of which twenty-eight days was considered the equivalent of life imprisonment.[12] January prayer week revivals often occurred in that church and the converts were unwilling to wait until spring to be baptized. Consequently, two- to three-foot-thick ice on Rush Lake was cut through, and in 1876 a total of thirty-two persons were baptized; in the winter of 1878, fifty-four persons.[13] To those people, Baptist doctrine was important, and they preached it in their churches. Lest you think these are fictitious cases or "preacher stories," we can assure you they are not. Ida Sundstrom was the mother of one of the authors, who grew up in that second church mentioned.

The point here is not whether Baptist doctrine is correct, or whether one ought to be a Baptist or something else. The point is that doctrinal beliefs were considered important in earlier generations. One did not make the choice of church primarily on the basis of geographical proximity, beauty of building, or quality of program or preaching. To many leaders of churches today, there must be change to meet the times, a concern that is basically correct in its emphasis. One of the changes envisioned, however, is that the church must not be so doctrinal, so doctrinaire, that it narrows the possible field of its appeal.

2. Some object that doctrine is divisive. Like many other concerns today, this stems from a correct and noble intention and desire, in this case, the desire for unity in the church. That this is important to our Lord himself is indicated by his prayer that his followers might be one as he and the Father are one (John 17:20–23). But, say some of today's church members and leaders, we are actually formally divided from other believers by our teachings and beliefs on such matters as the nature of sanctification and the order of events surrounding Christ's second coming. Because this is the case, we should avoid discussing such doctrines.

There is, of course, a large element of truth to this complaint. Sometimes the church has been divided into numerous smaller and smaller subdivisions over matters of doctrinal minutia. The youth pastor of one evangelical church asked the youth pastor of another similar church to consider having a combined activity of their two groups, in this case a wiener roast. The latter youth pastor replied that he could not do that, since some of the young people from the first church might not be premillennial.

---

12. Adolf Olson, *A Centenary History; As Related to the Baptist General Conference of American* (Chicago: Baptist Conference Press, 1952), pp. 106–7, n. 1.
13. Ibid., p. 109.

In actuality, this sort of division is not the result merely of doctrinal differences. In many churches today, the disputes are over more practical than doctrinal matters. One of these, which will probably be with us for some time, is the style of worship, particularly of music. Another is the role of women in the church and in ministry. While these may be related to and even based on doctrinal issues, they are primarily a question of practice. To some extent such differences cannot be avoided, and must not be, if the issues are important.

The result of this fear of the divisiveness of doctrine is not necessarily rejection of doctrine, so much as neglect of doctrine. There is a broad-based avoidance of any kind of doctrinal discussion, whether acrimonious or irenic. When, however, this is done, it leaves the way open for perversions to enter, which would be rejected by both parties to some of these minor disputes. It is something like avoiding changing the motor oil in a family's automobiles because various family members prefer different brands of oil, and changing oil using one of these brands would be divisive. Thus, the needed lubrication that all family members agree is important is neglected, with serious consequences.

3. A third difficulty for doctrine today is the tendency toward generic Christianity and even generic religion. One quality of the baby boomer generation is a lack of "brand loyalty" as consumers. If a baby boomer's father drove Chevrolets all his life, that has little effect on the boomer, who may change to another make of car if it seems to be of better quality or a better value for the money, or simply if the local dealer offers better service. This, in itself is wise consumerism. When applied to the choice of church, however, the considerations that bear most strongly on a selection are not doctrinal in character. They are the questions of convenience of parking, quality of educational program, or nursery facilities. In such an environment, the trend is toward doctrinally generic Christianity. That which distinguishes one church from another doctrinally, that is, the specifics, is not perceived as being important.[14]

At present, most persons seeking "consumer-friendly" religion tend to go to evangelical churches, largely because these are the churches providing aggressive quality programming. If that were different, however, in other words, if more doctrinally liberal churches had better recreational or counseling programs, persons of this type might not be terribly reluctant to make the change. Indeed, the trend toward deleting the denomination from the church name both reflects and contributes to this trend. More churches are becoming simply "community churches," or are even deleting "church" from their advertised name, instead identifying themselves as "Grace Christian Community" or

14. Leith Anderson, *Dying for Change* (Minneapolis: Bethany, 1990), pp. 81–83.

"New Hope Praise Center." The issue is larger than this, however. Those patronizing the full-service churches are traditionally Christian and so seek for their needs to be met in a Christian context. What, however, happens if other religions, some of which are now becoming quite aggressively evangelistic, come to provide the best-quality religious and educational programming? To date, of course, most of these competitive religions are more doctrinaire than much Christianity. Yet, these religions may well learn from the strategy of Christianity, becoming much more generic, emphasizing experience, personal health, and so on. They may even learn to use identities that are not clearly non-Christian. Does a religious or psychological experience in a Christian versus a Muslim religious context matter?

4. Another problem for doctrine in our day is the move toward a more feeling-oriented approach to the Christian faith, and indeed to life in general by those in the West. This represents a trend that has been in place for approximately two centuries. Friedrich Schleiermacher asserted that the domain of religion is neither doctrinal belief nor ethical activity, but feeling. This has grown and taken various forms over the years.[15] I can remember a conference held at a Christian college more than thirty years ago. During the testimony sharing time, one of the college students indicated his enthusiasm for Jesus by saying, "Jesus is the greatest!" He did not indicate the greatest "what," just the greatest. While some of the pastors present were at that time somewhat taken aback by this expression of vague piety, that young man was the vanguard of things to come. What he was expressing, of course, was not primarily something about Jesus, but about himself and how he felt about Jesus.

This feeling approach to Christian faith is both reflected by and encouraged by a type of worship that focuses primarily on the emotions. One has only to observe the type of congregational singing that is becoming increasingly popular in evangelical circles to note this trend. At one time, hymns were a primary means of teaching or reinforcing doctrinal beliefs. The lyrics reflected this. Each stanza of a properly composed hymn advanced the thoughts of the preceding stanzas. In many popular songs today, however, the content of the lyrics is minimal. A few words and sentences are repeated numerous times, often more than the songwriter called for. There may be an ascending shift of key. All of this has the effect of elevating the emotions, as any observer trained in social psychology or even a discerning although untrained observer, can tell. As important as the emotional dimension of Chris-

15. Friedrich Schleiermacher, *On Religion: Speeches to Its Cultured Despisers* (New York: Harper and Brothers, 1958), second speech.

tian faith is, it has a tendency to eliminate or minimize the need for any fine distinctions among beliefs. In so doing, this brand of Christianity makes itself exceedingly vulnerable to the traditional charges of intellectuals, particularly in the behavioral sciences, that this brand of religion is simply a matter of emotional expression, as well as the contention of persons like John Hick that all religions are essentially different expressions of the same experience, veiled under different thought forms.[16]

5. Some Christians are quite indifferent to, or insensitive to, theological differences. To them, the difference between an understanding of justification as something God does in declaring the person righteous, and something he does by actually changing the person's moral and spiritual condition, seems inconsequential. They are as insensitive to such nuances as tone-deaf persons are to the sounds of adjacent notes on the musical scale. Thus, the attempt to teach doctrine, with its inevitable distinctions, seems superfluous and counterproductive.

6. Some laypersons have a strong distrust of any kind of learning. As Helmut Thielicke has pointed out, this is not without some justification, on the basis of both principle and experience.[17] This is especially the case with theology, which appears to be the most abstract discipline.

7. A further problem for doctrine comes from what might be called the "prophetic approach" to settling the matter of truth in certain areas. By this we mean the approach that expects God's direct communication of his truth to those who are alert and sensitive to such manifestation. This is of course found in the various Pentecostal, charismatic, and Third Wave movements, where something like prophecy or a word of knowledge is considered an important way to apprehend God's truth. It is also, however, found in less officially charismatic groups in which lay Bible study is undertaken, with the expectation that one will find the meaning in the process of reading and meditating on a portion of Scripture. This approach short-circuits the hard work generally involved in getting at the truth in doctrinal matters, such as exegesis of Scripture, examination and analysis of all the viable alternatives, and evaluation of those in such a way as to identify the most probable. This approach purports to dispense with that, providing a quick and easy solution to complicated doctrinal dilemmas.

Such prophetic solutions often emanate from authoritarian leaders. All goes well until two or more of these supposedly prophetic ideas come in conflict with one another. Then the weakness of the approach

16. John Hick, *God Has Many Names* (Philadelphia: Westminster, 1982), pp. 64–66.
17. Helmut Thielicke, *A Little Exercise for Young Theologians* (Grand Rapids: Eerdmans, 1962), pp. 3–8, 21–24.

becomes apparent. If rational means do not enter into the original formulation of these views, they will not be easily mediated. Thus, some sort of power struggle between the holders of these opposed views ensues, however well concealed this may seem to be or what form it may take. Either one subdues the other, or a division of the group takes place. Indeed, this approach to identifying the truth is major raw material for religious splits.

8. Yet another major problem for doing doctrine, although not necessarily for holding doctrine, is tradition. By this is meant holding something because it has been taught or received, or because it is the status quo. The very familiarity of the idea creates an aura of truth about it, which settles matters, or even precludes the consideration of any different way of thinking about things. In many cases, there is a generalized conception that this idea is held because this is what the Bible teaches, without any concerted inquiry regarding the specific location of such references. In one church, a middle-aged woman came to her pastor after a service and asked, "Why don't you preach about the ———, like other pastors do?" "What ———?" responded the young pastor. "Why the ——— that is taught in the Bible," was the woman's comment. When the pastor inquired exactly where in the Bible this doctrine was taught, the woman hesitated, then promised to come the next Sunday with the texts listed. Upon seeing the pastor the next Sunday morning, the woman immediately exclaimed, "How could they have so misled me at ——— [a school she had attended]? The word does not even appear in the Bible." Not all holders of traditional views allow them to be corrected that easily, however. Tradition frequently substitutes for the hard work of doing theology.

Not all traditions are necessarily old, however. It is impressive to see how quickly some of today's young people, with their lack of awareness of or concern about history, absolutize a recently accepted idea, or allow a very old idea to become their belief, not recognizing that the church may have condemned the teaching centuries earlier. Sometimes the persons or groups that pride themselves on being the most innovative hold to their young traditions most tenaciously. Among the dozens of congregations one of us has served as interim pastor there were two that particularly thought of themselves as avant garde, innovative, and flexible. Yet in one, the interim pastor was told quite clearly that the congregation wanted him to perpetuate a practice called "the prayers of the people," which the previous pastor had introduced, in which he came down from the pulpit and stood among the people. In explaining the procedure to him, the church chairman actually said, "Here is where X [the preceding pastor] stood when he prayed." In the other church, the leadership strongly suggested to the interim pastor a partic-

ular pattern of topics for the advent sermon series, because that was
how it had been done the two previous years. Attempts to preach from
a different location than the customary place on the platform met with
no enthusiasm in either church, less so in fact than in almost any of the
other churches where such an innovation had been attempted. It was
almost as if these churches were saying, "We want to be innovative, and
our form of innovation is the right and the final way to innovate."

There is here, of course, quite frequently a doctrinal conception, albeit held for a poor reason. It may quite frequently be poor doctrine.
The real difficulty, however, stems from the fact that holding this doctrinal conception for this reason may prevent one from holding or
teaching a better version of such a doctrine.

9. Another obstacle to doctrine in our day is the presence of what
might well be referred to as bizarre conceptions. All sorts of strange
ideas, held for various reasons, affect people's thinking. These are frequently based on taking a single text out of its context and extrapolating
it without regard for other portions of Scripture. Such an idea is often
thought of as the very key to the Christian faith, and the resulting pre-
occupation frequently diverts people from the appropriate concern
with doctrine. For example, one church mailed to its entire community
an invitation to attend its vacation Bible school. A letter was received
from one person, objecting to the idea of mailing invitations and citing
a biblical reference that could be vaguely construed to relate to this. The
entire effort and concern of the person seemed to be focused on this
matter. Here was a case of drawing an extremely questionable inference from Scripture, and then making primary what, even if taught in
Scripture, would appear to be very secondary.

10. This is closely related to what might be called "formulism," or
"sloganism." By this is meant the tendency to place great confidence in
a single word or phrase, and to regard it as the measure of orthodoxy.
Apart from the fact that the expression may not really be understood,
the danger is that formal use of the language may divert attention from
what is actually believed and asserted, or what, in other words, is meant
by that expression. Formulism, in other words, short-circuits inquiry
and reflection in doctrinal matters.

11. A very real cause of difficulty for the doctrinal enterprise is the
increasing self-orientation of much popular Christianity. This has several manifestations. One is the primary concern for human welfare,
often conceived of in terms of personal pleasure or satisfaction. This affects to a large extent the doctrines of God, humanity, sin, and salvation. A second dimension is the tendency to consider our ideas right
and our judgment correct. The rest of doctrine is then construed in light
of this. For example, it is now fairly popular to object to the doctrine of

hell on the ground that it is offensive to moral sensibility. God therefore is evaluated by whether he conforms to my conception. It may mean that the biblical statements are interpreted in light of my ideas, so that God's love is understood in a more permissive fashion. Or it may be that God is seen as actually not fitting my understanding, and therefore is judged to be less than fully loving and benevolent. The underlying assumption in all of this thinking is the inherent goodness and integrity of human personality. The human is able to judge what is right and wrong, and Christianity's doctrines must conform to this. The human, in other words, has become his or her own authority. The result may be a severe distortion of biblical doctrine. What is needed, if that revealed truth is to be held and proclaimed, is a virtual Copernican revolution, in which God is made the center of our moral and spiritual universe, rather than we ourselves.

13. Closely related to this development is another powerful factor bearing on the formulation and proclamation of doctrine. In recent years there has been a strong emphasis within Christian circles on psychology, mental health, and related matters. This is frequently considered more important than biblical content and doctrine, at least in practice if not in overt theory. This then influences doctrine in several ways. One is the temporal character of this concern. Concern for mental health and emotional soundness is primarily a concern for that which is here and now. Doctrine, on the other hand, concerns matters that apply to eternity.

What this means is that a different set of categories is being employed and claimed to be completely adequate as means of description and explanation. For example, what was in the past considered self-centeredness and consequently labeled sin may now be treated as exclusively a psychological phenomenon, involving one's concern for adequate self-esteem or one's reaction to a situation of insecurity. This is aggravated by the tendency toward euphemism in Western (especially American) society. Thus, a student no longer does poorly; rather he or she "can do better." What formerly was an "F" grade for an extended case of the former now becomes "no credit" in the context of the latter explanation. In such a setting, no one is seen as "handicapped" or "disabled" or "abnormal." These terms are instead replaced by such concepts as "disadvantaged" or "challenged." Thus, persons who in an earlier period would have been thought of as short are "vertically challenged" and those who would have been referred to as overweight or even stout are now understood to be "dietarily enhanced" or "horizontally gifted." This type of language when carried over to discussion of other kinds of behavior virtually exterminates any thought of sin. Writing in *Christianity Today*, "Eutychus" offered a series of such redefinitions of sin, including spiritually dead as "eternal-life challenged," Satan as a "divinity-impaired being" and Anti-Christ as "alternative leader."[18]

14. A further difficulty stems from the fact that while doctrine is found throughout the Bible, it is not always stated in explicitly doctrinal form. Much of the Bible is narrative in form, a type of material that is the subject of considerable attention currently. Other portions are poetic. The difficulty is how to obtain the doctrine found in these portions, so that it can be understood as doctrine.

The formulation of Christian doctrine has never been easy, but that is particularly true in our time. Because doctrine is so important and helpful, however, the effort to find ways to develop and state doctrine today will be well worthwhile. We turn to this endeavor in the chapters ahead.

Clergy Factors

1. One obstacle to clergypersons being true pastor-theologians is that theology is hard work. Doing theology correctly and effectively requires a broad knowledge of Scripture, care in the choice and application of methodology, and reflection and deep thought. Given the time constraints and the multiple demands on the preacher, it is difficult to motivate and discipline oneself to do that for which most members of the flock are not clamoring.

2. For many pastors, there is a disjunction between theory and practice, a tendency to conduct their ministry without a clearly thought-out theological basis for what they do. This in turn frequently goes back to the nature of the theological education one has had. Just as universities tend to be pluriversities, with collections of noncohering and even conflicting disciplines, so do theological seminaries. The Issues Research Advisory Committee of the Association of Theological Schools in the United States and Canada sponsored research into the nature, problems, and improvement of theological education. At the end of several years of studies, underwritten by a major foundation, a conference was held to assess the results of that research. The chairman summarized by saying that the number one problem that had been reiterated throughout the studies was the lack of integration of the "classical" and the "applied" fields (e.g., New Testament and pastoral counseling, or theology and preaching). Given this lack of a theological basis for preaching, then, there will quite possibly be a tendency to deal with the myriad problems of the Christian life that the preacher addresses without regard for the theological basis of those issues.

18. "A Differently Sensible Idea," *Christianity Today*, 37, no. 2 (February 8, 1993): 6.

3. Finally, there are some preachers whose understanding of the nature of truth and revelation makes it difficult for them to abstract doctrine from the Bible, or to make the transition from the divine self-manifestation to declare that manifestation or discussion of the nature of that deity. While this factor goes beyond the scope of this treatise, it is one problem that a certain segment of the clergy find difficult to overcome.[19]

---

19. For a treatment of this issue by one of the authors, see Millard J. Erickson, *Christian Theology* (Grand Rapids: Baker, 1986), pp. 191–96.

4

The Place of Preaching
in the Life of the Church

The various aspects of ministries of a local church—worship, evangelism, education, pastoral care, and all related tasks—combine to form the "life" of the church. Each individual church prioritizes its ministries in order of importance. Worship usually is among the most important, for a number of reasons. The first is spiritual: Scripture teaches that God's people are to worship him (John 4:19–24; Heb. 10:24–25). The second, generally, is practical: Worship is the ministry that involves most of the members and potential members of a church at one time in the same place. Church growth studies indicate that persons choose a church on the basis of the style of worship more than by any other criterion. At the same time, more churches are making the worship service the primary, if not exclusive, means of evangelism. These practices underscore the need for churches and church leaders to reflect on the content of worship.

Reflections on worship, in turn, prompt some consideration of the importance of preaching. If worship is becoming the central feature of the church's life, what place does preaching have in that life? That is the question this chapter attempts to answer.

The schema for the chapter is to analyze the status of preaching as a component of worship, estimate the comparative value placed on preaching in the worship of the church, and provide a biblical rationale for retaining preaching as a major feature of worship. The aim of this chapter is to contend for the value of preaching in the life of the church. We begin with the role of preaching in worship because worship is a barometer of the life of the local church. What is more, among the aspects of the church's life, or ministry, worship is the most visible. Finally, most preaching is done in the context of worship.

The Status of Preaching in Worship

For much of the history of the church, especially since the Reformation, preaching has enjoyed a place of prominence in worship. That position has come under threat in the final decade of the twentieth century, for many reasons. First among them is that worship has numerous components, including music, video presentations, drama, and interviews, which the persons who attend worship find more appealing.[1]

The threat to preaching has developed slowly and almost imperceptibly, beginning with the use of complementary means of communicating the gospel. We may trace this practice to the late 1960s and the advent of the youth musical. Combining drama with music, youth choirs introduced different elements into worship, including new instruments and new rhythms. These presentations gradually changed both the content and nature of worship. They also changed the length of the worship service, since each musical required about forty-five minutes, not including time in the beginning for introductions and at the conclusion for public invitations. The musicals usually were scheduled in the evening. Pastors cooperated and helped by shortening the sermons, then, by omitting them altogether in order to provide the necessary time for the youth choir and still complete the service within an hour. "This, too, is worship," was the justification.

The most obvious change in the nature of worship created by youth dramas was the sound of new music. Guitars and drums came first, followed by electronic keyboards. Groups who lacked such instruments employed professional soundtracks on audiocassette for accompaniment. Soloists and other vocalists used the soundtracks and audio mixers to blend their voices with the instrumentation. The resulting sound was different, professional, as though the entire presentation were a recording.

Soon, another fact for worship became obvious: Professional soundtracks would also enhance the choir and congregational singing as well. Throughout the 1970s and 1980s the trend continued, as newer, better equipment and digital recording improved the quality of sound. Further improvements in transistorized circuitry made possible orchestral support programmed into a computer chip in the electronic keyboard. Churches with large memberships formed their own orchestras. The live sounds of strings, horns, cymbals, and drums began to fill worship centers and the praises from God's people changed.

The new music became a phenomenon in its own right, employed less in association with drama than as accompaniment for choral

---

1. In chapter 5 the authors discuss the loss of appeal of the sermon.

groups and congregational singing. Drama continued to gain in popularity also. Instead of lengthy plays, worship leaders presented short skits with biblical themes. All this was included in the morning worship and other services of the church. The innovations offered by the youth musical became a way of life.

In their worship, pastors now freely employ recorded music and drama; they have added slides, overhead projectors, video, art, and a number of other media. These, too, are forms of proclamation in the same sense as is preaching, the rationale goes, and they have far greater appeal to worshipers, so use them—even if their use means replacing the traditional sermon. Eventually, means of proclamation other than old-fashioned preaching assumed a greater place in worship; the sermon, a lesser place.

The sermon did not disappear from worship; it merely became one among many ways of preaching. Those other ways of proclaiming the gospel are more attractive to church attendees.[2] Less time for the sermon meant that preaching, in the form of sermon, was pushed to the periphery of the service; it yielded its traditional place and became marginal.[3]

These authors often preach on Sunday mornings, filling in for pastors on vacation. As a guest unfamiliar with the practices of individual congregations, each usually finds the person in charge of the service to look over the order of worship before the service begins. The following scenario is typical. After going over the order carefully, the minister of music says: "I will hand it to you at about 11:40" (the service begins at 11 A.M.), then adds: "The congregation is accustomed to having the service conclude at or before 12 noon." To meet that expectation the speaker has a total of twenty minutes for the sermon, the hymn of commitment, and the benediction. That usually necessitates a shortening of the sermon. If the relative amount of time assigned to it is an indicator, preaching, at best, has lost some of its importance.

A sermon of fifteen or twenty minutes may be long enough, to be sure, but not because that is all the time left. Shorter sermons are the order of the day, anyway, because preachers are learning to be more precise and succinct in preaching (i.e., say as much or more in less time).[4] At least that is the dream of homiletics professors. The trend in

---

2. This still begs the question of effectiveness.

3. The purpose of this chapter is not to discuss the pros and cons of the other forms, or to evaluate their value for worship. Instead, the purpose here is limited to an assessment of what the changes in worship content mean for preaching.

4. This is true, incidentally, because preachers have learned that the attention span of their listeners is short due to the influence of television. Also, those who study homiletics formally do hear from their professors' lectures on the importance of preparing sermons

worship, however, is toward adding other features, whether or not the length of the service is an issue. Given that the length of the sermon is not what it used to be, for whatever reason, the proportion of worship time allotted to preaching, generally, is less.

Perhaps the rationale for planning less time for preaching is that the spoken sermon is only one among many forms of proclamation. Music is essential for good worship. Various means of proclamation such as drama are valid and the traditional sermon is but one way to present God's message. Besides, the public responds more to the other forms of presentation of the gospel in worship. To paraphrase Harry Emerson Fosdick's quip that people in the pews are not terribly anxious to hear what happened to the ancient Jebusites,[5] people do not rush to church to hear a minister stand up and preach a sermon. They go to hear good music and see good drama.

The concern of this discussion, though, is to raise these questions: Are these new forms equal to the sermon in proclamation value? Are these forms, then, worthy substitutes for the sermon? Should the minister devote less time to preaching, as traditionally understood? The questions derive from a perspective on preaching that is defined as oral communication of the gospel done by a preacher standing before a congregation with an open Bible and declaring: "Thus says the Lord." That image underlies the entire discussion this chapter comprises.

The decision concerning the place of preaching in worship, no matter how one defines the term, as well as the manner in which to do proclamation, should be based on a correct understanding of the value of preaching, a consideration of what preaching can accomplish, and a proper distinction of the relative value of preaching and other forms of proclamation. Such understanding may give cause for new considerations about the form of preaching as well as its place in the worship life of the church.[6]

---

free from superfluous remarks and other uses of language that take extra time and add nothing to the content of their sermons. Professors of homiletics are inclined to ask, however, why the rule of shortened attention span is usually applied only to the sermon!

5. Harry Emerson Fosdick, "What Is the Matter with Preaching?" *Harpers Magazine* 157, no. 938 (July 1928): 135. Fosdick's exact words were: "Only the preacher proceeds still upon the idea that folk came to church desperately anxious to discover what happened to the Jebusites. The result is that folk less and less came to church at all."

6. The length of a worship service is not the primary concern here. That is a matter to be determined on the basis of the worship leaders' purposes in worship and the ways in which they attempt to accomplish those purposes. It also relates to a particular congregation's expectations, habits, and patterns. What's more, the sermon may assume forms other than the traditional monologue (explored in other chapters of this volume).

The Value of Preaching

Basic definitions of preaching stress that preaching is the communication of God's Word. Biblical metaphors for the communicating of that Word include proclaiming, teaching, speaking (on behalf of someone), and bearing witness.[7]

The value of preaching may be found, first, in its very nature: The essence of preaching is that it is a message to be told. The nature of the message—it is God's communication, his word to humankind—requires that it be told. Amos declared: "The Sovereign Lord has spoken—who can but prophesy?" (3:8). Moreover, the author of the message commanded that it be told (7:14–15; cf. Mark 3:14). Paul declared that he preached because Christ sent him to do so (1 Cor. 1:17) and, though unworthy, he must preach (1 Cor. 9:16; 2 Cor. 2:16). When the prophet Jeremiah decided he would no longer speak for God, he discovered that God's Word was a fire that burned in his bones, a message he could not refrain from speaking (Jer. 20:9).

The word or message from God is news to be reported. "I have a word from the Lord" is the motto of the spokesman (cf. Jer. 37:17). Hezekiah wondered if there was a word from the Lord about Judah and its threat from Babylon. Jeremiah replied in the affirmative. There is a word. Preaching is the announcement of good news. Jesus began his public ministry by preaching the gospel of the kingdom of God (Mark 1:14–15). Preaching offers forgiveness, reconciliation, fellowship with God, life with meaning (Rom. 10:14–15). Preaching is bearing witness to truth (see Acts 2:14–40, the sermon of Peter on the Day of Pentecost).

This message from God is such that it calls for a response. At the conclusion of Peter's sermon, the people asked what they should do. Peter replied that they should repent and be baptized for the remission of sins. Moreover, when Paul presented his testimony (preaching as witness, Acts 26:1–29), Agrippa responded that he was almost persuaded to be a Christian.

Preaching is spoken communication.[8] It involves a message source, a message, a channel or means of communication (words from a

7. These are based on the words of the biblical text we translate with the English word "preach," which are more numerous than this list. For each of these there is a corresponding metaphor to describe the one who does the preaching. Proclamation requires a herald, teaching requires a teacher, speaking requires a spokesman or advocate, and witnessing requires a witness. See Tom Long, *The Witness of Preaching* (Atlanta: Westminster/John Knox Press, 1989), pp. 41–47. Long contends that the very best of these is "witness."

8. See Myron R. Chartier, *Preaching as Communication: An Interpersonal Perspective,* Abingdon Preacher's Library, ed. William D. Thompson (Nashville: Abingdon, 1981), pp. 11–26.

speaker), and a receiver (someone to hear).[9] Some things may be done through oral communication that may not be accomplished in any other way.

What can preaching, thus understood, do? For one thing, it can give expression to the church's doctrine (as in Acts 2:42–47, the didactic kind of preaching) and provide interpretation of that doctrine. Second, as a corollary to the first, preaching can correct poor or false doctrine. Paul instructed Timothy to do just that (2 Tim. 4:1–5). Famous doctrinal battles of the early twentieth century were conducted from the pulpit. Harry Emerson Fosdick and Clarence Macartney articulated their theological viewpoints, as well as their differences with each other, through their sermons. Third, preaching can bear witness to the church's faith. This witness may take the form of apologetics, evangelism, or teaching. The Bible, the source of preaching, belongs to the church as well as to the individual.

A commitment to preaching as oral communication does not preclude the use of other forms of witness. Preaching, however, has a uniqueness about it. Moreover, preaching can accomplish some purposes that other means of proclamation cannot achieve. Thus, the sermon should not be relegated to a minor role or replaced in worship.

The investigation of the various forms of proclamation current near the end of our century leads to the certain conclusion that preaching is no longer understood exclusively as speech communication. The image of a preacher as a person who stands in front of a gathered congregation and speaks the message from God, with no additional medium other than the preacher's voice, is fading. This very image, though, is implicit in the nature of preaching.

Indeed, these changes in the media of proclamation have revolutionary implications for homiletics and may require a broadening of the definition of preaching. Preaching, as traditionally understood, can still have great value for the church today.

A second value of preaching may be found in the claims it makes for itself. Among those claims are the following: (1) Preaching has an authority that comes from God. The prophets often began their messages with "Thus says the Lord." (2) Preaching is done in response to the command of God. (3) Preaching claims God's promise that he will honor his Word (Isa. 55:8–13; 1 Cor. 1:17–25).

Third, preaching is personal communication, done on a person-to-person basis. As such, it allows for interaction, the dynamics of feed-

---

9. Ibid., pp. 24–25. This is the well-known SMCR model of communication, which is not limited to speech communication, but is applied in that manner in the current discussion.

back and emotion. The preacher dares to incarnate truth in human life and personality.[10] People who are accustomed to interacting with impersonal computers need and want a personal touch. They sit at home and make contacts for everything they want or need via computer, losing touch with other real live people. A sermon, though, can allow for questions, discussion, and participation on a level that another medium, such as a computer or television, cannot do.

A sermon may allow a spur-of-the-moment response to a need that occurs at that very moment—spontaneously. This quality of immediacy in preaching infuses authenticity into the sermon. The preacher, if need be, can change course in midsermon. Emotion may become a natural part of the event, too. A person can laugh or cry. A person may respond to an interruption such as a passing fire truck. An oral event has a dynamic about it other art forms do not have. For example, one may react emotionally to a video of starving masses, but may not interact with the screen. A certain detachment is built into the presentation due to the nature of the medium. On the other hand, a minister who recounts emotions felt when helping feed refugees with a team of other Christians may sense the emotional response among those who hear the story and respond emotionally—by weeping, for example. The same is true with the recounting of the story of the plight of the Israelites when they were under siege by the Syrians (2 Kings 6:24–7:20) or David's sorrow at the loss of his infant son (2 Sam. 12:15–23).

Fourth, preaching allows for interpretation as well as event. Video and audio, recorded earlier, present event only. Any interpretation, even oral interpretation, contained in a recorded message is done at the time of recording, not in response to a live congregation. Disclaimers, such as those used early in the history of videorecordings shown on network television, provide little or no help. "The preceding program was recorded before a live studio audience" added nothing to a television sitcom, except a laugh track, for those watching it in their own homes. Interpretation is related to content, to be sure, but preachers are to interact with those who hear the message as well as with the message itself. Impersonal media cannot get acquainted with their audiences; they have no personal contact. Loss of the personal is a tragedy of this generation. The best a preacher who is recording a sermon can do is to respond to an anticipated audience the exact nature of which she or he does not know—assuming the preacher is the one doing the recording. Each sermon, as an event in time and space, assumes a life of its own that can never be duplicated exactly.

---

10. As suggested by Clyde Fant in *Preaching for Today* (New York: Harper and Row, 1987). Fant contends for the incarnation as the model for what takes place in preaching.

Fifth, the sermon can be given organizational strength. A sermon may be so structured as to anticipate a particular response, and the preacher may determine by what is happening during the presentation whether that response is forthcoming. A single sermon can be structured in several different ways for various occasions with several different kinds of outcomes in mind. The minister prepares each sermon with a specific aim. He or she may build this aim into the sermon directly; the task is not easy or always possible with a video or other presentation. Producers determine those aims and the preacher's first task, after choosing which ones to use in worship, is to determine the purpose in each presentation and to ascertain whether it is the same as or compatible with what he or she has in mind.

Purpose is critical to good preaching. Clear and distinct purpose may not always be part of another artist's creation or, at least not be obvious. A preacher may appeal for action in one sermon, for understanding in another, and for a change of mind in another. A sermon may be dialogical or monological in form. It is not "recorded earlier for use at this time." A preacher may allow for questions and answers even as the sermon progresses. It can be adapted or customized, even made ad hoc.[11]

Sixth, preaching can give complete statements of meaning or make part of a sermon more complete. A preacher may sense whether understanding is taking place as the sermon actually is underway, and take as much additional time as necessary to express a given idea.[12] The minister may decide on the spot to continue a sermon at the next gathering— to make it into a segmented sermon or part of a series.

A statement emblazoned on a banner, on the other hand, is static; it stands for itself with no explanation. The message allows for as many interpretations as it has readers, as does a painting, a photograph, or a movie—even if its author had a purpose in mind when creating it. The perceived nature remains the same every time it is displayed. It may not change in response to feedback. A listener, viewer, may not frown in disagreement and change a picture!

During a national political convention that nominated a candidate for president of the United States, a banner prominently displayed carried the following message: "Promises Made Are Promises Kept." Of course, the party meant that they and their nominee would deliver on the party platform. With two marks of punctuation supplied in the imagination of

11. Calvin Miller has argued, in a recent volume, that the preacher may see that a sermon is not going well and make corrections even while the sermon is being preached. Miller describes this as "editing the sermon while it is underway." This certainly is not possible with other media. See *The Empowered Communicator* (Nashville: Broadman and Holman, 1994), pp. 187–96.

12. Ibid.

a curious reader, however, the meaning could undergo great change. "Promises Made. Are Promises Kept?" surely was not the intended message. The statement was meant to be declarative, not interrogative. Party speakers, with their speeches, clarified the meaning which the banner alone could not do. Conversely, the speeches could have accomplished the communication of the same message without the banner.

Compare the banner that displays the message "Hail to the King." The preacher may explain in a sermon that the King is Jesus, but the banner itself makes no such distinction. Without some form of explanation, each viewer, especially one who is not a follower of Christ, may think of a different king. A sermon portraying the Lord as King of Glory, contrariwise, may explain the Kingship of Jesus, or may employ word pictures to communicate the same message and leave no doubt as to his identity.

Seventh, preaching allows for saying the same thing, at different levels, without being repetitious. A sermon may appeal initially to the intellect by giving statistics, then move to the deeper level of emotion by telling a story, and aim its conclusion at the spirit or will by direct appeal, pleading for a response to the gospel.[13]

A drama, conversely, may also appeal to various levels, but publishes no advance call for specific intellectual response from each individual in the audience. Actors speak memorized lines, which are designed to reveal an author's message or develop an author's plot, to be sure, but much of the meaning is left to the imagination. Five different persons may come away with five different impressions from the same drama. Each is a valid conclusion, whether it is the same as the author intended. Dramas may be composed to provide commentary on a social or political subject or to promote some agenda, but do not usually call for action based on appeal to the will of persons who attend.

The preacher crafts a sermon, though, to communicate a particular message which that preacher deems to be inherent in the biblical text and which he or she did not compose, and usually states that message and its intention directly during the presentation of the sermon. The content of preaching, ultimately, is what sets it apart from all other forms of communication. The preacher does not always leave each listener the responsibility of coming up with his or her own meaning.[14]

---

13. G. Campbell Morgan, famous London preacher of the late nineteenth and early twentieth centuries, said that preaching was aimed at the citadel of the will. See *Preaching* (New York: Revell, 1937), p. 13. The eighteenth-century evangelist George Whitefield was a master at pleading with the unregenerate to come to Christ.

14. There are some exceptions. Fred Craddock, for example, contends for inductive preaching, which by its very nature leaves it up to each listener to make his or her own discovery. See *Overhearing the Gospel* (Nashville: Abingdon, 1978). Sermons, though, may be deductive and preachers may state directly the conclusion to which the listener

The preacher usually appeals for some decision or action predicated on the hearing of the sermon. He or she also acknowledges that a power other than the speaker is at work, the power of the Holy Spirit.

Arguments for Retaining Preaching

Faced with the growing popularity of other forms of proclamation, along with a diminishing interest in preaching, the preacher is tempted to feel less confident about the sermon in worship and yield all but a few minutes at the end to the other components.[15] The minister has good reasons, however, to retain preaching as a major feature of worship. They fall into two categories: spiritual and practical.

Spiritual

First, preaching is found throughout Scripture. Almost from the beginning of the Old Testament, God called on persons to speak for him. The prophets and the priests were the forerunners of the preachers and teachers of the New Testament, among whom were John the Baptist, Jesus, Peter, and Paul. Their messages we understand to be comparable to today's "sermons."

The preaching of John the Baptist and Jesus provide models for proclamation, although they did not preach in a "worship service." The example of Jesus in Luke 4:16–21 may be an exception. Jesus went into the synagogue, as he was accustomed to do, immediately following his temptation experience. While there, he read from the scroll a passage found in Isaiah 61:1–2 and gave a brief commentary. He employed the verb "to preach" three times within a few minutes.

The setting was a synagogue service of some kind. The rabbis were gathered for the usual service. Their custom was to invite guests to read from the Scriptures. Jesus was their guest, and so they asked him to read. His response in that exact setting is instructive, at least to a degree, for the reading and commenting on Holy Scripture. That his own mission included preaching is a significant precedent for understanding our own practice.

On numerous occasions Jesus referred to preaching, both his own and that of his disciples, as a primary feature of his mission (Matt. 4:17;

---

is expected to arrive. Craddock believes, as do other homileticians, that preachers should move beyond rational thought with preaching. Cf. Richard Eslinger, *A New Hearing: Living Options in Homiletic Method* (Nashville: Abingdon, 1987), pp. 95–132.

15. Perhaps we should remind ourselves that, if the congregation has no need for a sermon, they have no need for a preacher! That is not justification enough for retaining the sermon.

10:7, 27; 11:1; Mark 1:38; 3:14; Luke 4:18, 19, 43; 9:2, 60). In Matthew 4:17–23, Matthew 11:1, and Acts 15:35, the terms "preaching" and "teaching" appear together, apparently referring to the same activity. Jesus' greatest "sermon" is presented by Matthew (chaps. 5–7) as a lesson, yet is remembered as the Sermon on the Mount.

Jesus' preaching included doctrine. In the Sermon on the Mount, immediately following the Beatitudes, he launched into a succession of references to the Old Testament law (Matt. 5:17–48). He spoke of his own fulfillment of that law. Prayer and the kingdom of God dominate chapter 6. Judgment follows in chapter 7, then practical application of the entire contents of the sermon (especially 7:21–27). In his parables, especially those recorded in Matthew 13, Jesus emphasized the kingdom and the Word of God. Jesus came to establish the kingdom and the church (see especially Matt. 16:13–20). He came to announce that God had come to the human race in person. Indeed, doctrine was central in his preaching.

The church was born in preaching. On the Day of Pentecost, the first event after the coming of the Holy Spirit was a sermon (Acts 2:14–40). When Peter finished his sermon, the people immediately asked what they should do. Peter commanded them to repent and be baptized. That same day, three thousand souls were added to the church. In fact, day by day new converts were added to the number of believers. From the first, preaching has been prominent in the life of the church; it was the primary means of communicating the Good News about Jesus Christ.

Each major event involving the Holy Spirit also included preaching. Philip the Evangelist went to Samaria, where a great revival took place. Some have called it "the Samaritan Pentecost" (Acts 8:4–25). Simon Peter, the preacher of Pentecost, went to Caesarea Philippi and preached to those whom Cornelius had gathered in his house specifically to hear from the Lord (Acts 10:1–48, especially v. 33). When the sermon concluded, the Holy Spirit came and those who believed were baptized. This event often is described as "the Gentile Pentecost."

The church grew and expanded on the crest wave of its preaching. Indeed, the history of the growth of the early church is the history of its preaching.[16]

---

16. The sermons to which we refer in the Book of Acts are not recognized universally as sermons. Some scholars prefer to designate them as "speeches"; others question whether Peter and Paul actually delivered them. This discussion is not within the province of this work, but the authors acknowledge the issue. See Dennis L. Phelps, *Implications of Lucan-Peter's Pentecost Homily for Christian Preaching of the Old Testament*, unpublished Ph.D. diss., Southwestern Baptist Theological Seminary, 1990. Whatever one's position, preaching includes proclamation, evangelizing, teaching, witnessing, declaring, speaking, and the like, found so frequently in the Book of Acts.

Uppermost in the minds of the apostles was the telling of the Good News of the resurrection of Jesus. Following Pentecost, each time Peter and John confronted the crowds or the authorities, they gave witness to the resurrection (Acts 3:11–26; 4:8–12). The most notable convert in the Book of Acts, Saul of Tarsus, followed this same practice. He engaged in dialogue with the philosophers on Mars Hill (Acts 17:22–31) and testified to his own conversion (Acts 22:1–21; 26:1–23). These accounts we properly may label as sermons. Each makes specific application and calls for a response. Witness, then, was the distinctive feature of the first preachers of the first church. Preaching was central in the life of the congregation of the New Testament church.

The second spiritual reason for retaining preaching is that it relates to the nature of religion, of Christianity, of the human, of the gospel. The Bible speaks of universal truth—what is always and universally true. The preacher, who is the interpreter, searches for that eternal, the "always," of the Scripture as he or she prepares to preach. Sermon preparation is incomplete without the discovery of that eternal quality. This dimension is unique to preaching. It touches the eternal, the soul, the heart, the person. Such is the nature of Scripture. Its meaning is not frozen in words. It springs to life when read or spoken due to the work of the Spirit. God spoke to humanity about the eternal. Preaching alone among the forms of speech communication partakes of the Word of God. In a strange way the Spirit breathes life into the preacher's words and they live; they stand up and march into the consciences of those who hear. This dynamic quality of preaching is what preachers should remember and retain as they make or renew their commitment to the preaching of the Word of God. No other ancient words so live when restated. In our preaching, God speaks again. This does not mean that as we create our sermons we are creating new revelation or that our words are equal to or synonymous with Scripture. We are not adding to the Bible or creating a new Bible. We are retelling the words of God and he makes them live again, as he did the first time he spoke them. We help it happen. That is part of our calling and responsibility as ministers. We dare to speak for God.[17]

The third spiritual reason for retaining preaching is that it has nurtured, sustained, and brought revival to the church throughout the history of Christianity. History verifies the value of preaching for the various aspects of the life of the church. Some of the great advances of the church have come, in part, through preaching. Luther and Calvin recalled the church to the Word, thus precipitating a renewal and creating a reformed tradition in the history of the church. Luther's theme

---

17. See Wallace Fischer, *Who Dares to Preach?* (Minneapolis: Augsburg, 1979).

was justification by faith (Hab. 2:4; Rom. 1:17). Calvin's theme was the sovereignty of God. The Anabaptists stressed eschatological themes in their preaching. English Baptists were concerned to recover the "true church." The Reformers were disturbed that the church had strayed from the central issues, doctrinal issues. In their preaching and teaching they were dedicated to the recovery of the life and power of the church.

Eighteenth-century preachers continued the emphasis on doctrine. Jonathan Edwards, for example, followed the teachings of Calvin and contended for the sovereignty of God. He also preached on the judgment of God. His sermon "Sinners in the Hands of an Angry God" is one of the most famous in the history of preaching. Edwards' preaching also helped begin the First Great Awakening in America.

At the same time, across the Atlantic, John Wesley was promulgating the evangelical revival in England. His prominent theme was salvation. His revivals prompted numerous social and moral reforms as well. Wesley's method of teaching spawned a new denomination, the Methodists. Among his converts was John Newton, author of the well-known hymn "Amazing Grace." A contemporary of Wesley, George Whitefield, also became a famous evangelist, in both England and America. A distinguishing characteristic of his preaching was his call for repentance.

Throughout the nineteenth century preaching enjoyed a central place in the history of the church. Dargan referred to it as the greatest age of preaching.[18] Clyde Fant termed it the "golden age of preaching."[19] The one preacher who was most responsible for such glowing descriptions was Charles Haddon Spurgeon. At a time when life was good and doctrine was unpopular, thousands flocked to hear the new pastor in London preach. The doctrine of God's sovereignty was central in his preaching. His sermons and treatises on the fundamentals of the faith are well-known elements of the "Downgrade" controversy, which affected Baptists throughout Britain. To Spurgeon, the doctrines of the church mattered enough that he risked losing fellowship with other Baptists by expressing his convictions.

Doctrinal controversy continued well into the twentieth century. Harry Emerson Fosdick became the lightning rod for the struggle when he published his article "What Is the Matter with Preaching?" in 1928.[20] Clarence Macartney, among others, argued that the way to have a pure

18. E. C. Dargan, *A History of Preaching* (Grand Rapids: Baker, 1954–74), vol. 2, pp. 350–51.

19. Fant, *Preaching for Today*, pp. 350–51.

20. Harry Emerson Fosdick, "What Is the Matter with Preaching?"

church life was to hold correct doctrine. Thus he preached doctrinal sermons in an effort to make, or keep, the church pure.[21]

The common element in these historical references is the importance of doctrine. The church always loses strength and influence when it strays from the essentials of the faith. All the church's ministries should have their beginning in correct doctrine. When other themes control preachers and their preaching, the power of the church and individual churches wanes.

The history of preaching indicates that a revival of the church can come through a renewal of doctrinal preaching. It is necessary for the health of the church to declare the contents of the faith. Other themes, valuable as they are, should derive from, not replace, doctrinal sermons. Christian action springs from worship and knowledge of theology.

Practical

Primary among the practical values of preaching is its utility; it is universally usable. No special equipment or staging is needed; it can be done anywhere. Wherever one can stand up and speak, one can preach. There is no need for additional support or preparation. No set time is necessary. Day or night, a preacher may preach. Preaching accomplishes what it does by means of verbal proclamation alone. The delivery, not to mention the preparation, belongs only to the minister who speaks.

In addition, preaching can be responsive to the moment of delivery in a way that no audio- or videorecording, or group, can do. The preacher, during the actual presentation of the sermon, can sense a right moment to conclude more quickly than planned and move directly to an appeal for response. The preacher can pause and acknowledge an interruption, such as a baby's crying, or an emergency, or a sudden movement of the Holy Spirit. The preacher may invite spontaneous participation in the sermon. The personal element in preaching cannot be carried by impersonal presentations, or by groups in drama, for example. Preaching is not prepared or rehearsed in exactly the same manner as other kinds of proclamation. Preaching is a truly dialogical form of communication.

A third practical value of preaching is its applicability; it applies to human life. Evidence abounds, today as well as in the past, that the gospel changes life.[22] Also, people still testify that the study of the Bible and

---

21. Clarence Edward Macartney, *The Faith Once Delivered* (New York: Abingdon-Cokesbury, 1952), p. 5.

22. The recent conversion of Jane Roe of *Roe v. Wade* fame has intensified this discussion.

attendance at worship, even listening to sermons, make a difference in life. The current "Promise Keepers" phenomenon reveals the hunger for spiritual matters, at least in America. The program is unashamedly based on Scripture and scriptural teaching. Thousands of men and boys gather to listen to speakers tell them from the Bible how to be better men. Programs similar to Promise Keepers are springing up in other parts of the world. The international conference on women's issues in Beijing in 1995, though not a religious gathering, employed speakers for the presentation of the issues concerning women. Response and debate were done via oral communication.

The history of preaching also verifies the claim of applicability. Spurgeon heard the word "Look up and be saved." Wesley's heart was strangely warmed as he heard Luther's commentary on Romans 1:17. Moody responded to a Sunday school teacher. In our own century the conversion of Billy Graham, Charles Colson, and other public persons such as Johnny Cash validate the claims made first in Scripture.

Good preaching does that; it applies; it lasts; it requires some living out during the week; it creates pastoral ministry opportunities. Harry Emerson Fosdick found his office full of persons who needed counseling—persons who heard him preach and knew, from his sermons, that he cared. Other ministers have, or could have, the same experience.

Fourth, preaching also has value as a means of teaching doctrine. This function of proclamation undergirds and extends the education ministries of the church. Acts 2:42–47 states that the new believers "devoted themselves to the apostles' teaching and to the fellowship." C. H. Dodd's argument that preaching and teaching were completely different, that preaching was evangelism and that teaching was discipleship, was answered by Robert H. Mounce, who pointed out that often the words *didachē* and *kerygma* were used interchangeably in the New Testament to refer to the same event.[23]

The apostles' teaching ("doctrine" in the KJV) is a reference to the contents of the faith of the first believers, which the apostles felt an obligation to pass along to the new converts. The "doctrine" consisted of summaries of the teachings of Jesus, which they had received firsthand while they served with him during his sojourn on earth.

Thus the task of preaching continues beyond the point of conversion and baptism. Preachers also have a solemn duty to instruct believers in the essentials of the Christian life. Teaching is a function of preaching.

---

23. Robert Mounce, *The Essential Nature of New Testament Preaching* (Grand Rapids: Eerdmans, 1960), pp. 40–43. The purpose of this book will not be accomplished by rehashing that discussion. We note it here to stress that the two, preaching and teaching, are not mutually exclusive terms.

Evangelistic sermons are a necessity, but so are series of sermons on discipleship and the doctrines of Scripture. The numerous letters of the apostle Paul in the New Testament, perhaps sermons themselves, provide an example of this practice. He also urged Timothy to teach doctrine (2 Tim. 4:1–16).

Fifth, preaching is essential to the mission of the church; it is an integral part of the church's mission. Jesus came preaching the gospel of the kingdom of God (Mark 1:14–15, 38), and then sent his disciples to preach (Mark 3:14). Following the resurrection, the first apostles, who were scattered after persecution began in Jerusalem "went everywhere preaching the word" (Acts 8:4). Their story is a story of bearing witness to faith in the risen Lord. On his missionary journeys, Paul preached in the synagogues and in the streets, then established churches to continue the spread of Christianity. Local churches are established and nurtured by preaching.

Sixth, preaching is necessary for the establishment of the identity of the church. It is a part of the uniqueness of the church. Local churches still are known by their preachers and their preaching. If the church merely duplicates what other organizations in culture do, what makes the church different?[24] The church should be clearly distinct from other organizations that offer recreation, entertainment, stimulation, and a place to find release. The church alone speaks for God. The most popular television preachers still make preaching the centerpiece of their broadcasts. Billy Graham's organization edits video in order to broadcast the entire sermon. The most famous public preachers still preach.

Seventh, preaching continues to hold a prominent, if not central, place in the life of the evangelical church. Attendance in local church worship services that feature preaching furnishes proof that interest in preaching has not disappeared. Moreover, pastoral search committees in local churches continue to place a premium on preaching when they search for a new pastor.

Finally, the results of preaching stand as the starkest reminders of its effectiveness. From the days of the prophets who spoke for God the power of the spoken word is evident. Kings have trembled in response to it; God's own people have bowed in submission to it; entire nations have been revived through response to it. When Jesus preached and taught, even his critics stood in awe of his words. In response to the witness of Peter and John to the resurrection thousands believed, the crippled walked, and their opponents could not deny its effect.

We may conclude, on the basis of this examination of the value of preaching, that church life develops more completely when its preach-

24. See chapter 2.

ing is controlled by doctrinal orientation. This conclusion perhaps will prompt reconsideration of some current widespread practices in local churches. Omission of emphases on repentance, confession, salvation, and discipleship eventually will weaken the church. Though the church must be sensitive to those we attempt to reach, and though we must learn to communicate with our culture, we should not sacrifice the essentials of the faith in order to do so. Sermons, at times, must confront. Worship should include a balance of emotional emphases. Sorrow, remorse, and mourning reflect the mood of many of the psalms and confessions found in the Bible (see the Book of Lamentations), and provide a contrast to the joy, forgiveness, and praise. Worship that seeks only to bring affirmation, celebration, and anonymity for worshipers, and which omits altogether correction, condemnation, and instruction in righteousness so necessary for all, excludes some of the biblical teachings about humanity's relating to God. Worship, to be sure, should give worshipers a sense of belonging, happiness, and affirmation. To do so to the exclusion of confrontation, admonition, and exhortation, however, may be too great a price in order to boost sagging attendance or to create a new mood in a congregation.

The church, as an institution, no longer enjoys the fame and influence it once had, at least in American culture and other parts of the Western world. Allegiance to it appears to be waning. The church is held to have become antiquated, a remnant and icon of the past. Except for some political activism, the church appears not to be a formative influence in the life of the nation or of individuals. With old hymns, sermons filled with historical information, and church life constructed on the principles of a book thousands of years old, the church risks a plea of guilty to the charge of irrelevance.

What, then, should we do? Do we accommodate ourselves to culture in order to attract persons back to the church? The necessity of relating to the congregation[25] may overshadow the imperative to "preach the Word" as traditionally understood. Do preachers change the way we do preaching? Relational preaching, best done without the benefit of a pulpit, leaves the impression that a minister who stands behind a pulpit and thunders the message from God is a relic of the past and a reminder of "church." The thunder-and-lightning sermons of frontier revivalism surely would pose a threat to churchgoers of the twentieth century.

25. Often labeled "behavioral" or "relational" preaching. See D. Stephenson Bond, *Interactive Preaching* (St. Louis: CBP, 1991), by a pastor who is also a counselor. This work is reminiscent of Reuel Howe's *The Miracle of Dialogue* (Greenwich, Conn.: Seabury, 1963), and Clyde Reid's *The Empty Pulpit: A Study of Preaching as Communication* (New York: Harper, 1967).

Should we give up on preaching altogether? Preaching lends credence to the importance of the Word of God and the spoken proclamation of the gospel.

This chapter began with a consideration of the nature of preaching in order to raise the question: What is the preacher attempting to do and to say? The same question may be asked of the church. We wish to speak a word to our time, to contextualize the gospel, but to avoid becoming a captive of culture instead of a voice to it. God calls the preacher to speak for him. The church was put in place by Jesus to have a part in the extension of the kingdom (Matt. 16:13–20). The church's mission includes, among other tasks, preaching.

Local churches, indeed, prioritize their ministries. Some churches streamline their schedules of activities in order to decrease the demands made on faithful members, or in response to the reality that members select activities in which they participate. Churches may respond to the lack of participation by discontinuing programs. Others attempt more social action ministries instead of the traditional missions education organizations and study groups. The pastor eventually is confronted with difficult questions: "And what do I do about my preaching? What is preaching's relation to the other features of church life?"

Sunday morning worship, complete with preaching, may soon be the only major gathering of the membership for an entire week. Additional meetings take place in homes and other locations, such as counseling centers, food distribution centers, or halfway houses. Thus the pastor and other worship leaders have the additional responsibility of preparing for the one occasion on which they will speak to the gathered church. Minimal time for preaching in that one service means minimal opportunity to communicate the demands and contents of the faith, even to church members.

The pastor usually is the one person who, more than any other, decides the importance of preaching in relation to the other ministries of the church. If it is not of great importance to the preacher, then it very well may be lost as a significant factor in the life of the church. Have the world and the church changed so radically that we no longer need preaching, because it is no longer relevant or necessary? The Scriptures, the history of the church, and the testimonies of millions require us to say that we need preaching as much as ever.

Clyde Fant was right: There is a certain stubbornness about preaching. It refuses to go away.[26] We cannot give up preaching without giving up an essential part of the life of the church.

26. Fant, *Preaching for Today*, pp. 21–22: "Preaching, then, has a double stubbornness: it is stubbornly the same, and it is stubbornly there."

5

Obstacles to Preaching

In a previous chapter, we stressed that preaching is vitally important to the Christian life and the life of the church. In many ways, this is truer now than ever before. Yet, paradoxically, effective preaching is difficult to achieve, and perhaps more so now than ever because of the presence of numerous obstacles. Some of the obstacles the preacher must overcome are inherent in preaching, while others are products of unique factors of culture. The presence of these difficulties does not mean that preaching cannot be done successfully in our time, but knowing the nature of the problems can help us better prepare ourselves and deal with them. The difficulty manifests itself at several different points, which we need to observe carefully.

Listener Obstacles

The lifestyle and the mentality the worshiper brings to a sermon today may be quite different from that of thirty, twenty, or even ten years ago. Many of the changes in society and in individuals are positive from the perspective of preaching, but probably a majority are detrimental to the preaching process.

General Characteristics

1. Apathy. Members of congregations are concerned about practical matters. Doctrine is abstract, theoretical, and does not really "matter." Practicality is a primary consideration in almost every area of life. From self-diagnosis and treatment of medical problems to building a sun deck, families and individuals prefer to do it themselves. Local bookstores accommodate this preference by filling their shelves with

best-selling "how-to" books. Shoppers grab them and go home to "do" something.

Doctrine is not, by definition, utilitarian. Theology requires doing, but reflection and evaluation precede the doing. Thus, even church members develop an "I don't care" attitude. Without step-by-step instructions they lose interest, no matter what or how important the subject. Pastors who attempt to package the Christian life and offer guarantees for its success, as though it only required some assembly, complicate this issue further. The preacher who asks listeners to think appears laughable by comparison. Stated simply, church members have grown apathetic about spiritual matters due to the influence of our highly pragmatic culture. Society teaches them to enjoy life, not how to have life. The church comes off as drab, uninteresting, and irrelevant as it pleads with people to tend to the realm of the spirit.

2. Superstar mentality. Culture's worship of the superstar indirectly creates an obstacle for doctrinal preaching. Professional athletes have become the newest folk heroes of the American culture. Media have made them high-profile persons. Advertisers pay for the use of their names to sell everything from basketball shoes to rental cars. Entrepreneurs in other countries have learned from Americans. A tourist walking on a sidewalk in Berlin will see billboard pictures of Michael Jordan wearing a famous brand of underwear. Talk show hosts and hostesses dominate daytime and late night television programming. Talk radio radiates from the AM and FM dials. Dialogue is the order of the day, even in the print medium. Letters to the editor fill the opinion sections of major newspapers and national magazines.

The preacher, meanwhile, stands before the congregation and presents a message in a monological style, supported only by personal appearance and natural vocal production ability. Should the preacher adopt a talk show style in order to attract listeners? Should the style be less forceful because seekers will not tolerate a harsh, authoritative manner? Today's churches have the first generation of youth who had all their ministries conducted separate from adults, with Bible lessons presented in a talk show or other format designed to "communicate with today's youth," while their parents and other adults went to church. Now these youth have grown to adulthood and are sitting in the pews where their parents sat. They have a different perception of the role of the preacher. Thus preaching appears, to some at least, to be an antiquated activity; other media have become the primary means of communication.

3. Impatience. In the age of instant communication, listeners are anxious for speakers to get to the point without wasting a second. Television commercials introduce products, acquaint the viewer with them,

stimulate a desire to possess, and tell the eager customer where to find them at bargain prices, all in less than a minute. No one should wonder why persons who are conditioned by such fare grow increasingly impatient with preachers who plod through sermons, unfolding outline points that lead to a conclusion in about twenty minutes. The same listeners achieve quicker results in every medium of communication. Multimedia computers enable them to access databases for answers to the most complex problems within seconds. Interactive computers administer examinations and reveal test scores at the instant the student answers the last question. A university student took the Graduate Record Exam on computer and returned home with her scores in less time than it took a friend to take the written version of the exam in another university nearby. The friend waited six weeks for a report. Meanwhile, he decided that was too long, applied to take the exam by computer, and paid extra money in order to have the scores reported without delay. He completed the second exam before the results of the first one came in the mail.

Indeed, the preacher who announces a conclusion at the end of a sermon, even a short sermon, asks much from many in the congregation. The instant answer mentality poses a particular kind of threat to the minister who would preach a series and draw several conclusions in a final sermon.

4. Lack of commitment. At an earlier period of our history, commitment and loyalty were highly regarded qualities. In part this stemmed from a society in which most persons lived in small towns or neighborhoods of larger cities, where people knew each other and dealt with each other on a personal basis. People bought from the same merchant all the time. Some drove one make of car their whole lives. Because of the "reserve clause," a professional baseball player frequently stayed with one team for his entire career. Marriages were thought of as permanent commitments. Similarly, people joined a church and stayed with it, through good times and bad. People did not move very frequently, but if it was necessary to do so, one sought a church of the same denomination. Patriotism meant that one responded when one's country called for sacrifice.

These qualities are not nearly as present in our time, however. Persons change their shopping places when a store with lower prices opens. The make of an automobile is less important than its features and the "deal" one can obtain. Professional athletes become free agents and sell themselves to the highest bidder; teams release players because they can replace them with younger, less expensive players. Marriages are relatively temporary in many cases, as a spouse is exchanged for a

new, more desirable partner. Mobility among churches and denominations is the ecclesiastical manifestation of this lack of loyalty.[1]

5. Competition. Culture adds complications to the preaching of doctrinal sermons. One is competition. Due to the number of attractions
competing for attention, people, including church members, do not "attend" church as they once did. The church service no longer is "the"
event of the week as it once was in American public life. In colonial
America, for example, the general population gathered with believers at
the local meeting house in order to hear the preacher present the sermon. The preacher, after all, was educated and was a good public
speaker. Moreover, and of particular import for this book, the local par-
son was the resident theologian. The word emanating from the pulpit
carried great influence in village life. The pastor was personally influential as a community leader and the opinions he expressed helped
shape home and community life. The church, as an institution (joining
home, school, and government), was one of the cornerstones in the
structure of American society. Sermons provided instructions for believing and living.

Church and preacher no longer enjoy such prominence or influence
in social life today. The church building is one among many public
gathering places. The preacher is one among many outstanding, highly
educated professional speakers. Besides, with the advent of radio and
television,[2] those who formerly went to hear sermons now get them via
media. They often listen to them as they are driving to attend some
other event, such as a football game, or to visit relatives or friends in a
distant city.

These changes in religion are occurring at a time when the home is
also changing. Parents once received instruction in the faith at church
and taught their children at home. Now, parents relegate more and
more of the care and education of children to institutions outside the
home. Due to the changing nature of the institutions that have served
so long as cornerstones of our society, families now search for other
means of imparting values to family members. The function of the
church has been redefined as well. It no longer serves as a base for
learning.

6. Demands and concerns. Family, career, finances, world affairs,
and other concerns distract churchgoers. Decisions at every level of life
are made more difficult by the fragmentation of modern society. The
nuclear family is a thing of the past. With longer life expectancy, an individual may have up to three careers of twenty years or more. At a sem-

---

1. Leith Anderson, *Dying for Change* (Minneapolis: Bethany, 1990), pp. 46–50.
2. These are obstacles to preaching as well, and we discuss them later in this chapter.

inary where one of the authors taught, he had a student seventy-two years of age who had come for training in ministry. The man had already had two careers, had answered the call to the ministry, and wished to prepare for Christian service with the hearing impaired. The other author once had a seventy-four-year-old student, a retired public school superintendent who was now enrolled in the master of divinity program. This is not uncommon practice among business and professional persons.

Widespread economic hardship places great strain on individuals and families who incurred numerous debts when times were better. In some households every member holds a job; sometimes one family member holds down two jobs in order to meet financial obligations. When time comes to go to church, the need for rest or to take some time off prevents people from going to the meeting house. Even when they do go, they often are exhausted or stressed out, with their ability to listen to a sermon marginal at best.

The television age, with satellite transmission of news from around the world as it happens, creates stress for people that previous generations knew nothing about. With live coverage of the spectacular, people sit transfixed before their sets, their minds a long way from the service of the local church—and everything else local, for the moment. Those who turn off the news and attend worship often carry images and burdens with them that distract as they attempt to participate. For example, television riveted the pictures of starving men, women, and children in Somalia to the mind of the world. In homes, stores, and churches people were talking about the pitiable plight of the Somalis. Stress also ran high during Desert Storm, as families looked through the eyes of cameras at their own kin fight a war in real time. Viewers will not easily forget the sight of smart bombs finding their way into bunkers and buildings, with pinpoint accuracy. We shared the viewpoint of the pilots who flew the fighter bombers. What preacher hopes to capture the imagination of the congregation with descriptions of the "Holy Land" while the listeners recall images of the latest video reports from Jerusalem while it was under attack by SCUD missiles?

Characteristics Specifically Related to Listening

1. An aversion or, at best, an indifference to authority. At one time the preacher was considered an authority on religion, ethics, and various other subjects. This was true, in part, because in another generation the clergyman was frequently the best-educated person in the community. Thus, he was looked up to for his understanding of life as were few other individuals in the average person's acquaintance. Because the

preacher was better educated than the listener, the sermon was likely to be both informative and helpful. Certainly, he would be better informed than his listeners with respect to the contents of the Bible, which was regarded as a major repository of wisdom and truth. Indeed, even considerable culture might be conveyed in the well-read preacher's sermon.

All that has changed, and in several ways. For one thing, there are many more potential authorities whose insights are available to the average layperson today. The teacher, physician, and politician are as well educated as the pastor and in many cases more so. Like the child who has always regarded her parents as the source of all wisdom but now places as much or more stock in the pronouncements of her schoolteacher, the layperson today has many sources of authority from which to choose.

Moreover, the average layperson may choose to place his or her trust not in some external authority, but in oneself. The person who is the sage with the gems of wisdom is not the hero of today. Persons are learning to "trust the authority of their own experience," as one seminary student put it, rather than looking to the pinnacle of the all-knowing one. More and more persons are even choosing to make their own medical diagnoses, coming to the physician and stipulating what should be done. In some cases, this is accompanied by self-treatment. More and more popular journals and books are available to the public, and more medications can be purchased over the counter. One of the authors recently toured an American drugstore with a foreign physician. The doctor was appalled by the number of medications available without prescription.

This aversion to authority frequently results from the sense that everyone's opinion is as good as anyone else's, which is a sort of popular variety of relativism. This is reflected, for example, in the popularity of radio talk shows. People call in and express their opinion about any subject to a host or hostess, who is equally willing to hear and respond. When asked why they listen so eagerly to such programs, listeners give answers such as, "It's interesting to hear what different people think about things," or "You hear a lot of different angles on things." Opinion has become as important as fact.

In this situation, the preacher is perceived as someone who considers his or her word final. If the traditional view of preaching is correct, then the thoughts of persons other than the preacher are unnecessary. The idea that one person has the final truth is antithetical to the mood of the times. Thus, the word not only of the preacher but also of the God for whom he or she claims to speak is cast into suspicion.

2. Orientation to visual stimulation. Increasingly, the audiences a preacher faces have grown up on a visually stimulating diet. Television and multimedia presentations are common experience. Those who watch MTV may see several hundred images flashed on the screen within mere seconds. The viewer sees vivid color and movement, and constant change of scenes. The video-game craze fascinates young people. Some of them spend hours, whether in a video arcade or with their own games, engaged in battle, flight, or race (motorcycle or car) via computer joysticks. They learn to respond quickly to visual stimuli. By way of contrast, the sermon, even with movement and gestures, seems to be a rather static, slow-moving, dull event.

Influenced by the multimedia environment, people who attend church and listen to sermons have developed different expectations. So much of what they hear and see is entertainment-oriented that they expect something that entertains, or resembles entertainment, even at church. The preacher who insists on the traditional mode of sermon delivery risks losing hearers or having hearers who fail to comprehend the message because they fail to understand the medium. The one who fills preaching with heavy theological material encounters lack of interest in content as well. Minds massaged with images and words that leave nothing to the imagination can scarcely grasp concepts that require attention and thought. Cameras and editing techniques do all the work for them in movies and on television. They receive imagery, action, and speed in the messages.

What, then, is the minister to do? Perhaps we should understand preaching as an image event, as David Buttrick has proposed, in addition to thinking of it as a word event.[3] Building on the phenomenology of language, Buttrick suggests that the preacher employ "moves" instead of points in sermons.[4] Each move presents an image to the mind of the listener. His method, if followed, would require dramatic changes in preaching. Buttrick offers a method for preaching that takes into account the difficulty of communicating the message of the Bible to listeners who are accustomed to seeing as much as to hearing messages.

3. Movement, action. America's favorite pastime, baseball, has a low level of contact, proceeds slowly most of the game, and is a rather benign spectator sport. Football, basketball, hockey, and soccer, on the other hand, have fast-paced action with contact and provide excitement for the fans from the start. When viewed on television, their pace is intensified by numerous cameras that capture the action, instant re-

3. David Buttrick, *Homiletic: Moves and Structures* (Minneapolis: Fortress, 1989), pp. 113–25.
4. Ibid., pp. 23–28.

plays, and highlights of the most spectacular plays. Fans have a break only occasionally.

By comparison, the house of worship is a quiet, peaceful place, with a rather serious atmosphere. The preacher traditionally stands alone to present the sermon. Every word must be instantly intelligible, for no instant replay or rewind switch is available. All the action must come from the verbs and other elements of language employed by the preacher. The sermon is no team sport. Each individual present participates at a level that he or she chooses.

4. Attraction to the spectacular. The media generation has developed a love for the spectacular. Basketball players have slam dunk contests with high-flying stunts that border on the incredible. When compared to the nonstop gyrations of dunking, the game they play appears relatively mild.

The appetite for the spectacular also has a tragic twist. Detailed media reports of the sensational and bizarre have created a morbid curiosity. Home videorecorders capture plane crashes and tornadoes. News organizations pay premium prices for such tapes in order to render eyewitness accounts of destruction and death. Amateur photographers occasionally risk death to capture cyclones on film or tape. A public television station recently presented a one-hour program about tornadoes that consisted mostly of videos of actual storms. One of the reporters pointed a camcorder at a tornado that was coming toward the taping crew. At the last possible second before the revolving black funnel hit them, the reporter and crew dived under a highway overpass, where other travelers had already sought refuge. All the while the recording continued, enabling viewers at a later time to watch the tornado fly by, roaring, twisting, turning, and throwing debris in every direction. Capitalizing on the public appetite for the morbid, news radio stations report on the nationwide death toll during every holiday weekend.

A sermon may appear to be a ho-hum event alongside a report on the spectacular. The preacher faces the difficulty of maintaining the interest of persons who constantly are treated to the level of sensationalism they are willing to endure. The Bible has a message of a different kind, to be sure, and some of its stories are every bit as spectacular as today's news, but the preacher has no live report via satellite from a news reporter on the scene or pictures from someone who was present. Still, the preacher should have no desire to be sensational merely for the sake of doing so. The traditional sermon is still an explanation, illustration, and application of a text, presented for a purpose other than to titillate the senses.

5. Short attention span. Accompanying the inclination toward the visual is a short attention span. The average news story on CNN is only

about one minute in duration. The producers of a local television newscast in a major market inserted a feature summarizing world news with the caption: "Around the world in a minute." Soon a competing station in the same market followed suit, but their summary took only fifty-five seconds! Politicians, too, have learned that their messages must be delivered in "sound-bites," usually lasting only three to five seconds. A sermon, on the other hand, lasts twenty to thirty minutes and deals with one subject. A parallel event would be an entire news broadcast devoted to just one story, with no commercial interruptions.[5] This type of discourse frequently depends for its effectiveness on the listener paying attention to several steps in the development of the argument, demanding of the listener what he or she may be incapable of performing. Each listener must follow a logical presentation, carefully piecing together the bits of information as the sermon progresses toward a conclusion.

6. Lack of imagination. Earlier generations depended on radio for much of their entertainment. Some families today have one or more television sets running continuously. This medium is ever present and its effects on persons are extensive. Early radio featured serial dramas and required that listeners use their imaginations, creating images of what they were hearing and filling in details that otherwise could only be given in a book or visual presentation. Such use of the imagination is not required in the television age. Even with the visual stimulus of television, the cameraman and the director decide what will be seen and heard, the angle from which it will be viewed, and which characters become prominent. By contrast, the preacher, whether dealing with a narrative or a didactic passage, has to call upon listeners to form their own mental images of what they are hearing. Preaching seems strangely out of date, like a 1940s radio drama.

Preacher Obstacles

Just as there are difficulties for the preaching event from the listener's side, so there are obstacles from the other end of the communication process, that of the preacher.

External

1. Time and priority pressures, multiple demands. Time pressures bear on the minister's preparation. The number of separate speaking

---

5. The British Broadcasting Company in the United Kingdom still does this. Often they present an actor who tells a story, thirty minutes long, with only two camera angles and no background video or other support.

occasions in the preacher's week is now considerably fewer than in the past. Whereas most evangelical preachers even a decade or two ago had to prepare for two messages each Sunday and a midweek Bible study, that is rapidly becoming less common; many preachers now prepare only a Sunday morning message. Yet, paradoxically, we are in many cases getting less well-prepared sermons because the pastoral ministry has in recent years become considerably more complex; the minister has more difficulty finding uninterrupted time for sermon preparation.

One may account for this difficulty, in part, by noting the increase of social problems that make demands on a pastor's time. The average pastor is deluged with problems of a type, scope, and frequency seldom found in the past: marital and family problems, crime, drug abuse, and many others. Frequently, the pastor is the first person to whom people turn in time of need, the only one who will come in a time of emergency, and the only one many feel they can afford.

The changing pastoral role is also a major factor. The pastor as spiritual teacher and helper/healer is being replaced by the pastor as chief executive officer of a business, the local church. Success is measured less by changes in human lives than by numbers. Planning, leading, and managing take a higher priority than does study for sermons.

2. Pressure to succeed. The pressure to succeed, even in the church, has reached a feverish level of intensity in American culture. For the preacher this pressure comes at a bad time, because the culture is unresponsive as a rule. Researchers report that the population is rather cynical and skeptical about church, religion, and religious figures.

Temptation is strong to alter the message and even the nature of the church in order to attract and win people. The coffeehouse and dinner theater ministries of a former generation, usually mission outreach arms of local churches, have become churches. Groups now meet in vacant shopping mall buildings, hotel conference rooms, and other public spots—not to do missions as an outreach of a mother church or to start new units, but in order to avoid giving the appearance of "church." Discussions have replaced Sunday school lessons, group leaders and facilitators have edged out ministers, and topical presentations on current issues, both social and personal, have taken the place of sermons.

When one such ministry "succeeds," the person serving as executive pastor usually becomes a regular on the conference circuit, instructing others how to do ministry in exactly the same manner. Those who follow the pattern, naturally, expect to succeed, even though they are in different locations with different people and cultures.

3. Pragmatism. A corollary to success is numbers. The successful pastor has the numbers; they are always increasing. Should the numbers discontinue their unending spiral upward, the preacher feels pressure, perhaps self-imposed, to correct whatever problems caused them to stop and to get them moving upward again. A church in a large metropolitan area, whose senior minister performed dramatic healings as a regular feature of the church's worship, attracted large numbers of people. The minister was accused of paying indigents to come to services and "be healed" in order to maintain the attraction.

Internal

1. Lack of training. A minister of the gospel may have relatively little or no training in drama, literary theory, or the way people learn. Seminaries offer training in the classics and practical ministry. The typical curriculum includes a basic course in sermon preparation, followed by a practicum in which the student delivers one or two sermons. Only in elective offerings does the seminarian find opportunity to "experiment" with variety in the form and style of preaching. A few seminaries offer doctoral degree majors in homiletics, with programs of study and research in innovative preaching.

While the persons who attend worship grow more and more sophisticated in their listening habits and expectations, preachers continue to serve up sermons that resemble those prepared for homiletics class. The weekly fare comes from notes taken in Bible class, checked against the rubrics of systematic theology and filled with illustrations from life experience. The hermeneutics professor's lectures about the various genres found in the Bible and proposals for ways in which those forms could contribute to variety in sermons might be helpful, but the pastor has little time for creativity and innovation because of a crowded schedule and incessant demands to perform pastoral duties.

2. Uncertainty about role. The numerous hats the pastor is forced to wear may create or intensify uncertainty about his or her role. Church congregations expect the minister to serve as administrator, counselor, pastor, family person, community person, moderator, and role model for discipleship, in addition to being the master communicator of God's Word. A pastor who serves such a congregation can only admire and envy at a distance the megachurch leader who serves as executive minister and functions between preaching engagements as a kind of CEO.

Meanwhile, the prestige of the minister continues to decline generally in culture. No longer does the pastor of the county seat church enjoy instant recognition and a degree of fame throughout the entire region, as did preachers of another era.

Ministers themselves are to blame, one could argue. Some have tried literally to "be all things to all people." That attempt in itself has helped erect another obstacle as the preacher tried to determine how to relate to culture.

3. Ambiguity with respect to culture. How can a spokesperson for God be prophetic to a public that ignores preachers? Surely, one must participate in culture to some degree in order to address it.[6] Yet, one who accommodates culture cannot stand outside it and speak to it. The distance between "the voice in the wilderness" and the "echo" is substantial, and some ministers attempt to traverse it each week, seeking to affirm culture in one sermon and trying to exploit it in another.

4. Uncertainty about the relationship among style, form, and content. Our society emphasizes the importance of the communicator and elevates the role of style in the communication process. In television attractive people appear as spokespersons for products and causes. In radio the voice is paramount. A young applicant for a job at a local station was turned away with the comment: "You are just not the voice we are looking for."

The preacher's seminary professors, on the other hand, stressed the importance of the message, in particular the message of the Bible. Form is significant, but form is no good unless it delivers something. John the Baptist and Paul, according to the few references in Scripture to appearance, probably were quite unattractive. The Baptist warned his generation of the approaching wrath of God and had the privilege of introducing Jesus at the beginning of his public ministry. Paul cried, "Am I become your enemy because I tell you the truth?" and carries the distinction as the "apostle to the Gentiles." Message content was dominant in each ministry.

Thus the preacher faces another dilemma involving style as opposed to content. In fact, the minister should strive for both elements.

5. Lack of clarity about goals. A bewildering array of options for styles of ministry and preaching may cause a lack of clarity about the local church and preaching. For one thing, what can one hope to achieve in a sermon? The preacher must have more in mind than simply to communicate or to relate. Each sermon needs a specific aim. Sermon purposes may range from the evangelistic to a wide variety of pastoral aims.[7] The minister who serves up stories, personal experiences, topical discussions, current events, dramatic monologues, and interviews, as listeners want, should have a specific purpose for each ser-

6. See Clyde Fant's discussion in *Preaching for Today* (New York: Harper and Row, 1987), pp. 84–85.

7. See Jay Adams, *Preaching with Purpose* (Nashville: Abingdon, 1988).

mon. Listeners may not be able to comprehend purpose in sermons that are completely inductive or indirect.[8] The good sermon makes application to life, in addition to communicating a truth from Scripture. Unless the minister tells them directly, some listeners never will discover the meaning or application on their own.

While the crowds gather to hear the innovative preacher, the preacher who delivers traditional sermons watches the size of the congregation dwindle Sunday by Sunday. Dozens join the church with the creative pastor; few come in response to the same old sermons. People are talking all over town about the exciting church they attend and bragging about the minister there. Do the numbers alone make a church? One is left to wonder.

Perhaps the preacher can no longer believe that preaching can do the same things it previously has done. Culture has redefined the "good sermon." It is one that makes the listener feel good about self. The church where the preacher seeks to please the hearers has hundreds, even thousands, in attendance every week. What is a preacher to do? The choices seem clear: Maintain the traditional or change strategy and watch the numbers increase.

At the same time, the minister may ask whether preaching is merely intended to satisfy those who hear so that more people will come to hear the sermons. Will that kind of preaching, often aimed at the "unchurched," teach members the content of the Christian faith? Many members of local churches do not know what they believe.[9] This is a tragedy for both them and their churches. Perhaps the fault lies with preaching.[10] The crisis "has resulted in large measure from the loss of a persuasive message clearly proclaimed in the power of the Holy Spirit."[11]

Preachers should seriously consider these claims and, if they are true, find a remedy. If church members do not know the content of their faith and if preachers are partly to blame, then we should resolve to take corrective measures immediately. One step in the right direction is to preach each sermon with a clearly defined purpose in mind. One such purpose should be that church members know what they believe.

8. This raises a major question related to biblical authority. How much of the Bible must a sermon contain to have biblical authority? Conversely, if a sermon clarifies and applies a teaching of the Bible, is it not a good biblical sermon? The authors address these issues in other chapters. For example, is the topical sermon, in fact, a biblical sermon?

9. This is the thesis of a book by William J. Carl III, *Preaching Christian Doctrine* (Atlanta: John Knox, 1985).

10. A charge made by Timothy George, in "Doctrinal Preaching," in *Handbook of Contemporary Preaching*, ed. Michael Diduit (Nashville: Broadman, 1992), pp. 93–102.

11. Ibid., p. 93.

Christianity risks losing its distinctiveness as people sample religions from around the world and select the tenets of their belief from numerous sources. This eclectic approach to formulating one's faith has led to increasing levels of tolerance and blurred the distinctive nature of Christianity.[12] One very good reason to preach doctrinal sermons is to delineate the unique character of Christianity.[13]

Church Obstacles

The church has created a number of obstacles to doctrinal preaching for itself, even if inadvertently.

Internal

1. There is a lack of emphasis on doctrine, that formal expression of what the local church believes. Some churches subscribe to a general statement of doctrine, or confession, which may be denominational in nature, but these same churches never precisely state or recite their beliefs in an orderly fashion. Conversely, they never require individual members to express the essence of their faith. How, then, can one know the content of the faith of an individual church? Pastors and churches can no longer assume that people who currently hold membership know what a church believes. Churches that carefully compose and advertise requirements for membership, job descriptions for staff members, policy manuals, and constitutions and bylaws fail to publicize their doctrine.

Some practices at the local church level and beyond, such as ordination of ministers and annual doctrinal sermons, have, in the past, stressed the importance of belief for individuals and churches. These exercises have been changed or eliminated and the change of practice creates the impression that basic doctrines held in common by the churches now hold less importance. Commitment to such a body of beliefs, however, is the very foundation of church and denominational identity.

2. In fact, denominational identity itself is a critical matter in the present generation. Lack of denominational loyalty, now common among even the largest of denominations, is a second internal obstacle

---

12. As one of us points out in another chapter of this book, church members no longer declare what they believe, that is, what they have in common with other believers, and form their congregations on the basis of common doctrine. This loss of commonality surely undermines unity.

13. See the discussion of this point in chapter 4, "The Place of Preaching in the Life of the Church."

worthy of consideration.[14] Young singles and young family members consider style of worship as one of the primary criteria in the choice of a church—if, in fact, they even go to church.[15] Denomination has little or nothing to do with the choice. In response, some ministers and churches are dropping those parts of their names that identify them with a particular denomination; they have, for all practical purposes, become nondenominational.[16] Given no clearly defined denomination, a preacher will have difficulty articulating a characteristic theology. Some observers have declared that denominationalism is a thing of the past. If they are correct, the set of beliefs that unite individual churches becomes less important. The doctrinal sermon becomes less necessary; the church loses one of its high-profile forums. One of the ways of expressing those beliefs, the doctrinal sermon, also loses one of its reasons for existence.

The "community" church trend and the identification of churches by names other than denominational labels enlarge this obstacle. Words such as "Temple," "Tabernacle," "Fellowship," and "Assembly" now identify places formerly known as "Churches." These are good words, but they are generic. A church sign that includes the word "Presbyterian," "Methodist," or "Baptist" makes a statement about the theological persuasion of the body that gathers there. The emphasis, with the designation of "Community" for example, is on gathering instead of believing. While the gathering of persons before God is important, an assembly ought also to believe something, ought to have a theology. That being true, a church should be identifiable by its "beliefs."

The idea of community clearly is a biblical one as Acts 2 makes clear. At the same time, the sense of belonging in the first New Testament congregation was created, to a great degree, by adherence to the "apostles' teaching and doctrine" (Acts 2:42). Belief does matter. If a congregation

14. A survey conducted among the student body of the world's largest seminary indicated a very low level of loyalty to the denomination. Most of the students are from the South, where denominationalism is more alive than in many other parts of the country, and more than 90 percent of them are from the Southern Baptist Convention, which has traditionally had a very high level of denominational loyalty and even exclusivism.

15. See the discussion of this subject in the chapter on the place of preaching in the church.

16. In an article published in an official news organ of the Home Mission Board of the Southern Baptist Convention prior to the annual meeting in 1993, the president of the Convention was quoted as saying that, if he were just beginning his church, he would probably not call it a Baptist church. Response to the statement was low level and the president was elected to a second term without a serious question during the Convention session in which he was elected to the customary second year of service. Mike Livingston, "Houston's Exciting Second," *Missions U. S. A.* 64.5 (May–June, 1993): 14.

should say it does not matter, that community surely offers something as the unifying factor of church life.[17] Doctrine, as well as fellowship, makes a church—and a denomination.

Lack of loyalty to a denomination or a church carries over to the commitment to a particular preacher as well. The ease with which churchgoers may choose everything else applies to the local preacher whom they go to hear. Should the listener hear one somewhere he or she likes better, then it is only a matter of driving in a different direction the next Sunday to hear another kind of minister. This practice of choosing on the basis of likes and dislikes can create a special kind of difficulty for the pastor who preaches series of sermons or through a book of the Bible, as is the case with expository preachers. The listeners who go to a different church each time they attend will never hear all of a series and may never know the whole of which one sermon is a part.

3. A third obstacle the church has erected for itself is the provision of multiple activities that are not exclusively or distinctively Christian. Many are duplicates of services offered by other agencies. Churches often fill their schedules with softball games, golf tournaments, pizza sales, and car washes while relegating spiritual matters to a smaller space. Worship planners often devote more time to announcements and promotion, usually repetition of the calendar of events, than they do to public reading of Scripture.

These practices may signal yet another change in the identification of churches, redefining them by what they do instead of by what they believe, hence lessening the need for doctrinal preaching. A church defines its character by doctrine.

Those activities that are, in fact, duplications of those offered elsewhere, may find competition from agencies that offer only activities. This underscores that some agencies are identified by what they offer. Should the church, then, worry that it will alter its identity by offering something to believe and a way to live?

Christians should be concerned about ministering to the whole person, not to the "soul" alone. This conviction doubtless drives the ministries of churches with multiple activities. At the same time, activity alone does not complete ministry.

---

17. In another chapter, one of these authors addresses the question of "easy believism" so prominent currently and provides an assessment of the perils it poses to unity. What, he asks, keeps the seekers from going to another location if one church fails to offer what they are seeking? Conversely, what is to keep a seeker from attending a different "church" service each week, in the same manner as the seeker attends theater or opera?

External

Some obstacles to preaching have been created by culture.

1. The first of these is the demand for instant relevance, for something that makes a difference "right now." People who do attend church do so for reasons other than to hear sermons.[18] Worship planners may worsen the plight by preparing the service in such a manner as to "give them what they want," thus decentralizing the sermon as the focal point of worship. Instead, worship matches the expectations of those who attend, which is a different style of worship. Other elements dominate; the sermon is but a small part of the entire service, coming in the middle of choruses, drama, and media presentations. Even if it is labeled "important," the sermon comes off as rather anemic when compared to the other elements. For that reason, some preachers have begun to employ different means of communicating the sermon, such as dramatic monologue, dialogue, and interview.[19]

2. Lack of interest in religion in general. Recent surveys around the world indicate that, except in a few countries where revival is taking place, people do not take religion seriously. They surely know very little about it. That is one reason they need doctrinal preaching.

3. Mobility. Travel is easy in the Western world. People who wish to hear sermons are willing to drive great distances to hear their favorite sermons. If they hear about a more popular preacher in another part of the city, they motor across town next time to hear for themselves. This practice lends itself to a lack of attachment to a specific church. Loyalty to a local congregation hardly exists with the ease of travel. Families may drive past five neighborhood churches to get to church. Moreover, some churches and pastors encourage the commuter mentality by locating their buildings near freeway interchanges and providing ample parking space, complete with security police to direct traffic and patrol the parking areas while car owners attend church. Others provide shuttle bus service from the parking lots to the main buildings. Location, not doctrine, becomes a major factor in the choice of church.

4. Changes in means and content of communication. Instantaneous communication on a global scale via cellular telephones, fax machines, and the information superhighway means that news more than five

18. Harry Emerson Fosdick declared, in a now famous 1928 article, that folks are not terribly anxious to hear what happened to the ancient Jebusites. "What Is the Matter with Preaching?" *Harpers Magazine* 157, no. 938 (July 1928): 135. He aimed that barb at preachers who never made contemporary applications in their sermons. No contemporary critic has repeated the charge in exactly the same language, but no one has to repeat it; people in this generation merely ignore the church and the sermon.

19. See Harold Freeman, *Variety in Biblical Preaching* (Waco, Tex.: Word, 1987) for a discussion of possible ways to present biblical sermons in innovative forms.

minutes old is old news. Consumers look for the latest information, and are conditioned to retrieve it for themselves. At the church, however, the preacher comes to the front and announces the news to them. Though this information is vital, the delivery may interfere with its reception.

Preaching today, however, must do more than overcome some external obstacles if it is to survive. Such things as television, computers, and other distractions are threats, even formidable obstacles, but what they have done to condition the minds and thought patterns of listeners may have more serious implications for the preacher.

Preachers may have to become willing to evaluate the content of their preaching. Are we willing to proclaim doctrine, even if it means rowing against the current, to risk being unpleasant? Some doctrine, such as the doctrine of sin, does not make people feel good until they face the bad. The emphasis on the moment, "be happy now," neglects some aspects of life. The one who speaks for God contends for a more holistic view of existence. Doctrine talks about sin before it speaks of forgiveness and restoration to wholeness. Scripture stresses the eternal rather than the temporal. How, then, do we formulate doctrinal sermons and present them to our generation? These are the concerns of the following chapters on sermon preparation.

Part **2**

Gathering the Doctrinal Content

6

Getting Doctrine from Didactic Passages

One type of final examination essay question one of the authors has frequently used is to imagine oneself moderating a debate on one of the major issues of theology. Exponents of several different views set forth their own views, then each criticizes the views of the others, after which each responds to each of these criticisms. Then the student, the moderator of the panel, is asked to summarize the debate, explaining the differences and the reasons for them, and indicate his or her own view. It is often challenging for the student. What is especially trying to some students is that each of several speakers may appeal strongly to the Bible in support of his or her view, yet they differ greatly. There may be at least two reasons for such a difference. Either the speakers may appeal to different passages, or they may deal with the same passages but draw radically different conclusions from them. How can this be, however?

If this is confusing to a seminary student, it is even more so for the average layperson. Imagine a debate on a subject such as baptism or sanctification, in which several speakers address the biblical basis for different positions. To the layperson, unable to evaluate the sophisticated arguments, such a discussion might seem not only confusing but unsettling as well. In the last two decades, a number of books have appeared that are symposia on various important theological issues of the Christian faith, such as the millennium, sanctification, human freedom, and divine sovereignty.[1] To the pastor-theologian, these are

---

1. E.g., *Predestination and Free Will: Four Views of Divine Sovereignty and Human Freedom*, ed. David Basinger and Randall Basinger (Downers Grove, Ill.: InterVarsity, 1986); *Four Views on Hell*, ed. William Crockett (Grand Rapids: Zondervan, 1992); *Christian Spirituality: Five Views of Sanctification*, ed. Donald Alexander (Downers Grove, Ill.: InterVarsity, 1988).

helpful in sorting out the alternatives, but also challenging, to make sure that one's own formulation of doctrines is both competent and accurate.

We noted that there may be two reasons for the differing conclusions of those who claim to base their doctrine on the Bible, either the selection of different passages or varying interpretations of those passages. A third would be somewhat different conceptions of the nature of the Bible and its authority. Each of these will need to be explored and resolved in the process of formulating one's own theology and the content of what one will declare to others.

The Nature of Didactic Doctrinal Passages

It is important that we distinguish between obtaining and formulating a doctrine and expressing it in a sermon. Irrespective of the method or the style of sermon employed, it is crucial that we determine the content of the doctrine taught by Scripture and to be expressed. It might seem this is most important when doing expository or more formal discursive preaching, and less so when giving a narrative or a dramatic sermon. Actually, the exact opposite is true. In a more discursive type of sermon, such as an expository sermon, the preacher consciously calls attention to the doctrinal issues to be dealt with. This in itself serves as a check on the agreement of the doctrinal content of the sermon with the doctrinal teachings of the Bible. There is an overt linking of the sermon with specific data of Scripture and a continual attempt to bridge between the two. In the narrative or dramatic sermon, on the other hand, there is not quite the same attempt to call attention consciously to specific data of the biblical text. Thus, "slippage" may more easily take place.

Doctrine can be obtained from different types of biblical passages. Some passages are narrative in nature, describing the occurrence of historical events. There are also didactic or teaching passages, in which the speaker or writer is definitely intending to teach something, often doctrinal in nature, to his audience. We should note as well that there are several different kinds of doctrinal assertions or didactic material. In so doing, it will become apparent that the distinction between narrative and didactic portions of Scripture is not quite so clear, sharp, and definite as we might think. This is because teaching portions of Scripture were addressed to specific situations and given in historical settings. We may have a considerable amount of detail regarding the setting, occasion, or flow of events surrounding the giving of that teaching. We have in mind here, however, those portions of the Bible in which prominence is given to what is said rather than to what is done. Generally, the statement will be prolonged, and the speaker will be conscious of what he is saying or writing and intentionally convey that.

Types of Didactic Passages

Having said this, we may note several types of didactic material in the Bible.

1. A didactic passage may be a statement from God. A message may come from God audibly, as in the case of Samuel (1 Sam. 3); more frequently, a prophet or apostle says something like, "The Word of the LORD came to me, saying . . ." (e.g., Jer. 1:4; Hos. 1:1; Jonah 1:1). God's appearance to Moses and the subsequent discussion in Exodus 3 would be a case of this, as would the voice from heaven, saying, "This is my beloved Son," or "You are my beloved Son," at the baptism of Jesus (Matt. 3:17; Mark 1:11) and at the transfiguration (Matt. 17:5; Mark 9:7; Luke 9:35).

2. Didactic material may come in the form of the Scripture writer's personal testimony of an experience of God. An example of this would be Isaiah's account of his vision of the Lord, high and lifted up (6:1–5).

3. Sometimes the didactic passage is an account of a sermon given by a spokesperson for God. Peter's sermon in Acts 2 would be an example. This sort of passage may include the citation and interpretation of another portion of Scripture (in this case, Joel 2).

4. Perhaps the most common type of doctrinal didactic materials is the letter of instruction, either to a church (Romans) or to an individual (1–2 Timothy), in which a doctrine is asserted and expounded.

5. Our Lord's formal teachings during his time on earth are a very important type of didactic doctrinal material. A significant example would be the great eschatological discourse in Matthew 24–25.

6. Editorial comments and explanations of a doctrinal nature by the author of a Gospel or other narrative-type material also are significant, if somewhat briefer, instances of didactic material. Examples would be the prologue to John's Gospel and Matthew's statements relating a narrative occurrence to a didactic, usually prophetic, passage from the Old Testament.

Initially it would seem that obtaining doctrine from didactic passages would be relatively simple. In these passages the speaker or writer is definitely setting out to teach something, often doctrinal in nature, to his audience. The writer's immediate goal is therefore similar to ours in formulating doctrine and preaching doctrinal sermons. There is a correspondence between the author's type of endeavor and ours. Surely, all one needs to do is to determine what the writer or speaker was saying and incorporate this into one's doctrinal beliefs or declare this in a doctrinal sermon. Yet the task is deceptively simple. Certain considerations need to be borne in mind in attempting the transition.

Problematic Considerations in Utilizing Didactic Doctrinal Passages

The first consideration is the fact that much of Scripture was directed to specific situations. Although phrased in the form of categorical statements, these passages had in mind very particular, even local, problems. Frequently, the exhortation was a corrective to one extreme. To apply the statement to a situation where the opposite extreme is the difficulty, or to translate it into a universal, where this is the seemingly unqualified objective, is to say something quite different. Such an emphasis may be only part of the whole, and to make it the whole is to introduce distortion. One can see this in the history of Christian thought. Frequently, a heresy was condemned. Yet the heresy had simply taken part of the truth and made it the whole. In the reaction, however, the next development was to neglect that part of the truth that had been absolutized by the heresy, and instead, to absolutize the opposite, thus falling into an opposite heresy. For example, at the Council of Nicea, Arianism, the view that made Jesus somewhat less than fully equal in deity with the Father, was condemned. However, one of the champions of the orthodox position, Apollinarius, desiring to maximize the divine factor, concluded that Jesus was fully human in his physical aspect, but that in his psychological makeup, the divine took the place ordinarily supplied by the human soul. Thus, Jesus' full humanity was compromised.

The second consideration is that the statement is in a definite cultural setting. What is being said in that setting can only be understood within that setting. If we do not investigate that culture sufficiently, we may fail to understand that. If we take the statement as if it were being written or spoken in that language and imagery to our present time we may hear it saying something quite different from what was really meant. To read Moses' statements about the law as if he was speaking to us today will result in grave distortion.

A third consideration requiring great care in the task is that the biblical revelation was progressive in nature. By that we mean that God revealed his message over a period of time, as the people were prepared to receive it and as the events that had transpired made possible the more complete revelation. In so doing, the later did not contradict the earlier, but advanced it, completing and deepening it. Thus, Jesus on several occasions said, "You have heard . . . , but I say to you. . . ." He also, however, stated that he had not come to destroy the law but to fulfill it. He had not come to set the law aside, but rather to fill it out, to complete it. The apostles, then, were the interpreters of what Jesus had done, applying those teachings to specific cases. Jesus gave relatively little interpretation of how his death was to achieve salvation for those who believed in him. That was left for Paul and others to expound. Similarly, Jesus' statements about his identity are relatively incomplete compared with passages like Philippians 2:1–11, Hebrews 1:3, and others. Difficulty ensues if we fail to take this into account. While the Old Testament discussion of atonement is true, it was not the final revelation on the subject. If we stop our consideration with the biblical theology of the Pentateuch, we will miss some of the most important considerations about the work of salvation.

A further problem comes from the fact that we are historically situated as well. As we read and seek to interpret the Bible, we do so from a particular time and place. We cannot help being who we are. We look at biblical passages through our historical glasses. Around each passage has accumulated a whole series of teachings we have received, which in effect amount to tradition. This may cause us to hear something quite different from what the original Scripture writer said or perhaps than he would say if he were writing to us today. An example is the question of justification by faith. We must reckon with the fact that we live on this side of the Reformation, and how we hear the passages in Romans and Galatians is affected by the fact that Martin Luther lived, preached, and wrote. This may make it very difficult to hear Paul rather than Luther when we come to those passages. Beyond that, however, there are nontheological influences on our understanding of the didactic portions of the Bible. To a person living in the late twentieth century, the conception of authority, even religious and theological authority, is inevitably affected by current attitudes toward authority in general, our situation generation-wise, and our exposure, conscious or unconscious, to general philosophical and cultural movements, such as existentialism. Similarly, any discussion of God the Father will be colored by the relationship each of us had to his or her own earthly father.

Further, even the didactic passages may not be fully doctrinal in their teaching. Some of them, although not narrative passages as such, are reporting historical or factual occurrences. Paul's statement that "God sent his Son, born of a woman, born under the law, to redeem those under law" (Gal. 4:4–5), or Peter's statement that "he has given us new birth into a living hope through the resurrection of Jesus Christ from the dead" (1 Peter 1:3) are examples. The doctrinal statement includes the interpretation of the event, its meaning. That Christ died, or that he rose from the dead, are historical statements. That he died for our sins, or was raised for our justification, are doctrinal statements.

Yet even these are not fully developed doctrine. How did Christ's death serve as atonement for our sins? What did it mean? How did Christ's resurrection relate to our justification? These dimensions of explanation are essential today for us to form a fully rounded theology, whereas Paul or Peter may not have needed to include them in speaking and writing to audiences whose needs were not exclusively or even primarily doctrinal.

One form in which this problem arises is in ethical teaching. Paul, for example, writes to the Corinthian Christians, exhorting them to live holy lives and to flee from immorality. He bases his appeal on certain doctrinal truths, such as that their bodies are the temples of God (1 Cor. 3:16) or the Holy Spirit (1 Cor. 6:19). Similarly, he reminds the Philippians to care about others, not being primarily concerned for themselves, their own needs, their own welfare. He does so on the basis of the model or example of Christ (2:1–11). This includes a powerful statement of the incarnation. We must be prepared, in dealing with didactic passages that are primarily ethical, to distill the doctrinal elements from these passages and utilize them in constructing our own doctrine, which will in turn, of course, be the basis for our ethical teaching and preaching in the present time.

Finally, the use of didactic passages for formulating doctrine is problematic because the language is not always literal. Various types of language are used, and even such concepts as the verbal inspiration and inerrancy of Scripture do not preclude the use of metaphorical and symbolic language. It is not always easy to determine what the metaphor in these passages is, and what is being expressed—or, to put it differently, to distinguish what is an illustration or an example of a truth and what is the pure form of the truth per se.

The Methodology of Constructing Doctrinal Statements

In view of these problems, it is important that we have a definite methodology for doing our theological work. This will be essential to our being able to be true doctrinal preachers, proclaiming the Word of truth for our time. There are basically four steps involved, each of which has a number of substeps that we elaborate further later:

1. Determine the exact meaning and application of the original teaching in that culture and to that audience.
2. Assess the place of this particular teaching in the whole of the doctrine. In other words, place the passage in the universal setting by asking if this is the whole of the truth or simply one aspect of the truth of this doctrine.

3. Isolate the principles that are the underlying permanent or eternal basis of this particular statement. This is the factor that is to be carried over in any recontextualization of the statement.
4. Finally, place the passage in the setting of the present time and context. This means saying to this particular target group the equivalent of what was being said to that group at that time, or what and how the speaker or writer would have expressed it if addressing our target group.

In the remainder of this chapter and in the next, we will be examining especially the first two steps. The latter two will be dealt with more completely in later chapters.

Obtaining the Meaning of the Passage

Careful exegesis is in order whenever a passage is studied. This is especially important when one is dealing with doctrine where a slight shading may make a considerable difference in meaning. It is important to use good tools in the craft of deriving doctrine from the Scripture. Ideally, the exegete should work with the biblical text in the original language. One who is not able to do that with confidence and skill will need to use several good Bible translations and commentaries that work with the original text and interpret it for English readers. Here, however, as we emphasize later, it is important not to consult commentaries too soon, so that one's own exegetical work is cut short. Also, one will want to obtain as much help with the background material as possible. Some of the biblical background books, Bible dictionaries, and Bible encyclopedias will be of help, as well as general and special introductions to the specific biblical book being studied.

In addition to these materials for direct study of the text, there are others that will be of help with respect to the doctrinal content. The *Theological Dictionary of the Old Testament* [2] and the *Theological Dictionary of the New Testament* [3] are very helpful in doing doctrinal word studies, as is the *New International Dictionary of New Testament Theology*,[4] which gives a more conservative or evangelical alternative to *TDNT*. In addition, one or more biblical theology books should be available, as well as one or more good recent systematic theologies.

2. *Theological Dictionary of the Old Testament*, ed. G. Johannes Botterweck and Helmer Ringgren, 6 vols. (Grand Rapids: Eerdmans, 1974–).
3. *Theological Dictionary of the New Testament*, ed. Gerhard Kittel, 9 vols. (Grand Rapids: Eerdmans, 1964–74).
4. *The New International Dictionary of New Testament Theology*, ed. Colin Brown, 3 vols. (Grand Rapids: Zondervan, 1975–78).

The average preacher will not, of course, be able to purchase a large number of these books. What one should do, however, is have a systematic plan for library acquisitions, emphasizing quality in the purchases. These are the tools of the preacher's trade. A mechanic would not attempt to work without mechanical tools, a golfer without golf clubs, or an accountant without computers and accounting programs. Neither should a preacher. Without the proper tools, the task is not likely to be done well.

One important step is choosing the passage or passages, which follows the selection of the doctrine to be dealt with. To some extent, this may take care of itself. When preaching through a biblical book and coming to a didactic doctrinal passage, one will of course need to deal with that. At certain seasons of the year, topics tend to be self-evident, such as the incarnation at Christmas, the atonement on Good Friday, and the resurrection on Easter Sunday. Passages about these topics will often be narrative passages, but there are important doctrines related to these periods of the year, and in the effort to vary one's preaching at these times from year to year, use of a didactic passage will often be in order.

Let us assume, however, that one has settled on a given doctrine with which to deal and wants to investigate it. Various means of identifying the passages to examine are available. One of these is the use of a concordance or a topical concordance, or perhaps a Greek or Hebrew lexicon, or a grammar that illustrates the various uses and occurrences of a given word. Here we should note that more resources are becoming available to the pastor-theologian. The computer software developed by the Gramcord Institute is of real value. Not only will it perform electronically the work of a concordance with either the Greek or Hebrew text or the English translations included, but it will also do the work of an analytical concordance.[5] Every occurrence of a particular grammatical form in a given range of text can be found, as well as every combination of two words, for example, within five words of one another in the biblical text.

One will need to determine that the passage or passages being dealt with really refer to the doctrine under consideration. This means that out of the possible passages that show at least some superficial indication of such reference, one will need to do at least some preliminary exegesis. This means that when a preaching program is planned some time in advance, either the passages should not be finalized too early or they should not be publicized too specifically. In one seminary preach-

---

5. Information on the Gramcord program can be obtained from The Gramcord Institute, 2218 N.E. Brookview Drive, Vancouver, Washington 98686, U.S.A. (360) 576-3000.

ing class the students were assigned to preach on a given subject from a given passage. Based on their knowledge of that passage from another class, a number of them were convinced that the assigned passage did not really deal with the topic. They were finally able to persuade the instructor to let them prepare a topical sermon on the subject. A similar but less easily negotiated problem arose when one seminary professor was asked to speak to the annual meeting of a denominational group on four specific subtopics from a particular Old Testament passage. Unfortunately, as he began closer study of the chapter, the professor became convinced that this chapter really did not address these four topics. A slight fudging of the topics in the messages was the result. Where no one passage seems to deal adequately or inclusively with the doctrine under consideration, it may be necessary to create a sermon series on the doctrine, enabling a well-rounded treatment. One should be prepared to either shift passages or change the doctrinal theme.

Actually, the choice of a passage may occur in any one of several stages in the process. One may choose a passage first, as when preaching a sermon series or at a particular time of the church year. Then, in the process of preparing the message, the decision to make it a doctrinal sermon, or the decision to preach on this particular doctrine, or both, may need to be made. On the other hand, the decision to preach on a specific doctrine may be made first, and then the passage is selected. Or the preacher may first decide to preach a particular type or style of sermon (i.e., narrative, expository, etc.) and then select the passage. This is perhaps the least common sequence of events.

To some extent, there will be a relationship between the choice of passage and the style of the message. For example, a narrative passage will lend itself more readily to a narrative sermon than will some other types of biblical material. A single didactic passage will conduce to an expository sermon, and a collection of several passages dealing with the same doctrine will more likely lead to a topical sermon. This is only a partial correlation, however, for one may take a passage of poetry and do a first-person dramatic presentation on a portion of the life of the author, especially if the setting of the poetry can be identified fairly exactly. A narrative passage can also be developed into an expository sermon.

The doctrinal teaching of the passage may actually be only one of several topics that can be developed from the passage. It may not be the only or even the main thrust of the passage. In fact, the passage may not be primarily doctrinal. This leads to the observation that a sermon that is not primarily doctrinal will contain doctrinal elements. Such a sermon can be declared in this connection, a doctrinal mini-sermon within an ethical sermon, or can become the basis for another, primarily doctrinal, sermon.

As an example, we may note that the primary purpose of Paul writing what he did in Philippians 2 seems to be practical, namely, that the readers might have the same mind as Christ, thinking more about others than about themselves. Yet the argument offered in support of this is profoundly doctrinal in nature. There is a school of thought that seems to say that, in effect, only one sermon can be preached from a given passage, namely, one that appeals on the basis of the central thrust.[6] On that way of thinking, one could only preach a practical or ethical sermon, not a doctrinal sermon, from the passage. This appears to be too narrow an approach, however. Anything may be taken from the passage that is being affirmed, whether the conclusion of the argument, or as here, one of the premises of the argument. These premises frequently are established on other grounds, or they can be considered proved by virtue of having been asserted here. Thus, several complementary sermons might be preached from the passage. If we bear this in mind, we may well find fruitful sources for doctrinal teachings in passages where the doctrine in question is not being primarily expounded. An example is Jesus' statement in Matthew 10:29–31 that not even one sparrow can fall to the earth without the Father's knowledge and permission. His major point is the Father's concern and care for his human children. Yet this rests on the declaration of his protection and care of these small members of his creation, and the fact that humans are of far greater value to him than birds. So one can, on the basis of this passage, also declare that God cares about and watches over other members of the creation.

A major consideration in abstracting doctrinal teaching is lexical studies. It is important to determine the exact meanings of the terms involved, for often fine gradations of meaning turn on which term has been translated into English in this way. This can, of course, best be done with the use of the best lexicons of the original languages. If one has sufficient control of the respective language to be able to consult those lexicons, that will facilitate the process. Beyond that, we may be able to find some help in cognate sources. One Old Testament professor told his class, "The margin of the Bible translation sometimes says something like, 'the Hebrew is obscure.' Actually," said the teacher, "it is often not the Hebrew that is obscure. We may know exactly which Hebrew word is written in this place. The problem is to know the meaning of the word, so that we can translate it into another language. In a

---

6. E.g., Haddon Robinson, *Biblical Preaching: The Development and Delivery of Expository Sermons* (Grand Rapids: Baker, 1980), pp. 41–44.

sense, the English is obscure." There are cases, especially in the Old Testament, where we have very few occurrences of a particular word, so there is considerable difficulty in determining contextually what it meant. Here the use of cognate languages may be especially helpful, for one or more of those languages may contain a word that bears such strong resemblance to our word that we can learn from its usage something of the meaning of our term. In practice, however, few pastors have a knowledge of Aramaic, Ugaritic, Syriac, Coptic, Akkadian, and other such languages. More likely is the possibility of using a Hebrew lexicon that includes reference to such cognate languages. Similarly, in the New Testament, the availability of classical Greek and Koiné Greek will help us. The papyri, which contained numerous occurrences of some of the rare biblical terms, shed light on the meaning those had in more general cultural usage.

But what if the pastor-theologian is not able to read the original languages? By no means is all lost. Tools have been developed that enable such a person to do word studies. One of these is *Strong's Concordance,* which can be used in connection with Thayer's lexicon. Words are identified in the former by number, which may then be found in the latter. Thus, one is able to look up the meaning in a Greek lexicon without actually knowing Greek. Other sources do this type of thing more directly, including *Word Studies in the New Testament* by Marvin Vincent,[7] *Word Pictures in the New Testament* by A. T. Robertson,[8] the *Word Study Concordance* by George V. Wigram and Ralph D.Winter,[9] and the *Word Study New Testament* by Ralph D. Winter and Roberta H. Winter.[10]

Further, one should consult theological dictionaries. These will often be in English, but if one can work with the biblical languages, sources such as the *Theological Dictionary of the Old Testament, Theological Dictionary of the New Testament,* and *Dictionary of New Testament Theology* are especially helpful. Yet one should not simply accept the pronouncements of these sources as final and authoritative. Like any other type of

7. Marvin R. Vincent, *Word Studies in the New Testament* (New York: Scribners, 1911).

8. Archibald Thomas Robertson, *Word Pictures in the New Testament* (New York: Harper and Brothers, 1930–33).

9. George V. Wigram and Ralph D. Winter, *The Word Study Concordance: Modern Improved, and Enlarged Version of Both* The Englishman's Greek Concordance *and* The New Englishman's Greek Concordance, *Expanded to Include Key Numbering, an Alpha-numeric Index, a Word Family Index and the Cross-Reference Headings* (Pasadena, Calif.: William Carey Library, 1978).

10. *The Word Study New Testament, Containing the Numbering System to the Word Study Concordance and the Key Number Index to Standard Reference Works, based on the Authorized Version of the Holy Bible,* ed. Ralph D. Winter and Robert H. Winter (Pasadena, Calif.: William Carey Library, 1978).

human work, they are subject to the biases and perspectives of their authors. It is important to be aware of these and of their possible influence on the position taken. If not, they will have an unintended impact on the outcome of our research. Like an error in a compass or a gunsight, they affect the conclusions, perhaps far removed from the beginnings. One should find out as much as possible about the author of the article. For example, an article written by Rudolf Bultmann can be expected to have an existentialist twist. Being aware of this will often make one more skeptical about the assertions made.

One way to guard against such a subtle influence on one's conclusions is to have more than one source. So, for example, *The New International Dictionary of New Testament Theology*, alongside the *Theological Dictionary of the New Testament*, provides a balance to the information. If one cannot afford multiple sources, then one should probably attempt to work with a source whose basic presuppositions agree with one's own. If this is the case, however, one should be more demanding of the evidence presented, as it will tend to seem more plausible.

The next step, after completing lexical studies, is to determine the grammar and syntax of the passage being studied. This is a matter of discovering how the meanings of the words relate to one another and is a key factor in determining the meaning of the passage. An example would be Hebrews 6:4–6, where the statement made of these persons who had "tasted" of salvation, is literally, "falling away." How one renders those words, whether "if they fall away," "when they fall away," and so on, goes far toward determining the true meaning of the passage.

There are a number of ways of isolating grammatical and syntactical issues and conclusions. One is through diagramming the grammatical structure of the sentences. While this is best done with the original languages, it can also be done with the English text. The virtue of this endeavor is that it forces us to look for the relationships between the words. Ambiguities become much more evident than might otherwise be the case.

Especially when working with the original languages, one should consult competent grammars. One will probably want to have a variety of levels of grammars, from the handbook type of intermediate grammar to the advanced grammars such as A. T. Robertson's *Grammar of the Greek New Testament in the Light of Historical Research*.[11] In many cases, the indexes of these grammars include references to specific verses, so that one may find what the author had to say about the grammar of the passage one is working with.

---

11. A. T. Robertson, *A Grammar of the Greek New Testament in the Light of Historical Research* (Nashville: Broadmans, 1934).

At this point, and preferably not earlier, one should also consult commentaries, beginning with critical commentaries on the original text. More expository type commentaries should be brought in only after synthesizing one's own preliminary understanding of the doctrinal statement of the passage being studied. If possible, one should endeavor to have more than one commentary, so that any bias is neutralized. In the acquisition and consultation of commentaries, however, quality is to be sought. There are certain biblical scholars, such as F. F. Bruce, Leon Morris, and others, whose work is of such quality that anything they write is worth owning and reading. It is also wise, for the purpose of extracting doctrine from these passages, to rely especially on more theologically oriented commentaries.

The next step is to endeavor to summarize and state, in one's own words, the doctrinal affirmations of the passage as clearly and specifically as possible. This is an effort to clarify and simplify what the passage says. While the task of actually having to write something or trying to explain it verbally to someone else is difficult, it forces us to sharpen what we have to say. It forces, us, in other words, to think through what we hear in the passage and to understand it.

This is doctrinal interpretation, as contrasted with merely exegetical interpretation. For example, Paul says of Christ, "though he was in the form of God, he did not count equality with God a thing to be grasped, but emptied himself, taking the form of a servant, being born in the likeness of men" (Phil. 2:6–7). What does that mean? The meaning cannot be determined merely by examining the text. What does the text say? It says that Christ emptied himself. What does the text mean, however, or what is it really saying? That is a question which in effect goes beyond the text in its search for explanation. Similarly, Paul wrote, "Lo! I tell you a mystery. We shall not all sleep, but we shall all be changed, in a moment, in the twinkling of an eye, at the last trumpet. For the trumpet will sound, and the dead will be raised imperishable, and we shall be changed. For this perishable nature must put on the imperishable, and this mortal nature must put on immortality" (1 Cor. 15:51–53). What this says is in one sense quite clear: The dead will be brought back to life in such a fashion that they will never die or be able to die. What does this mean, however? That question will not be answered merely by additional lexical or grammatical studies of the passage, although those must be used to the maximum extent possible. The exegete is limited to the choice either of saying we cannot determine this from the text or of some highly sophisticated eisegesis. Interpretation must, in other words, be more than merely textual or exegetical interpretation, going on to doctrinal interpretation.

This will require us to reflect in some depth on what is being asserted. In a class, it is possible to get the benefit of this by the persistent probing inquiry of the professor, who asks the students, "But what does that really mean?" This may be done by providing the students with several alternative interpretations of the passage or concept, and then asking which is most nearly correct and why. Pastor-theologians do not have the benefit of a scholar in residence, a personal professor, to interrogate, and thus to force thought and interpretation. Yet it is important that they perform that role for themselves. Sigmund Freud spoke of the human superego, which was the teaching and judging of the parent now taken by the child, internalized or introjected, so that the child now serves as her own parent. Something similar will need to be done by the pastor-theologian.

It is notable that such questions of doctrinal interpretation can be asked on different levels. One is the level of the layperson, the nonprofessional student of the Bible. Here there are several sublevels: the chronologically young or spiritually young person, the biblically uneducated, the long-time student of the Bible who can quote numerous verses from memory, the relatively simple person, the sophisticated thinking intellectual. The second is the level of the pastor or the seminary student, the level of study attained in most first degree level courses in seminary. This is the professional pastor-theologian, but not a person occupied full-time in doing theology. The next level is the professional theologian, the person engaged in teaching pastor-theologians whose entire life centers on the mastery and communication of this discipline. Finally, there are the theological geniuses, those few who pioneer in the study of theology and whose research and reflection become the objects of study for the other professional theologians.

It will be tempting, because the product of one's theologizing is expressed sermonically on the lay level, to do one's own thinking on that level. This has the advantage of facilitating communication, since it is already understandable by the laity. The disadvantage, however, is that there is little that is stimulating, that challenges the hearers to grow, in a sermon of that type. If we are to facilitate intellectual and spiritual growth on the part of our people it is important that we function at least at the level of the pastor, and preferably be reading and reflecting one or even two levels above that. That is the way fresh and challenging insights are brought to the congregation.

What must be done, of course, is to bring that work to the level of the audience for purposes of expression. That is hard work, and sometimes is done poorly or not at all, so that the audience is perplexed, bored, or frustrated. The preacher is not alone in this. It is proverbial that some of the greatest scholars are some of the poorest teachers of their subject, and one of the reasons is that they fail to express their knowledge at a level accessible to their students. We address later the difficult problem of speaking great insights so that laypeople can understand them. We simply want to say here that this is a key factor in being fresh, stimulating, and challenging: to do one's thinking beyond the level of one's hearers or even of one's own comfort level, and then to find ways to preserve that content but express it to the layperson.

Part of what we are saying is that we must separate the study from the pulpit. We should bring to the pulpit the results of that study, not the actual details of that study itself. Some persons in the audience will have the interest and ability to deal with that research and we will want to share such with them on a more personal basis, but this is not for everyone. The pastor-theologian is like an architect. The architect does a great deal of calculation and perhaps even testing in designing a building. When he meets with clients, however, what he shares is the results of that calculation, the proposed building, not the actual calculation with formulas and figures, unless the client wishes to see that documentation.

This endeavor will help us avoid oversimplification. While the adaptation of the doctrinal content into a sermon especially involves simplification, it must not say more than is justified, by saying less than could be said. The kind of rigorous reflection we are talking about must be thorough enough to know the qualifications on a statement. While it will not always be necessary to express every qualification, one will not make unqualified statements.

Placing Meaning in Perspective

The second major step is putting this doctrinal affirmation in perspective. We need to ask the extent to which what this passage states on this subject is the whole of the doctrine. We are not yet asking whether this is the way we would state it to people in their unique situation, but rather whether this is to be regarded as *the* biblical doctrine on this matter. We must ask ourselves whether the writer was even trying to answer all of the questions that those readers had on the subject, to say nothing of what others might have.

There are steps that can be taken to assess the degree of generalizability or universalizability of the statement. Part of this involves asking about the situation in which it was written, or the *Sitz im Leben*, as biblical scholars like to term it. Who was the audience? What do we know about them and their situation? This question, of course, should have been asked in the process of trying to determine the meaning of what was said. Here, however, it is asked in terms of whether those first readers can be treated as if they were all persons at all times. We will want to ask about the geographical location, economic status, and ethnic characteristics of the audience. We will want to ask for clues in what the writer says as to the issue being addressed, and what he was seeking to correct. If, for example, the readers were too far left on an issue, then the writer may well be emphasizing the more right-oriented perspective, and only that. Whether the readers are legalists or antinomians goes a long way toward knowing what status to assign to a particular message. We would not want to focus on only what the writer emphasizes here in a different situation, however.

An example would be the question of the biblical teaching regarding faith, works, and justification, as dealt with by Paul in Galatians and by James in his letter. These two writings have sometimes been considered contradictory. When, however, one begins to see the different problems being dealt with by the writers, the conflict declines or ceases. It is quite likely that each author would have written what the other did, if writing to the audience that other was addressing.

One way of finding out if this is the whole truth, or just a particular perspective on it, is to compare this statement with others this author has written. This would include other statements within the same book, but also in other books by this author. Thus, for example, while extolling the virtues of grace for justification, as over against any self-righteous fulfillment of the law, Paul considers the objection that some may take this to an extreme. He says: "What shall we say then? Are we to continue in sin that grace may abound?" (Rom. 6:1) Here is a case where Paul supplies his own corrective to a misunderstanding of what he has said.

Whether we are working with the same book or another book by the same author, it is especially important to identify the context and avoid taking the statement out of that context. This means the context of the passage, as well as of the book (the occasion of its writing). It also means the context of the author or his *Sitz im Leben*. What Paul had to say doctrinally in Philippians should be interpreted in light of the fact that he was imprisoned and may have sensed that he would never be able to leave prison to resume his missionary ministry.

Further, we must compare the statements in the passage under consideration with other statements in Scripture, even by other authors. Underlying this prescription is the assumption of the unity of the Bible, that it is, in other words, really one book with many sections, rather than a collection of books. In our case, we are working with the principle that God, or specifically, the Holy Spirit, is the primary author of Scripture, so that there is a consistency among the several things he has communicated in the various books. Again, we will compare what is said in this passage with what is said elsewhere and formulate our understanding inclusively, rather than in isolation.

What is the point of this endeavor? It is not to use the teachings from elsewhere in Scripture to modify the meaning of this passage. We are not endeavoring to do eisegesis, to read into one passage what is found elsewhere. We also must avoid Procrusteanism, the effort to make all statements in Scripture say the whole thing. What we are attempting to do is to see the whole picture. We are trying to avoid absolutizing the relative or generalizing the partial. If we find that the interpretation we give to a particular passage is different in light of other passages supplementing what it says, then we may have a clue that we were totalizing a partial statement.

Let us take as an example the issue of what is required to receive salvation. One might make a single case the paradigm for the answer to this question. In Acts 16, Paul is asked this crucial question by the Philippian jailor: "What must I do to be saved?" Certainly the answer would be our answer as well. He replied: "Believe in the Lord Jesus, and you will be saved" (v. 31). Note that there is no mention here of repentance. Accordingly, some have concluded that repentance is not essential to salvation. However, earlier in the book, Peter is asked a similar question: "Brothers, what shall we do?" Here he replies, "Repent and be baptized, every one of you, in the name of Jesus Christ for the forgiveness of your sins" (2:38). Here repentance is clearly mentioned, but there is no explicit prescription of faith. We might conclude that the two are in conflict with one another. Or we might conclude that we have misinterpreted the first passage, so that repentance is actually the same thing as faith. It might be better, however, to understand the two passages as complementary. Thus, both repentance and faith are necessary, but only that which needed to be emphasized and practiced was mentioned in a given case. The Philippian jailor was sufficiently repentant, so he did not need to be told to repent. Peter's hearers may have come to believe in Jesus as a result of what Peter had just preached to them, but they needed to repent in view of the charge he had just laid on them, that they had crucified Jesus.

There is one other help when endeavoring to form this well-rounded understanding: the consulting of one or more good biblical theologies, not simply to see how they regard this passage, but also to find out what other passages deal with this same matter. These theologies should be investigated with as great care as we have given to our treatment of this passage. Again, of course, it is important to be informed regarding the presuppositions of the author of a particular biblical theology. To combine the interpretations of differing passages given by authors of radically different orientations will almost surely lead to internal inconsistency.

All of this says as well that if we are going to do an expository doctrinal sermon from a given passage, it may be necessary to qualify what we say. This may be done in terms of the degree of universality or the degree of dogmatism we display in connection with it. It may also be done by calling attention to the existence of other facets of the doctrine, or by pointing out other passages and how they relate to what is being said in this passage.

7

Getting Doctrine from Narrative Passages

I pulled my car into the parking lot, got out, and walked over to the guard rail. Below me was an open-pit iron mine, one of the largest in the world. I looked at the reddish-colored iron ore, then turned and looked at my automobile. I thought of how a large part of that car, sheet metal, mechanical parts, even some of the trim, had begun with un-mined, unrefined ore such as I saw below me. Between the raw ore and the finished vehicle a number of carefully planned and executed steps had intervened.

Steps to the Doctrinal Sermon

There are basically three stages involved in the process of making a car. The first is the actual mining of the iron ore, the extraction of it from the ground. That provides only raw materials, however. The process of making steel is a complex one, which involves removing impurities from the iron and combining it in a process known as alloying, with other elements, to produce steel. The result at this stage is finished steel, in the form of bars or sheets. The next stage is reforming the steel into particular shapes, as automobile parts. Bars are transformed into fenders, gears, knobs, and other parts. Finally, these parts are combined with others to produce an assembled automobile.

The process of preparing a doctrinal sermon follows a course somewhat analogous to that of producing a car. There is first exegesis, which is the process of determining the meaning of the relevant biblical passage(s). This corresponds to the process of mining the iron ore. What is obtained here is meaning and truth, including doctrinal assertions, but not necessarily theology as such.[1] The second stage is theology, both biblical and theological. This is, for our purposes, the process of refining, of extracting the theological material from the other types of material (e.g., devotional, ethical, etc.) and casting the doctrines into contemporary expression, not unlike the production of bars or sheets of high-carbon alloy steel. The final stage is homiletics, the shaping of these contemporary expressions of doctrine into sermonic form. This corresponds to the actual fabrication of automobile parts. This chapter and the previous one are primarily concerned with the exegetical task, although they do not deal with specific topics of exegetical methodology. Rather, they address the question of how to do exegesis in such a way as to obtain the theological result from that process. Chapters 8 and 9 concern themselves with theology: how to formulate doctrines in a contemporary and relevant fashion. Chapters 10 through 13 deal with homiletics—the casting of these doctrinal truths into sermons of various types.

The Nature and Role of Narrative

In addition to a large amount of didactic doctrinal material, there is an even larger and potentially very useful body of material, namely, the narrative portions of the Scriptures. There is a large amount of this material, found in different settings and covering a long period of time. Some theologians, practicing what they term "narrative theology," have even made this the normative source of doctrine. In some ways, this is a carryover from a view of revelation according to which historical events constituted the primary variety of revelation. Whether we concede that this is the primary mode of revelation, we would probably agree that it is one of the modes God utilized in making himself known. This is also a primary form of communication used by some theologians and others today. For example, rabbis today often answer a question, not by a direct affirmative answer, but by telling a story. We will want to ask ourselves whether this is also closer to the ancient Hebrew mind as well.

Biblical Narrative

It is important that we make clear that it is biblical narrative that we are referring to. Currently, there is a great deal of emphasis on narrative in theology as well as in preaching. There are various conceptions of the role of narrative. One is that it is basically a communication device. An-

---

1. Charles Hodge appears to have held that what we find in the Bible are the "facts of theology," and that the task of the theologian is simply to arrange them in systematic fashion. Charles Hodge, *Systematic Theology* (Grand Rapids: Eerdmans, 1952), pp. 18–19.

other is the hermeneutical use, as the key to unlocking the meaning of the biblical message. The final use is heuristic. This is the idea that narrative has certain inherent powers of discovering truth. Indeed, narrative as a literary form is sometimes thought of as having certain inherent capacities for enabling knowing. Stories, simply because they are stories, are better means of revealing truth and creating insight than are propositions. When this move is made, story as such takes on theological significance, even when drawn from outside the biblical canon. Dialogue between persons is thought of as generating truth. "Tell me your story and I'll tell you mine" is often the slogan that underlies this approach. Biographies drawn from outside Scripture may reveal truth.[2] Underlying this approach is, of course, a particular conception of the relationship of truth to revelation and of general revelation to special revelation. We cannot here discuss at length the issues involved in this approach. We do, however, want to make clear that the narratives we are referring to as the source of our doctrine, and ultimately of our preaching, are those found in the Bible.

If narrative is a primary mode of revelation and of communication, is it a means of conveying doctrine, and if so, how? This will be a clue to the answer to an even more important, and in many ways, more difficult, question: How do we identify, isolate, and extract doctrine from such passages? For if this is a large lode of useful raw material for doctrinal construction, the problem is that the ore, in this case, is difficult to extract and then to convert into doctrine of a more conventional sort.

Narrative and Special Revelation

Our justification for the use of narrative for obtaining doctrine is found in the nature of special revelation. God has revealed himself through the use of several modes or modalities. One of these is what Bernard Ramm has called divine speech.[3] This includes the visions and dreams that came to biblical prophets, as well as the direct address by God we sometimes find reported in Scripture, and the concursive action or inward speaking of God guiding the Scripture writers' thoughts as they wrote. Alongside these are the divine acts of God as self-revelation. These are those historical events in which God acted in such a way as to make known something of his nature and activity. It is the report of these that constitutes narrative. Because they are revelatory, they are proper subjects of our doctrinal exegetical endeavor.

2. James McClendon, *Biography as Theology: How Life Stories Can Remake Today's Theology* (Nashville: Abingdon, 1974).
3. Bernard Ramm, *Special Revelation and the Word of God: An Essay on the Contemporary Problem of Revelation* (Grand Rapids: Eerdmans, 1961), pp. 53–69.

There are many examples of this, and numerous cases where Scripture writers identify the events as revelation of God. One of those most frequently cited is the exodus and the complex of events associated with it. Here God demonstrated his power, both in the series of plagues culminating in the Passover and then in the miraculous crossing of the Red Sea.[4] Here God was showing his benevolence by his provision for and deliverance of his people. He was also showing his judgmental or destructive power in the death of the firstborn of Egypt and in the destruction of the Egyptian army. This event was referred to on several occasions by the psalmists and other Scripture writers as evidence of God's power and goodness (e.g., Pss. 66, 78).

Another passage that clearly is a manifestation of the nature and especially the power of God is the account of the contest between Elijah and the prophets of Baal on Mount Carmel (1 Kings 18). Elijah and the 450 prophets of Baal agreed that whichever god was able to send down fire to consume the sacrifice would be established as the true God (v. 24). Then Jehovah revealed himself by sending fire (v. 38), and the people acknowledged that he was indeed the true God (v. 39).

In the New Testament, we have a coalescence of two modalities of revelation in Jesus Christ. Here we have both divine speech and divine act coming together in the fullest revelation of God. Jesus' words were God's words and Jesus' actions were God's acts, for he was God in human form. John refers to Jesus' mighty acts as "signs." They were divine action. Jesus indicated the revelatory character of his miracles when he said to the Pharisees, "But if it is by the Spirit of God that I cast out demons, then the kingdom of God has come upon you" (Matt. 12:28). He made this point even more clearly when he said, "He who has seen me has seen the Father" (John 14:9).

The event regarded by the Scripture writers as God's supreme act of self-revelation is the resurrection of Jesus. Time and time again, the apostles refer to the resurrection as God's work and indicate the revelation that was involved. An example is Paul's speech in the synagogue in Antioch in Acts 13. He recited the history of God's Old Testament working and promises to Israel, and then shows that these were fulfilled in Jesus Christ, as evidenced by the resurrection: "And we bring you the good news that what God promised to the fathers, this he has fulfilled

4. The authors are aware of the contention of some that it was not the Red Sea that was crossed by the Israelites, but the Reed Sea, a much shallower body of water. The miracle then becomes, as someone has put it, "that God could drown all those Egyptians in three inches of water." For a recent thorough discussion of the issues and defense of the traditional view, see Robert L. Hubbard Jr., "Red Sea," in *International Standard Bible Encyclopedia*, rev. ed. (Grand Rapids: Eerdmans, 1988), vol. 4, pp. 58–61.

to us their children by raising Jesus; as also it is written in the second psalm, 'Thou art my Son, today I have begotten thee'" (vv. 32–33).

Values of Narrative Passages

There are certain advantages or benefits to taking doctrine from narrative passages. The most significant is that doctrine is in a more usable form than in didactic passages, at least in terms of our ability to preach it. This may seem like a contradiction of what we have just said, but while doctrine may not be as easy to identify in this form, it can nonetheless be more easily communicated. It makes the task of doctrinal preaching easier.

There are two major problems in doctrine: intelligibility and credibility, or, in other words, the problem of understanding the meaning of the doctrine and the problem of believing it. Sometimes we have one of these without the other. Frequently, persons understand a doctrine, but do not believe it or are not convinced that it is true. Sometimes, a more devout person may believe that something is true without fully understanding it. A common example of the latter is the doctrine of the Trinity. Yet we can have both understanding and belief, and they are facilitated by being presented in narrative.

Enhancing Credibility

It is possible to believe doctrines that occur in narrative because the very fact of the narrative, if true, demonstrates the reality of the doctrine. If something is actual, it obviously is possible, and narrative provides a demonstration, not just a discussion, of the doctrine at issue. For example, take the doctrine of the power of God. When we look at the miracle narratives, such as the Passover, the crossing of the Red Sea and the destruction of the Egyptian army, or the birth of Isaac, we see that the God who did those things is indeed powerful—more powerful than the most powerful things we know in this world, including the laws of nature.

Facilitating Understanding

Beyond that, however, the doctrines come illustrated. If we ask what the omnipotence of God means, we find out by seeing it connected with actual human circumstances. We are thus able to relate it to our own experiences. These may not always be the same, but at least we can often find some congruence or parallel between what happened then and what is happening today or what persons in that time and place experienced and what we experience today.

Problems with Narrative Passages

Having said this, there are some special problems or particular difficulties in attempting to deal with doctrine in narrative passages. We recount them here, not as a discouragement, but to alert us or prepare us for what we will need to do.

Normativity

One problem centers around the question of whether a passage is to be regarded as normative. This is how it was, on that occasion, but is this how it is to be, how it always is? To put it another way, can this passage be taken as universally true, or is it only true on that occasion and in that situation? The question concerns the nature of the authority of narrative material. Is it only historically authoritative, that is, reliable as an indication of what indeed happened on that occasion? Or is it normatively authoritative, that is, binding as an indication of what will and must happen in other situations, at all times? In fact, this may be a negative case. It may be the exact opposite of how things are to be. Take, for example, the dispute between Paul and Barnabas in Acts 15:36–41, when they were unable to agree whether to take John Mark with them. Is this to be understood as part of the normal variation within the doctrine of sanctification, or as a case of one or both of these men acting in an unsanctified way? That problem must be wrestled with before the passage can contribute to the understanding of sanctification.

Induction

Part of the problem is that we are dealing with inductive logic. In inductive logic, one instance alone does not establish a law. It is necessary to have more instances, until a sufficient degree of probability has been reached. In the case of didactic passages, on the other hand, we are dealing with deductive logic. There is a universal truth, now to be applied here. The nature of inductive logic, however, is such that trying to establish correlation by finding positive instances of agreement has a major shortcoming. How many positive cases, where a particular situation is accompanied by a certain consequence or evaluation, are required to validate the connection between the two? On the other hand, where there are negative situations, where the absence of one factor is accompanied by the absence of the other, then the method of difference enters in, and this is a more powerful factor. In the nature of the case, however, what we are generally dealing with in these cases is the method of agreement, rather than that of difference.

Need of Interpretation

Further complicating our use of narrative passages for doctrine is the fact that this approach involves a different modality of revelation than do didactic passages. This is a matter of revelation as divine acts, whereas the didactic is a case of revelation as divine speech. This means that there will need to be a considerable amount of analysis of the events in order to be able to interpret them correctly. For example, when an event occurs, we need to determine who is the ultimate cause of the event, and whether this causation is direct or indirect. Which occurrences are God's doing and which have been satanically inspired?

These conclusions may not be immediately evident on the surface. We will have to find a way of distinguishing them. For example, when some great disaster strikes in Scripture, such as a famine, how is this to be understood? Does this mean that God maliciously sends harmful experiences to the human race? Does it mean that God is weak, and unable to prevent certain events that he might wish to? Does this argue for the character and power of Satan, or of the forces of evil in general? Does it mean that God allows a considerable amount of leeway to human beings, that he simply maintains a sort of loose control over the creation? Or does it mean that nature is capricious, rather than following some sort of natural laws? Or does it indicate that nature, however personified this may be, has some sort of inner directive force, which responds in certain ways to human actions, so that if humans treat it unwisely it "fights back"? Another way of putting this is that nature is so structured that unwise human use of it, or human exploitation, results in adverse consequences.

All these questions may lead us to the conclusion that in order to interpret these matters we must bring to bear on the passages some of the insights gained from didactic passages. It is common to say something like, "Just let the facts speak for themselves," and some would want to cite that principle here. The one thing that facts cannot do, however, is speak for themselves. In themselves, they are frequently mute. They do not always come interpreted for us, nor do they always interpret themselves.

This caution is necessary even with respect to the supreme case of revelation, the incarnation. In the incarnation the divine acts and the divine speech coincided. Jesus was truly God in human flesh; what he did was God acting in human nature, and his words and teachings were God's own words. Yet, with respect to any given action, was this a manifestation of Jesus' deity or his humanity? If deity, then it does not tell us directly anything about the human nature and the human condition. On the other hand, if it is a manifestation of Jesus' humanity, it can give us insight into ourselves and enable us to imitate Jesus, but it does not really give us direct knowledge of God. Beyond that, however, suppose he truly was the God-man and this was a true incarnation, so that his deity was never separate from his humanity and he never acted simply as God in abstraction or as human alone. Then were any of his actions really usable revelations of deity, such as we find it in God the Father, and were any of his actions really revelations of humanity, such as we find it in ourselves?

The dilemma can perhaps be grasped by considering a problem posed by a paper read at a professional society several years ago. The thesis was that a given practice is not normative for a believer unless it is found in the life of Jesus. This means, for example, that since Jesus is never spoken of as praying for his own forgiveness, this prayer is not mandatory for a believer today. Since there is no recorded instance of Jesus ever speaking in tongues, how can this be an expectation of the believer today? These and other problems point out the difficulty of using Jesus' life as a direct revelation of the nature of humanity, and thus as an example for us.

Contradictory Narratives

A final difficulty in using narrative passages as a basis for doctrine is the existence of apparently contradictory instances of a given doctrine. For example, Clark Pinnock, in commenting on Acts 4:12, "Neither is there salvation in any other; for there is no other name under heaven given among men, whereby we must be saved," maintains that this salvation includes physical healing, which he observes is present in this passage.[5] It may be possible to argue that from this passage, although that is, to say the least, not beyond dispute. There are other passages that appear to support this contention. For example, Jesus said to the man who asked for healing for his son, "All things are possible to him who believes" (Mark 9:23). We are not told, however, that this person possessed salvation in terms of eternal life.

The biblical testimony is not so clear in every case, however. For example, Paul prayed three times for removal of what he terms a "thorn in the flesh" (2 Cor. 12:7). While there has been much debate about the nature of this "thorn," it appears that it was a physical illness that he experienced. It might have been a disease of the eyes, since he writes to the Galatians that it was because of a bodily ailment that he had first preached the gospel to them and testifies that if they could, they would have plucked out their own eyes and given them to him (Gal. 4:13–15).

---

5. Clark Pinnock, "Acts 4:12—No Other Name Under Heaven," in *Through No Fault of Their Own? The Fate of Those Who Have Never Heard*, ed. William V. Crockett and James G. Sigountos (Grand Rapids: Baker, 1991), p. 109, n. 6.

Yet although Paul was certainly a born-again believer, apparently a rather sanctified Christian at that, and a specially significant servant of Jesus Christ, the threefold request was denied. Instead the response came back, "my grace is sufficient for you." Instead of removal of the ailment, that is, healing, Paul was promised grace to be able to endure the difficult condition.

How, then, are we to reconcile this passage with the hypothesis drawn by Pinnock from Acts 4, which he states, not as a hypothesis, but as a dogmatic fact? If we are to make an induction of all the passages of Scripture that seem to bear on this in narrative fashion, it would have to be as follows: Healing is sometimes given to those who are believers, but sometimes it is not. Its presence is not correlated with the spiritual maturity of the believer, the amount of requesting that is done, or the degree of faith of the asker. It also may come at times to those who are not believers. There is, in other words, no invariable connection between salvation and spiritual healing, and the latter should not be considered a part of the former.

Need of Transitional Doctrine

Part of what we are saying is that we cannot simply make a transition from a biblical narrative to our own narrative, and apply the passage directly. We must ascertain that the two narratives are commensurable, in other words, that they are dealing with the same issue. Unless the question is the same, we cannot necessarily utilize the same answer. But this means that ultimately the narrative must be translated into some sort of propositions, which can then be carried over and applied to the new narrative, that of our lives today. To fail to do this will result in inaccurate and even unfortunate consequences.

A vivid illustration of this is the story of the farmer who decided he would seek to ascertain what he should do by the old method of closing one's eyes, opening the Bible at random, and placing one's finger somewhere on the page. He did so, and his finger landed upon 2 Corinthians 9:6, "The point is this: he who sows sparingly will also reap sparingly, and he who sows bountifully will also reap bountifully." Concluding that this was a message from God, he went out and rented additional acreage and planted intensively. It was a good year, and it was apparent that the bumper crop was more than he could store in his existing barns and granaries. He needed another message of guidance from God regarding what he should do, so he used the closed-eyes-finger-in-the-Bible method again. This time his finger fell on Luke 12:18: "And he said, 'I will do this: I will pull down my barns, and build larger ones; and there I will store all my grain and my goods.'" Since this was obviously a divine indication that he should do the same, he demolished his old barns and replaced them with new, larger ones, even though the old barns were in quite good condition. This enabled him to store his large crop, but it also saddled him with a large debt. The next year was not nearly so favorable; in fact, because of a drought, the crops failed. Soon the bank demanded payment on the loan, and he had nothing with which to pay. He decided to use his time-tested method of determining God's will once again. This time, when he opened his eyes, he found his finger resting upon the words: "chapter 11." Although we might not use this haphazard approach to biblical interpretation, we must also make certain that the lesson to be drawn from the passage parallels our situation. This involves getting at the specific doctrinal import of the passage. From that we can then derive a more abstract doctrinal principle, which we can then again apply in a specific fashion in the present time.

The Method of Doctrinal Exegesis of Narrative Passages

These foregoing observations should make us sufficiently aware of the difficulties of obtaining our doctrine from narrative passages. We must now ask, however, what procedural processes we should follow in order to make usable those materials that are available to us in this form. While it need not always be done in this step-by-step fashion, there is value in enumerating the aspects of the method in this way.

1. A first step will be to make sure we have interpreted the passage as thoroughly and accurately as possible, apart from the question of its doctrinal content and affirmation. It is not that the doctrinal content is unimportant, or that doctrinal issues are not part of the interpretative process; simply put, we cannot begin to deal with the specifically doctrinal issues until we have understood the entire meaning of a passage. We should be especially careful to avoid drawing doctrinal conclusions prematurely. That would be like attempting to apply a practical application before ascertaining what it is that is being taught in the passage.

In particular, we must work very hard at determining the cultural background. If we do not, we may find ourselves mistaking the event for what it would be and mean in our own culture. Was this a social custom or a business transaction, and whichever it was, what did or would it mean in that setting?

2. Having done this, we should then ask what doctrine or doctrines are involved in this passage. The question of the passage's doctrinal content should always be asked, rather than simply when we are primarily looking for doctrinal teaching of the Bible. This will frequently reveal to us fruitful passages for doctrinal preaching of which we might otherwise not be aware. We should ask whether this illustrates actions of

God, and if so, which actions. We should also ask about whether the relationship between God and humans is illustrated here, and if so, what
aspects of it. Further, to the extent that humans are involved in the passage, which will most certainly be at least partially the case in virtually
every instance, what do their actions reveal about humanity, whether in
the natural state or in the state of grace? Or, if both God and humans
are involved, what can we learn about the relationship between the two?

Not all narrative passages will be equally fruitful for all doctrines.
The doctrines for which we can more confidently turn to narratives are
those that especially involve the intersection of the divine person, nature, and working with history. This means that doctrines such as providence, redemption, sin, and judgment are likely candidates. One might
well develop a checklist of doctrines to look for. This is logically and
methodologically separable from the question of just what is said about
this subject.

3. Once we have identified who is acting in the passage and what they
are doing, we need to push the process a step further. If our focus is on
one or more humans, who was each, and what sort of person was each?
Is this person a believer or an unbeliever? Was this an outstanding
Christian, or a merely nominal one, based on what else we know about
the person? Was this an Old Testament believer? Was this an unbeliever, and if so, what type of unbeliever? Was this a hardened, determined opponent of the things of God, or was this a person who showed
openness to the God of Israel, or perhaps was even a "god-fearer"?

This means finding out all we can about the person under consideration. One way in which this is done is through the use of a concordance, by looking up every reference to the person. That will provide us
with some additional narrative passages that shed light on the person's
life. In some cases, we find, not additional narrative, but discursive
statements about the person that may give us God's evaluation. Another
way is to use a Bible dictionary or encyclopedia, making sure that the
inferences the author of the article draws regarding our subject person
do not go beyond the data or evidence.

4. If we are dealing with an action of God, we should ask what this
action presupposes in terms of the qualities of God necessary to produce it. Similarly, where the narrative involves the historical person of
Jesus, what can and must we deduce from his actions to account for
those actions? What sort of being must he have been to have performed
such acts? Here we are going beyond the "functional" theology that was
so popular a generation or so ago,[6] which focused on the "mighty

6. E.g., Oscar Cullmann, *The Christology of the New Testament* (Philadelphia: Westminster, 1963).

deeds" of God, but did not really ask about the fundamental character of the God who so acted. With its anti-metaphysical bias, it avoided such inquiry into more ultimate questions of "nature" or "being." Yet those questions cannot be avoided, and with the resurgence of interest in and confidence in the discipline of metaphysics, they no longer need be ignored.

5. We must also ask about the conditions that brought about this situation. For example, in the case of the Tower of Babel, what led to God's action to scatter the people and confuse their languages? What preceded the great flood in terms of calling for such action? A similar case could be made in connection with the destruction of Sodom and Gomorrah. In each of these, the unusual and intense evil of the persons involved led to God's destructive judgment. The action, therefore, is a demonstration of God's righteousness, wrath, and judgment. What we have in mind here are actions of the persons involved. We also, however, should examine the resulting factors. For example, when Moses interceded with God on behalf of the people of Israel, what change in God did this bring about, and what does this tell us about the nature and activity of God?

6. We should ask what interpretation or evaluation of the event may be given within the passage, and by whom. To what extent can we say that God has supplied the word of divine revelation to go with the revelation through divine act? Whether in this passage or elsewhere, this is what frequently enables the narrative to function as narrative. As we noted earlier, in themselves events may have been relatively mute, but facts seldom if ever come to us uninterpreted. Indeed, Bernard Ramm, in discussing historical event as a modality of special revelation, examines several significant events of redemptive history and contends that without the revealed word of interpretation, those events would be opaque. This is true, for example, of the crucifixion of Jesus or the events of Pentecost.[7]

7. We will also want to look for other places in Scripture where there is a word of explanation, interpretation, or evaluation of the event(s) described in this passage. Usually this will be a passage following this one chronologically. Sometimes, however, it will be a passage that comes from an earlier point historically. In this case, it is prophecy, rather than history, as in the former instance.

Examples of this former type of reference can be found in a number of places. For example, when we seek to use the narrative of the conversion experience of Saul of Tarsus (Paul) (Acts 9:1–22), we will also want to examine the two passages in which Paul later refers to the event and

7. Ramm, *Special Revelation,* pp. 77–83.

interprets it (Acts 22:1–21; 26:1–23). Similarly, one may attempt to use the story of the conversion of Cornelius (Acts 10:1–48) to determine whether persons can be saved based on a knowledge of general revelation alone, without exposure to the special revelation. Here, Peter's reference to it may well shed light on this (Acts 11:1–18).

Some references that interpret an event may not even refer to it overtly. For example, as one seeks to grasp and interpret the dispute between Paul and Barnabas over whether to take John Mark with them, 2 Timothy 4:11 is helpful. There Paul asks Timothy to bring Mark with him, because Mark is profitable to him. There is no reference to the earlier incident, but there is certainly aftermath here, which tells us something about Paul's reaction and assessment.

If we have done the type of comparative research described in point 3 above, we will also have helpful and fruitful insight into these issues. For what really was happening will often be interpreted by the nonnarrative references to persons elsewhere. Hebrews 11, for example, sheds considerable light on the actions of a number of Old Testament characters. One of these is Abraham's taking Isaac up onto Mount Moriah, there to offer him as a sacrifice to Jehovah (Gen. 22:1–19). The writer to the Hebrews gives us some additional insight into what Abraham might have been thinking with respect to how Jehovah was to keep his promise of a son (11:17–19). There also is an interesting reference to Rahab's action in concealing the spies from her own countrymen (Josh. 2:1–6). Was this a sinful action on her part, or a commendable and right action? It appears from the statement that it was "by faith" that she did this (Heb. 11:31), that this was a right action, which of course leads us to the issue of how to interpret just what it was that she did (i.e., was it a justifiable lie, the lesser of two evils, or a legitimate ruse of war?).

This last point brings out a matter that needs more complete treatment. We should look for indications in Scripture, whether in the immediate context or elsewhere, of divine approval or disapproval of what is done and said by persons in narrative situations. For example, Job's "friends," who sought to offer him counsel in his predicament, had a great deal to say about God. One might attempt to build a theology on the concepts that emerge out of the narrative. That would be a risky business, however, for there are indications of disapproval of these men and their ideas in Scripture. On the other hand, we have Thomas' famous confession, "My Lord and my God" (John 20:28). If this was an incorrect assessment of Jesus' person, here was the perfect opportunity for him to correct Thomas, and it would have been very desirable and even mandatory for him to do so, if Thomas was mistaken. Jesus did not do this, however. He simply accepted what Thomas said. This constituted a certification of his confession of faith and the theology it contained.

8. We will want to make certain that, since this is an inductive use of Scripture, we have done a sufficiently complete induction. We must ask ourselves whether we have looked at all the instances of this type of doctrine in the narratives, so that we know that this case is representative of the entire biblical testimony. There are three possibilities of what may emerge as we begin to compile these. One is that the other instances may confirm this particular teaching. The second is that there may be other instances that contradict this particular view. The third possibility is that the others may supplement it, thus helping round out our conception of this doctrine.

There are various ways in which we may identify those passages that deal, narratively, with the same topic. One way is to consult a good systematic theology text, or preferably, several, and look at the index. This will lead us to the topic that we believe our passage is dealing with. It will also give some indications of other passages that the author of the systematic theology text we are examining thinks deal with this same doctrine. Some of these will be narrative in nature. We will, of course, want to look at each of these to make sure that they do indeed pertain to the same topic.

9. We will look for didactic statements about this kind of action. Once we have classified the doctrinal topic or topics of the passage, we can consult didactic passages written on this subject. This can be done with a concordance, a topical concordance, a topical Bible, or a theological wordbook, such as the *Theological Dictionary of the Old Testament*[8] or the *Theological Dictionary of the New Testament*.[9] Since didactic material is generally clearer, more easily identified as to its subject, and more direct, this serves as an important check against our incorrectly identifying or overextending the teaching in this passage.

It may be helpful to illustrate this methodology in connection with a sample passage, Acts 16:6–10. Let us suppose that one is preaching through the Book of Acts and comes to this passage. What is the doctrinal teaching of the passage? The first step would be to interpret the passage as clearly as possible. Having done that, the next step is to identify the doctrine or doctrines involved. This involves the relationship between God and a group of Christians, in which God directs the latter. Thus, it seems to be a matter of providence, or the form of providence

---

8. *Theological Dictionary of the Old Testament*, ed. G. Johannes Botterweck and Helmer Ringgren, 5 vols. (Grand Rapids: Eerdmans, 1974–88).

9. *Theological Dictionary of the New Testament*, 6 vols., ed. Gerhard Kittel and Gerhard Friedrich (Grand Rapids: Eerdmans, 1964–69).

proper sometimes referred to as government. Specifically, it appears to be a case of God giving guidance to some of his children. We then ask who these people were and what kind of persons they were. Here it is apparent not only that these were Christians, but that they were rather outstanding Christians, persons whose commitment to the Lord involved their serving in missionary work, and even risking their lives for the sake of the gospel. It therefore renders it likelier that they were correctly understanding and interpreting God's action than if they were unbelievers or carnal Christians. Further, this account is presented in the first-person plural, so that the description of what happened is from the standpoint of one of the participants, who then also is the Scripture writer. Paul, as we know, went on to become the great missionary to the Gentiles, and many of the churches to which he wrote his epistles were founded during this particular missionary journey.

When we ask about what qualities and abilities of God underlie this action, this would include both his knowledge and power. Knowledge would enter in terms of his ability to know what is good, to know the future, to know the need of the different areas and persons, and to know the specific characteristics and abilities of the person involved in ministry. As to the immediately preceding incidents, we are not told enough about the situation in any of these regions to have basis for knowing which would be more in need of Paul's ministry than would others. We do know that Paul has just had a disagreement with Barnabas about whether to take John Mark with them, and that he and his group have been traveling among the established churches, delivering a message to them and seeking to strengthen them in their faith and usefulness.

What is of special help to us in interpreting this incident, or actually two incidents, of God's direction, is that we are given a divinely inspired interpretation by one of the participants in the drama, the Scripture writer Luke himself. Thus, it presumably is an accurate explanation of what actually occurred.

We must also look for other places in Scripture where some word of explanation or interpretation of this passage is given. Here we may turn to two passages that may give us some light. One is Galatians 4, where Paul speaks of how he first came to preach the gospel to the Galatians. He says that it was because of an illness that he first did this preaching (v. 13). There also seems to be some hint that this may have been an affliction of the eyes, since he says that the Galatians would have plucked out their own eyes and given them to him, if they could (v. 15). If this understanding is correct, the means by which Paul and his companions were turned aside from their original plans and went to preach in Galatia was because of a physical ailment. We may also turn to 2 Corinthians 12, where Paul describes a "thorn in the flesh" that he experienced. He there tells us, not that it was sent by God, but that it was "a messenger of Satan" (v. 7). Although not sent by God, it was apparently used by him to accomplish his purpose in Paul's life, which was to keep him from being unduly exalted. Thus, we may be able to form a hypothesis that the doctrinal thrust of the passage is that God is capable of using all sorts of factors, even evil ones, to accomplish his purpose, in this case, specifically, to guide people into his desired course of action.

We would then want to look at other portions of Scripture, to see whether they support this idea or whether the opposite may emerge. Here we may indeed find that not all instances of adversity are to be understood as meaning that God is telling us to desist from or avoid a particular course of action, and follow a different one. For example, in the Garden of Gethsemane it was apparent to Jesus that his disciples would not stand by him in the moment of trial. In the temptation of Jesus, his attempt to carry through on the Father's will meant that he encountered difficulties, such as intense hunger, and even danger, such as being placed on the pinnacle of the temple. We therefore should understand this passage as teaching, not that God also uses adversity or that he and no one else (Satan) can, but that he is capable of using all things, even the actions of evil beings, to accomplish his will.

Another narrative passage that bears on this same matter is the story of Joseph in Genesis 37–50. Here a whole series of wrongs was done to Joseph by humans, some intentional, some inadvertent or careless. Joseph's brothers sold him into slavery. Then Potiphar's wife, whose advances had been spurned by Joseph, falsely accused him of the very thing she had in effect been attempting, and her husband had him cast into prison. There one of the king's servants, whose dream Joseph had interpreted, promised to remember Joseph to the king when he was restored to favor, but neglected to do so. Eventually, however, Joseph was made the second in power over the entire kingdom. When his brothers came to him, Joseph eventually revealed himself to them. They feared that he would take advantage of his position of power to take revenge, but instead he expressed his understanding that God had used their evil intentions to accomplish his good will. Twice he expressed this. In 45:8 he said, "So then, it was not you who sent me here, but God." In 50:19–20, he told his brothers, "Don't be afraid. Am I in the place of God? You intended to harm me, but God intended it for good to accomplish what is now being done, the saving of many lives." Here is a clear understanding that God uses even the evil deeds of wicked persons to accomplish his good.

Finally, we can look at some of the clear didactic statements in Scripture. One of these is found in Romans 8:28: "And we know that in all things God works for the good of those who love him, who have been called according to his purpose." Notice that the promise is that God works not simply in the obviously good things, but in *all* things, good and evil. Lest we apply too broadly this lesson that God's providence can be exercised to provide for and guide us even through the evil things of life, rather than just the obviously good things, note to whom the promise is given and to whom this providence was extended in the narratives. It was not just to anyone, and so not everyone can claim these. It is believers, God's spiritual children in the fullest sense, who are the recipients of both the promise and its fulfillment.

Conclusion

We conclude that the large amounts of narrative material found in the Bible provide a rich resource for formulating doctrine. Although the task is not easy, when we make the effort to apply an appropriate method of exegesis to these passages, they can prove very useful to us as a basis for preaching doctrinal sermons.

In this chapter and the preceding one, we have considered how to obtain the doctrinal content of didactic and narrative passages. In the next two chapters, we will examine the next step: bringing that doctrinal content into a form more understandable for the context in which we plan to preach or teach it.

8

Universalizing Doctrine

Imagine you are in room with a number of people. A foreign-looking gentleman comes over to you with a very serious look on his face. In his hand is a clear glass containing a colored liquid. He says to you, "Gift." Looking at his serious expression and not wanting to offend him by refusing his generosity, you take the glass and empty it completely. If, as you assumed, the man was speaking English, you have just graciously shown your appreciation for his kindness. If, however, he was speaking German, then you have just consumed poison, which is exactly what the man was trying to tell you it was.

In this rather dramatic incident, we see just what serious consequences a misunderstanding can have. The problems of moving from one language to another are not unlike the problem we have when we attempt to move from the Bible to a contemporary statement of what that doctrine really was that we were trying to express. For when we simply try to express that doctrine in the same form it has been expressed in at points in the past, something similar can result. The problem can be seen, for example, in the changes of meaning of words in the English language. The words "ghost" and "spirit" have basically reversed meanings since the seventeenth century, which produces problems when parents, steeped in the King James Version, speak of "The Holy Ghost" to their children who are not. Similarly, the English word "prevent" meant in the seventeenth century roughly what "precede" means today, which is helpful in understanding Paul's statement in 1 Thessalonians 4:15 that believers who are still alive when Jesus returns will not "prevent" (King James) or "precede" (most modern translations) those who have already died.[1] A similar problem is involved in translating one language into an-

1. I once met a very zealous King James advocate who thought that "prevent" meant in 1611 what it does today, so that Paul was teaching that those alive will not obstruct the resurrection of those who have died.

other. There may not be exact equivalents in the two languages, which is part of why we recommend that preachers be able to work with the original biblical languages. Beyond that, however, the terminology used by the church to seek to understand and explain the biblical teaching may convey a slightly different meaning than it had in the day that it was used. For example, a formula often repeated for the Trinity is that this is the teaching that there is one substance and three persons in God. The English word "person," however, does not express exactly the same meaning as did the Latin word *persona*.

Types of Hermeneutics

What we are after, then, is retention of the basic meaning of the biblical teaching, not omitting, adding to, or distorting any part of it, but expressing it in a fashion that is understandable to people today. This is hermeneutics in the broadest sense. In light of this kind of hermeneutics, we may observe several different versions of the hermeneutical process.

1. In a one-step hermeneutic, one simply takes the biblical statement, including any application, and utilizes it directly. Thus, one would go out and buy a sword, because Jesus commanded such an action (Luke 22:36). In practice, many persons who claim to utilize such a hermeneutic do not do so consistently. Thus, although the Bible prohibits eating anything that swims in the water but does not have scales, few Christians feel compelled to abstain from eating catfish, bullheads, and sharks. Those who interpret 1 Corinthians 11:1–13 as teaching that the husband should be the "head" of the family do not ordinarily insist on women wearing veils in church (when "praying or prophesying") or prohibit them from cutting their hair.[2] Similarly, most of those who believe that 1 Timothy 2:8–15 forbids women to be pastors or teachers of men do not similarly speak out against women in the churches wearing jewelry or costly apparel. Similarly, Christian pacifists usually base their position on a direct utilization of Jesus' teachings such as turning the other cheek (Matt. 5:39; Luke 6:29), but do not cut off their hands (Matt. 5:30; 18:8) or pluck out their eyes (Matt. 5:29; 18:9). Whatever the reason, a different hermeneutic is applied to portions of each passage than is applied to others.[3]

2. See, however, as an exception, John R. Rice, *Bobbed Hair, Bossy Wives, and Women Preachers: Significant Questions for Honest Christian Women Settled by the Word of God* (Wheaton, Ill.: Sword of the Lord, 1941).

3. The point here is not to discuss whether the position taken on the role of women is right or wrong, but to note that virtually all interpreters go beyond a one-step hermeneutic at some points.

2. A two-step hermeneutic recognizes a difference between the biblical situation and ours. It believes, however, that this difference involves meaning and application. Thus, the meaning of the biblical text is to be applied to our different period and situation.[4]

The question, however, arises: How much of the material in the original text is to be applied to us today? If this question is not wrestled with, we are in the same dilemma referred to in connection with our discussion of the one-step hermeneutic. In practice, the advocates of this type of hermeneutic actually seem to be smuggling an additional step into the first of these steps. So, for example, I once asked an Old Testament professor to give me the two steps of meaning of Genesis 22:1–19 (the account of Abraham's command to sacrifice Isaac). He responded by saying that there were two primary teachings in the passage: that God expects us to give up everything for him and that he always supplies what is needed. I replied that it seemed to me those were second-step or second-level meanings. The meaning of the first step is that God commanded Abraham to sacrifice his son and that God provided a sacrificial animal in Isaac's stead. The two-step hermeneutic at least spares us from putting our children to death, as a consistent follower of the one-step hermeneutic might do. It is doing this without a sufficiently self-conscious effort to do so. That professor saw the second step (the meaning for now) as being that we should be willing to give up wealth, fame, and even family, to follow God, and that God will give us satisfactions that will more than compensate for them, a teaching given quite literally by Jesus in Matthew 19:16–30. I would say that is the third step.

3. The intermediate step, then, is to find the universal or timeless meaning of the specific teaching given in a particular passage of Scripture. A three-step hermeneutic would then consist of determining the meaning for that time and place, abstracting the permanent essence of that meaning, and finally making a contemporary application of that truth that parallels for our time the application being made in the biblical passage. To use the passage just referred to, the three steps would be something like this:

Step 1. God commanded Abraham to sacrifice Isaac and then provided a sacrifice to substitute for him.
Step 2. God expects us to be willing to place him before everything else, and will more than compensate us for anything we give up.
Step 3. [One application] If God calls a person to be a foreign missionary, he expects that person to be willing to leave family and

4. Berkeley Mickelsen, *Interpreting the Bible* (Grand Rapids: Eerdmans, 1963), p. 56.

loved ones, but will supply joy and satisfaction that far exceed the sacrifice made.

But what is the doctrinal import of this? We need to be very careful in defining the method. On the one hand, we must make certain that we retain the whole essence of the biblical message, not allowing any of it to be disregarded. On the other hand, we want to be certain that we are not insisting on something that is a particular interpretation attached to the doctrine, but not really something integral to the biblical revelation. Examples can be cited of both errors.

In the sixteenth and seventeenth centuries, the church found its tradition challenged by the Copernican revolution in astronomy. The traditional view was the geocentric view, the idea that the earth is stationary and the sun (as well as the other planets) moves around it. In the Copernican view, however, the sun is the center of the solar system, and the earth and the other planets revolve around it. This seemed to many of the theologians of the time to contradict the teaching of Scripture. Thus, they resisted the new teaching, condemning as heretics those who taught it. Eventually, evidence for the new view became so overwhelming that the church had to revise its view. It had been guilty of defending what it thought to be the essence of the teaching, whereas it was actually defending a particular interpretation of those passages, based on the views of Ptolemy and, ultimately, Aristotle.

The opposite kind of error can be found in a number of modern theologians. One who set out to modernize the faith by understanding in contemporary categories that expressed the abiding experience underlying them was Harry Emerson Fosdick. He took, for example, the doctrine of the second coming of Christ. This, he recognized, had been held by many Christians for a long time. Yet, he insisted, this is an untenable idea. It was simply part of the primitive way of thinking that the New Testament writers held. We can no longer believe this way, but must rather ask about the abiding experience that was expressed through this idea, namely, that of the hope for the victory of righteousness upon the earth. Is there a category that we can now use to express this experience of hope? Fosdick believed that there was, and suggested the use of the idea of the transformation of society in which humans participate, but which is ultimately God's doing.[5] We must ask, however, whether this is a new way of expressing an old hope, or if we are here dealing with a fundamentally different idea and experience. It appears to me that the latter is the case.

5. Harry Emerson Fosdick, *The Modern Use of the Bible* (New York: Macmillan, 1933), pp. 104–10.

Decontextualizing Ourselves

To be able to identify the essence of the doctrine from our own perspective is not so easy, however. For we bring to the examination of Scripture and reflection on doctrine a certain set of assumptions that we may then actually read into Scripture. We are talking about an unconscious and pre-reflective sort of eisegesis. It is as if one viewed a scene through tinted glasses. One of the contentions of the postmodern age is that the absolute objectivity that science idolized in the modern period is deceptive. We all bring some preconceptions to the intellectual task. To say this, however, is not to concede it and accept it as inevitable. We can and must take all possible steps to minimize this effect, since what we are ultimately after is to hear God's Word, not our own.

It is easy to see the presuppositions and biases of others from an earlier time, or even from our own time. It is not so easy to see them in ourselves, however. Until we are able to understand something of the perspective from which we think and speak, we will be unable to isolate the permanent within the many varieties of expression.

There are, however, some exercises that can enable us to grasp something of this self-understanding. One of the most useful that I have found is to debate the issue, taking both sides. One of the most helpful courses I ever took was one on discussion and debate that I took during my freshman year in college. It was not a very good course and the instructor was not very competent, in terms of his knowledge of the field or his teaching ability, but the subject proved extremely important and helpful. We were forced first to defend one side of an issue and then the other. What this exercise does is reduce dogmatism and opinionation. One can no longer simply hold an understanding as if it were the only possible position on the subject. There are other endeavors that also help with this problem. One is to expose oneself to other perspectives. This may mean first, those of different cultures. What seems to us to be of the essence of a particular doctrine does not seem to others to be taught in the very same portion of Scripture. As the third world church grows not only numerically, but also in doctrinal sophistication, it will increasingly make us aware of alternative ways of viewing certain issues. It is also helpful to gain the perspective of other historical periods. The study of church history, particularly historical theology, should help us see that the same issues have been framed in different ways at different times. Finally, exposing oneself to those holding different current perspectives is helpful in identifying our own presuppositions. Reading rather radically different theologies, while sometimes frustrating and even irritating, is a wholesome endeavor.

It is also helpful to seek to understand the forces that are currently influencing us. There are treatises that regularly assess the current milieu. Books like Robert N. Bellah et al.'s *Habits of the Heart,*[6] Alan Bloom's *The Closing of the American Mind,*[7] and in an earlier period, John Herman Randall's *Making of the Modern Mind*[8] help us grasp something of the milieu within which we are working and why certain things seem as they do to us. Our own biography, intellectually and religiously, also offers clues to assist us in self-understanding. For example, if we are able to recognize and acknowledge the forces against which we are reacting, we may gain insight into why we view matters as we do. Several years ago I participated in a conference of Christian sociologists, in which two philosophers and two theologians had been invited to participate. The other theologian presented a paper, analyzing what he termed "The Old [name of a seminary] school" of biblical inspiration. He identified what he thought was the major set of presuppositions of that school of thought. During the discussion time, I asked him, "One hundred years from now, when persons discuss 'The Old [name of his seminary] school' of biblical inspiration, what will they say were its presuppositions?" He seemed utterly unable to comprehend the question. The sociologists, however, immediately saw the issue, and continued to press the question.

Failure to recognize our presuppositions may lead us to identify our own view with the timeless essence of a doctrine, rather than a time-bound form of expression. I once heard a Roman Catholic theologian trace the history of the doctrine of revelation. He then announced that he would state the essence of the doctrine, and proceeded to state a mid-twentieth-century neo-orthodox version of the doctrine!

Decontextualizing Biblical Statements

Decontextualizing biblical statements involves understanding that the original writings were themselves already contextualizations. While they may at times appear to be purely essential or uncontextualized statements, this, in varying degrees, is not always the case. We, therefore, are not always working from pure raw materials, in the case of the biblical sources, but rather from something that is already in a manu-

6. Robert Bellah, et al., *Habits of the Heart: Individualism and Commitment in American Life* (New York: Harper, 1985).

7. Allan Bloom, *The Closing of the American Mind: How Higher Education Has Failed Democracy and Impoverished the Souls of Today's Students* (New York: Simon and Schuster, 1987).

8. John Herman Randall Jr., *The Making of the Modern Mind: A Survey of the Intellectual Background of the Present Age*, rev. ed. (Boston: Houghton Mifflin, 1940).

factured condition. Thus, it is not a matter of simply taking the biblical material and giving it a contextualized form, or of changing the biblical material into the present form through a small modification. Rather, the biblical contextualization of the statement must be reduced to a more raw or essential condition.

Continuing to bear this in mind, we must also then seek to isolate and eliminate or at least neutralize the elements peculiar to this particular passage. We must ask what local factors may have colored the specific expression of this truth. Here it would be good to think of this issue, not as a matter of distortion of the truth, but rather as an inevitable and necessary coloration of that truth. We will want to know as much as possible about the situation from which and to which the author was writing. Was there some particular heresy or problem that he was attempting to counteract? For example, one might get the impression from John's presentation of the person of Jesus Christ in 1 John that what is really important is the humanity of Jesus, and that his deity is not so crucial. To draw that conclusion, however, would be to make a false inference. We can see this by looking carefully at the situation that he was encountering. It is apparent that there was a problem with certain docetists, who denied that Jesus was genuinely and entirely human. This can be seen from 4:1–6. It might seem as if this is using the book in a circular fashion, understanding its statement in light of itself. In actuality, however, this is not the case. It is as if John is stating the question and then giving us the answer. The meaning of the answer is definitely strongly affected by the question to which it is the answer.

Decontextualization means that we should look for differing images for the same doctrine. These variations are not of the essence of the doctrine. For example, in terms of the doctrine of angels, these are often thought of as having wings, with which they fly. It is true that in Isaiah 6 they appear this way, if we may consider seraphs to be angels. Actually, these beings are pictured as having six wings. Yet in several other places in Scripture angels are pictured differently (for example, an angel appearing as a young man in a white robe in Jesus' tomb in Mark 16:5).

Decontextualization also involves the study of the unique emphases of different writers dealing with the same account. This is best done in the case of parallel accounts, such as are found in the Synoptic Gospels. While redaction criticism has been somewhat controversial in some conservative circles, it need not be so. It is an attempt to identify the variations in the several accounts, with the assumption being that each of the authors has made certain variations of selection, order, inclusion, and exclusion of material for the sake of giving a particular emphasis. What can be done is to determine, as a result, what the original material was with which these authors were working. While this is usually a matter of narrative details, it also relates to doctrinal concepts. Knowing the audience to which the writer was directing the writing helps us understand both the writer's statement and the underlying essence. For example, knowing that Matthew was writing to a predominantly Jewish audience helps us understand why he uses the expression, "kingdom of heaven" whereas the other Synoptists use "kingdom of God." To the Jew, the name "Yahweh" was so sacred that they would not pronounce it. Thus, they would substitute the word "heaven" for "God." This can be seen elsewhere in Jesus' statements, as in the parable of the prodigal son (Luke 15:18, 21).

We will also want to eliminate any variations that are found in the writing of a given writer in different situations. Paul, for example, emphasized different aspects of the doctrine of salvation in different situations. For example, he emphasized the dimension of justification by faith alone in his writing to the Galatians. He also, however, emphasizes the necessity of living in a certain way. These observations suggest that either form of expression alone is not the whole picture, and that the truth must embody both.

Once we have sought to eliminate the variations in the doctrinal statements in various parts of the Bible, the next step is to look for the positive essence. This may come to light in various ways. One is simple noticing, in our comparative study, the common factors found in the various statements. This may be in the several references by the same author, or it may emerge from the treatment of the same subjects by several different authors.

The identification of a common theme or motif may not be as difficult as we perhaps think. We do something of this nature in various areas of life and experience. Take dreams, for instance. There are certain generic themes that can be found in numerous varying dreams. For example, I fairly often dream something like this: I am scheduled to teach a class or speak at a church worship service. I am not quite ready. I am not dressed, or have not shaved. I rush to try to get to the place in time to fulfill my obligations, but cannot quite make it. Sometimes I cannot get to the airport in time to catch a plane. The interesting thing is that my wife has a recurrent dream in which she has dinner guests coming, and she is frantically, but unsuccessfully, attempting to get all the items prepared in time to serve them. Further, my travel agent told me when I called her one morning, that she had dreamt about me, and several of her other clients, the previous night. This dream occurred during one of the sales that the airlines periodically have, and she was attempting to get all of her clients' flights ticketed before the deadline expired. It seems to me that her dream, my wife's dreams, and mine are really generically the same dream. If dreams are conscious manifestations of unconscious desires, fears, and other thoughts, then all of these are really expressing the same anxiety.

I believe that one can develop skill in this task of identifying a common essence of a doctrine. Some of the analogy tests in the Graduate Record Exam or the Miller Analogies Exam are in many ways similar to the issue we are discussing here. There are books and computer programs that have as their purpose preparing one for the type of examinations we have just mentioned. Engaging in this type of exercise can potentially sensitize us to identifying the parallels among motifs and to being able to determine which are significant and which are insignificant. This skill is at least in part an art rather than a science, so it may not be possible to teach it completely, or to obtain it through learning a series of steps or procedures, but this does not mean that nothing can be done to acquire increased ability.

Criteria of Essence

One criterion for the essence of a doctrine is constancy across time periods. It is true that the revelation that God gave and that is recorded in Scripture is progressive. That is to say, the details of the revelation were not all revealed at once, but became greater in number and variety as time passed. This does not mean that certain doctrines were unknown at an earlier period and only subsequently shared with the people of God, but rather that the doctrines were described more specifically in the later stages of the revelational process.

One example is the nature of salvation. It is sometimes thought, on a popular level, that salvation is by grace through faith during the New Testament era, but that in Old Testament times the people of God were saved by performing works of obedience to the law. This, however, is not supported by Scripture. In fact, Paul makes it very clear in Galatians that no one is saved that way, and that this has always been the case. He goes out of his way to explain, that even Abraham, the father of the Jews, was justified by faith, rather than by works. It is true, of course, that the New Testament statement of the belief is more detailed than that found in the Old Testament, and these details are themselves normative, but that does not negate the fact that the Old Testament salvation was essentially the same experience. It is not likely that one would first turn to an Old Testament text for a sermon on salvation, but when preaching from the Old Testament one will develop a passage dealing with salvation in a way harmonious with and in many ways similar to, the New Testament doctrine.

Another factor to look for in seeking to identify the common essence of a doctrine is a commonality across cultures. We are fortunate in this regard in the fact that the biblical revelation was addressed to, and expressed in, a variety of such cultures. Most prominently, this involved both Hebrew or Jewish cultures, and Gentile or Greek cultures. We may identify, to some extent, those places where Paul preached to predominantly Jewish audiences, versus preaching to primarily Gentile audiences, as well as the letters written to Hebrew Christian congregations as compared with those addressed to congregations of Gentiles. The common factor found in each of these will then be the essence. For example, when discussing the issue of atonement, there is no real variation in the message from one of these cultural settings to the other. While there are differences in emphasis or in imagery, throughout all of these there is an agreement on the substitutionary nature of the work of Christ in his death.

On the other hand, when we work with the doctrine of the church, specifically, the government of the church, we do not find quite this same sort of uniformity. There are references in the Book of Acts to something that sounds like an elder form of government, and even something like an episcopal type of government. This is seen in the fact that Paul and Barnabas appointed elders in the churches (Acts 14:23). On the other hand, there are references in Paul's letters (Phil. 1:1; 1 Tim. 3:8, 10, 12, 13) to deacons, which carries a connotation of service rather than ruling. When a successor to Judas was to be selected, the apostles presented this to the entire assembly of believers, which at this point numbered about 120 persons (Acts 1:15–26). Further, when it was necessary to convene in Jerusalem to discuss the question of circumcision of Gentile believers, the congregation in Antioch appointed Paul and Barnabas and sent them to Jerusalem, where they met with the elders. The elders then sent representatives to the congregation at Antioch. It is almost as if the church in Antioch was functioning with a more purely democratic or congregational form of government, while the Jerusalem congregation was governed by elders. There even is a specification that at Antioch there were prophets and teachers in the church (13:1). When the need of the Jerusalem brothers became apparent, the disciples in Antioch sent Paul and Barnabas to bear their gifts to the elders.

What are we to make of these phenomena? Some have attempted to solve the problem by combining the concepts, so that the churches have both elders and deacons. There are other possibilities, however. The Jewish churches, which functioned against the background of the synagogue, were more likely to have elders than the Gentile churches, which had no such background. Another possibility is that in the earlier stages of the development of the church, a more top-heavy approach was needed; Paul appointed elders in all the churches initially, but as the various members of the church became more sophisticated, they were able to assume a greater degree of responsibility for the functioning of the church. Whether we follow either of these approaches, it is possible to affirm that certain factors do seem to emerge: There is a recognition of the need for leaders of some type, possessing authority that is to be recognized by the body of believers; there also is to be concern for each of the members, all of whom are important.

Another way to identify the underlying essence is to look for the supporting reasons offered for the particular concept that is presented for belief. When the reason is not merely some temporary or local factor but instead is rooted in a permanent matter, such as the establishment by the Lord or a feature of the very creative act itself, then this may be an indication that this doctrine or this feature of a doctrine is of the very essence of the doctrine, and therefore is to be maintained. An example of this may be found in the fact that God made the human as the last and presumably the highest of the creatures, that he made both the male and the female in his image and entrusted to both of them the task of dominion-having, or tending and ruling over the creation. At no point prior to the fall is there an indication of subjugation of either the woman or the man to the other. This is then an indication of the full and presumably equal humanity of male and female. Further, if Adam and Eve were the entire human race at that point, if all humans have descended from them, then all humans are made in the divine image and are objects of God's love and potentially are to share in fellowship with him.

A further factor in identifying the essence of a doctrine is that what is stated in a universal setting is to be considered essential, permanent, and binding. One doctrine that can be classified this way on the basis of this criterion is baptism. The command to baptize was given by Jesus in a very universal setting. The disciples were to go into *all* the world and preach the gospel to *every* creature. That this command was not just to this one generation of believers is indicated by his statement, "I am with you always, even to the end of the age." Consequently, this must be regarded as not simply a temporary practice, but of the essence of the doctrine. To determine the mode of baptism will require demonstrating that a particular mode was entailed in the command, or that its meaning is lost if the mode is changed. Contrasted with the instituting or ordaining of baptism, however, is the Lord's establishment of footwashing. That was not given in a similarly universal setting of the baptism command. For one thing, there was no indication that this command extended to anyone beyond the immediate group of disciples who heard it. Further, it is not stated as being of perpetual endurance or application or of universal geographical pertinence. The underlying principle there, the importance of each believer being a servant and being willing to subjugate himself or herself to every other, does carry the flavor of permanence and universality associated with essentiality, but the particular act does not.

Another criterion that needs to be noted and utilized is the final position within the progressive revelation. If one asks, for example, whether the atonement made by Jesus Christ on the cross is the universal basis of salvation or whether animal sacrifice such as was practiced by the Old Testament community of believers is still an option for salvation, the answer must be the former alternative. The reason for this is that the death of Christ succeeded and supplanted the sacrificial system, and that, indeed, the salvation of the Old Testament believers actually was accomplished by Christ's death, not by animal sacrifices.

Some Test Cases

If our methodology is sound, then it can be applied, and its success in those cases will be evidence that we are on the right track. We will try a few of these concepts, to determine the permanent and indispensable essence, as well as to separate this from the possible variant expressions they have been given.

The Transcendence of God

In many different places and in a number of images the Bible affirms the otherness and the superiority of God to humans and the rest of creation. He is the originator of all that is, the one who is the embodiment of all truth and wisdom. He is not limited in any of the ways that we are. He is infinite.

This teaching appears in a variety of places throughout Scripture. It is seen in Jehovah's appearance to Moses in the burning bush (Exod. 3:5–6). The very ground was holy, so Moses was to take off his shoes. Similarly, the presence of God in the mountain and in the Most Holy Place in the tabernacle was so sacred that only Moses, in the former case, and the high priest, in the latter, were allowed to come near. Places, objects, and special ministers were separated and made holy to God. In Isaiah, we see a similar picture of God's transcendence, in the vision that Isaiah has of him as high and lifted up, and his realization that he is "a man of unclean lips" (6:1–7). In chapter 55, Isaiah reports God saying, "For my thoughts are not your thoughts, neither are your ways my ways, says the LORD. For as the heavens are higher than the earth, so are my ways higher than your ways and my thoughts than your thoughts" (vv. 8–9). Here the point seems to be the superiority of God's knowledge and action, whereas the earlier references pertained more to his moral superiority to humans.

God's superior power is demonstrated in numerous ways throughout Scripture. When Moses questions whether Pharaoh will listen to him, God offers a demonstration of his power as proof of the divine commission and origin. Pharaoh's magicians were able to match these up to a certain point, but ultimately Moses prevailed with plagues that only God could inflict. Numerous passages indicate the superior military power of God over all the foes of Israel. One of these is 2 Kings 6, where God shows Elisha's servant the great number of warriors that are on their side against the enemy, and then strikes those enemy soldiers blind.

The New Testament also teaches this truth about God in numerous ways. In his discussion with the Samaritan woman at Jacob's well, Jesus emphasized the limitlessness of God, when he said, "the hour is coming when neither on this mountain nor in Jerusalem will you worship the Father. . . . God is spirit, and those who worship him must worship in spirit and truth" (John 4:21, 24). A similar idea had been expressed by Solomon at the dedication of temple: "But will God indeed dwell on the earth? Behold, heaven and the highest heaven cannot contain thee; how much less this house which I have built!" (1 Kings 8:27). It was repeated by Stephen (Acts 7:48–50) and Paul (Acts 17:24–28). The Book of Revelation contains several scenes in which God is praised for his greatness (4:1–11; 7:11–17; 15:1–4; 19:1–8).

When we apply some of the criteria we listed earlier, we find that this matter of God's superiority in moral goodness, power, and knowledge is indeed an essential doctrinal point. It fulfills the criterion of constancy across time periods, being found all the way from the earlier portions of the Old Testament to the scenes of the future in Revelation. It also is found in a wide variety of cultures, being proclaimed to the assembly of Israel and to the Gentile audience at the Areopagus. Further, the statement of the doctrine is clearly made universal. The pictures in heaven are of all people. Solomon's speech was clearly intended for the entire congregation of Israel. Paul's message refers to how God has made all nations on earth. These were not simply occasioned by or intended for a merely local situation. And certainly this truth was offered as the basis of experiences of worship, trust, and obedience, which are essential parts of the Christian life.

What, however, of the specific imagery of transcendence sometimes used? Quite frequently this has been made spatial in nature, as in the idea of "God up there" which John A. T. Robinson has criticized.[9] In a

---

9. John A. T. Robinson, *Honest to God* (Philadelphia: Westminster, 1963), pp. 29–44.

period of time when the earth was thought of as flat, it was natural to think of God simply as the one who is at a higher elevation than we are. This was encouraged by the reference to the heavens being above the earth in Isaiah 55. In our time, however, we now understand "up" and "down" to be relative terms. What the North American may think of as down is quite the opposite to the Australian or South African. Need this concept of God's transcendence as spatial be taken literally and retained in that form in our time?

Actually, it should be noted that the Isaiah 55 reference is a simile: "As the heavens are high above the earth, so are my thoughts above your thoughts." This was apparently intended as an illustration, a figure or an image, rather than what was being affirmed per se. Further, it is only one of several images employed, such as a burning bush, the inability of any human structure to contain God, and so on. It appears that what is being affirmed about God's transcendence with respect to space is not that he is very high up, or of very great size, but that he is immeasurable. There is nowhere that God is not. He is not restricted to any one space. His transcendence is also seen in relationship to time. He is not restricted to a particular time. He is the Alpha and Omega, the beginning and the end. He simply has no beginning or end. Transcendence is God's infinity, as contrasted with our finitude, and several images may assist us in grasping and expressing this great truth.

Human Nature

One issue of special relevance for our time because of the wide interest in the human is the question of the constitutional nature of human beings. When we look at Scripture we find that, on the one hand, persons are regarded or treated as unified entities.[10] It is the person who sins and the person who is redeemed, not the soul or the body as such. References such as "the flesh" are seen to refer, not to physical nature as such, but to the sinful tendencies of the person, the tendency toward self-gratification and independence. The person is thought of as sinful in mind, thoughts, feelings, and so on.

On the other hand, it appears that there is such a thing as existence in some sense apart from the kind of bodily existence human beings ordinarily experience. There is rather clear teaching of the reality of death and a resurrection of the body. Yet there is also evidence of the existence and persistence of the person during the intervening time between these two events. This is a conscious state, involving experience and interaction. For example, Jesus said to the repentant thief on the cross,

10. Bruce Reichenbach, "Life after Death: Possible or Impossible?" *Christian Scholar's Review* 3.3 (1973): 235.

"Truly, I say to you, today you will be with me in Paradise" (Luke 23:43). In Luke 16:19–31, in what is either a parable or an actual account of the intermediate state, the persons of the story are in conscious existence following their deaths. Paul on two occasions spoke of being absent from the body and present with the Lord (2 Cor. 5:1–10; Phil. 1:19–26). These references seem to argue for some sort of existence without the usual embodiment that requires a greater complexity of human nature than naturalistic views allow.

In the history of Christian thought one common way of conceiving of these two sorts of states has been the categories of body and soul.[11] In this scheme, the body is the physical nature of the person; the soul is the immaterial aspect, the "real person" that frequently takes on a body, but need not do so. In more recent years, however, this body–soul model has been questioned. There is a strong aversion today to any sort of metaphysical dualism. More important, the biblical data do not really support this sort of separation. There is reference to the body in such a way as to leave the impression that the word is a synonym for "person," and the same is true of the soul or spirit.[12] Thus, a person is to glorify God in one's body and to recognize that the body is the temple of God or of the Holy Spirit. It is not merely a vehicle of the soul's activity, nor the source of the soul's temptations and sin, but is virtually the person.

This conception of two different states or modes of existence seems to be an essential part of the doctrine. It meets the criterion of a variety of cultures. Jesus spoke of it to his Jewish hearers, and Paul wrote to Gentiles about this intermediate state with its conscious personal existence. It is true that there is no very clear conception expressed in the Old Testament of this sort of nonmaterial existence, but on the criterion of later position in the progressive revelation, this qualifies as part of the essence, for there is no point at which this idea is replaced or supplanted. It is necessary that we hold this view of human nature that allows for an intermediate state, but without making it dependent on a traditional but possibly unbiblical view of body and soul.

---

11. E.g., William Newton Clarke, *An Outline of Christian Theology* (New York: Scribner, 1901), pp. 182–83.

12. N. P. Bratsiotis, "בָּשָׂר," in *Theological Dictionary of the Old Testament*, ed. G. J. Botterweck and Helmer Ringgren (Grand Rapids: Eerdmans, 1977), vol. 2, pp. 325–27.

9

Particularizing Doctrine

After we have identified the permanent element of a doctrine, we must express that essence in a form that will be intelligible and relevant to our contemporaries. It may be helpful to observe the nature of our endeavor at this point. What we are attempting to do is move from one contextualized situation to another. We do so by decontextualizing the biblical doctrinal teaching so that it can then be recontextualized.

The Nature of Contextualization

Contextualization is translating, not from one language to another, but from one era or conceptual framework to another. This is similar to what is done in language-learning work, where the student does not learn the semantic equivalent in the target language of a word from the source language. Rather, the student grasps the object represented and then thinks of the word in the language to which he or she is translating. This enables learners from a variety of native languages to learn the same language together. Thus, for example, an instructor teaching German to a group of English-speakers does not say, "'The dog' equals *der Hund*." Rather, he shows them a picture of a dog and says, "*der Hund*." This is not word-to-word translation, but concept- or image-to-word translation. The aim is to break free of the language one customarily thinks in. It works the same way in the opposite direction. When the instructor says, "*der Hund*," the student should think of a dog, rather than the words, "the dog."

This is in some ways parallel to the endeavor that is made in translating original books of the Bible into various languages. The aim is to get back to the Greek, Hebrew, or Aramaic, rather than translating the biblical language into another language, such as English (or taking the product of someone else's work in doing this), and then translating into the new language. Occasionally, this is not done. For example, there is a New Testament translation in simple German entitled *Die Gute Nachricht*. This, however, is not a translation from the Greek, but from a simple English translation entitled *Good News for Modern Man*. What has happened is that some vestiges of English idioms have been carried over into the German. Actually, this is what Roman Catholic scholars faced for many years, since they had to work from the Latin Vulgate, a translation, rather than being able to go directly from Greek and Hebrew to their own languages.

What we are striving for is to express the same content, but in a different form. This places our labors in the classification of what William Hordern termed the "translators," as contrasted with the "transformers," who are willing to alter the message in order to make it intelligible and acceptable to modern hearers.[1] It is in some ways fairly easy to make something intelligible and relevant by saying something different, but sometimes the message is lost in the process.

Some readers may at this point become fearful that changing an expression is somehow threatening to the doctrine of biblical authority and inspiration. We do not have in mind as radical a reexpression as might be unintentionally connoted by this discussion. An example may help relieve this anxiety.

The doctrine in Scripture is frequently expressed in concepts drawn from a primarily agrarian or agricultural society. That served very well as recently as the beginning of the twentieth century, when as high as a third of the workforce of the United States was engaged in agriculture. By 1980, however, that figure had dropped to 3 percent.[2] Even those who live in what are still agricultural communities are becoming "rurbanized," taking on the thinking patterns of urban dwellers.[3] For example, the doctrine of providence is often conveyed using the imagery of the shepherd and his sheep. Jesus liked this concept very much, using it on numerous occasions, such as the shepherd who goes out seeking the one lost sheep. That image was very meaningful to his hearers, and to many Bible readers and hearers for most of the history of the church up to the present time. Many, at least in certain cultures, had enough contact with sheep so that they understood experientially something of their helplessness and what a shepherd did in relationship to sheep. That is no longer true. The truth is still unchanged, that God watches

1. William Hordern, *New Directions in Theology Today,* vol 1, *Introduction* (Philadelphia: Westminster, 1966), chapter 7.

2. John Naisbitt, *Megatrends: Ten New Directions Transforming Our Lives* (New York: Warner, 1982), p. 14.

3. Russell Chandler, *Racing toward 2001: The Forces Shaping America's Religious Future* (Grand Rapids: Zondervan, 1992), pp. 20–23, 305.

over his children with great knowledge, power, and care. It is important, however, to find imagery to convey for our time what the image of shepherd and sheep did in Jesus' time.

We are talking about contextualizing the truth for specific situations today. This contextualizing, however, involves three different dimensions of truth, or of changed situations.[4] The first is what we might term the dimension of length. This is translation along the line of temporal change, bringing the truth from the past to the present. There are successive, although frequently overlapping, epochs. Our aim is to go back to the biblical period, decontextualize the message there, and then reexpress it for our time. We must be certain that we get all the way back to the Scriptures, so that we are not merely reexpressing something from another century that falls between the biblical time and ours.

The second dimension is that of breadth or width. This is the cross-cultural factor, the movement from one culture to another. At any given time there exist a number of different frameworks or mentalities, of various expressions. It is likely, as cultures become more complex, fragmented, and unstable, that the number of these is increasing, and that within each major culture there are numerous subcultures. Too often in the past we have identified a particular culture with the inherent character of theology, and have exported that to those of other cultures. When those members of other cultures study theology, because the teachers and books are frequently oriented to that one culture, they become "Westernized," "anglicized," "bleached," or something similar. With the rise of third world Christianity, whose growth rate and vitality are far outstripping that of Western Christianity, this will have to change. Indigenous theology will need to be done, and is beginning to be done.

The third dimension of contextualization is what I would term height. This is the adjustment of the concepts for different levels of sophistication. The age, intelligence, background, education level, knowledge of Scripture, and several other factors cause persons to vary greatly in their ability to handle abstract and more refined or advanced concepts. The ability to express a concept at these different levels is necessary to facilitate making the doctrines intelligible and relevant to such varied persons.[5]

4. I have developed these concepts at greater length in *Christian Theology* (Grand Rapids: Baker, 1986), pp. 75–77.
5. I have sometimes given an essay examination in which students are asked to relate how they would explain a doctrinal concept like the Trinity to several different persons, such as a first-grader, a college student, and a Hindu.

The Search for Appropriate Contemporary Concepts

In selecting features of contemporary culture to which to relate the message, it is important to assess their appropriateness and helpfulness. We should decide which features are positive from the standpoint of the Christian message and therefore ought to be encouraged and reinforced by being utilized; which are neutral and therefore may be used; and which are negative and therefore ought to be avoided. We will examine some representatives of each of these classes.

Positive Concepts

It is true that the world has changed, both in terms of how it actually is and in terms of how we perceive it. One of the early discoveries in the modern era was the heliocentric view. Because some theologians felt that the biblical revelation taught a geocentric view, the church resisted the new view. With the passage of time and with more information, most Christians now understand that the Bible does not affirm the geocentric view for belief, and that it was actually derived more from secular thinkers such as Aristotle than from the Scriptures.[6]

Another area where understanding has changed is in the field of geology, particularly concerning the age of the earth. For a long time, it was popular to attempt to date the earth by adding the figures in the genealogies in the Old Testament. The most popular and widely held of these dating schemes was that devised by Bishop Ussher, which placed the creation at 4004 B.C. This approach has been rendered unlikely for two reasons. Various methods of dating, such as radioactive dating, lead to a much higher figure for the age of the earth, such as about 6 billion years. Further, from our study of Scripture we now know that it is not possible to use the genealogies in this simple fashion.[7] Thus, it is not necessary to resist or reject this development.

There also is belief that there has been development of various biological forms from less complex forms. In its most complete version, this theory of evolution sees all life as having developed from the simplest forms by a process of natural selection. This has been strongly resisted by conservative Christians during the years since it was first propounded. Yet it should be noted that the Genesis creation account, if taken as a somewhat literal description of creation, does not require us to hold that all of the species were directly and immediately created at

---

6. John Herman Randall Jr., *The Making of the Modern Mind* (Boston: Houghton Mifflin, 1926), p. 234.

7. See T. H. Green, "Primeval Chronology," in *Classical Evangelical Essays in Old Testament Interpretation*, ed. Walter C. Kaiser (Grand Rapids: Baker, 1972), pp. 13–28.

the beginning. There is basis for objecting to total evolution, that all forms have arisen through the process of evolution, including human life, but the word translated "kind," the Hebrew word *min*, is simply too general to lead us to conclude that it is speaking of species. It simply means kind, as a sort of subdivision of what is.[8]

Another twentieth-century discovery is the unconscious dimension of human personality. Sigmund Freud, the founder of psychoanalysis, was the person who first popularized the idea that much of human belief and behavior is motivated and caused by unconscious factors. This is widely referred to in terms of the "Freudian slip," in which a person says something unintentionally that reveals something going on in his or her mind.[9] While it is not necessary or desirable to accept all the details of Freud's particular version of this idea, the basic concept is not only not contrary to Christian doctrine; it is potentially very useful as a basis for understanding how inspiration of the biblical authors by the Holy Spirit could take place.

A concept now very widely accepted is Einstein's special theory of relativity. According to this, such basic concepts as space and time, once considered absolute, must now be understood as variable or relative. This represents a major change from Newtonian physics. A corollary of this theory is the convertibility of matter and energy. These are not two different things, but simply the same thing under different conditions. When matter is accelerated to the speed of light, it is converted to energy, which has been dramatically demonstrated in the case of the atomic or fission bomb.[10]

Since theology was for such a long time related to Newtonian physics, some Christians are tempted to insist on and defend that set of concepts, thinking they are thereby defending biblical doctrine per se. The objection to cremation, for example, may be a result of interpreting the resurrection in Newtonian categories. It does not appear that the Bible requires belief in the fixity of space, time, matter, and energy, or whether one is free to do his or her theology in a framework in which space and time are relative and matter and energy are convertible into one another.

These, and a number of other concepts we have not mentioned, need not and should not be resisted. To do so is not necessary. It is not required by the Bible, correctly interpreted. Defending something that

8. The derivation is from a verb that means literally, "to split the earth." The noun can also mean heretic or schismatic. See Francis Brown, S. R. Driver, and Charles A. Briggs, *A Hebrew and English Lexicon of the Old Testament* (Oxford: Clarendon, 1955), p. 568.

9. Sigmund Freud, *A General Introduction to Psychoanalysis* (New York: Washington Square, 1960), pt. 1.

10. Lincoln Barnett, *The Universe and Dr. Einstein* (New York: Mentor, 1952), pp. 67–71.

need not be defended is a waste or a least a poor utilization, of time and energy, which could be better employed elsewhere. The Christian may have other reasons for opposing some of these theories, but that need not be because of commitment to the authority of the Bible. To do so, furthermore, actually does not advance truth, but may actually impede it. If general revelation is a reality, then it can assist us in understanding special revelation. Rejecting these scientific discoveries, if they are correct, closes off a source of understanding and a means of conveying to our present time the meaning of the biblical concepts.

Neutral Characteristics

There are also more general cultural characteristics that are neutral in their import. These also may be utilized, in both our formulation and expression of doctrine. In particular, these characteristics of our culture need to be taken into account in our presentation of the message, because doing so will help ensure that it will be heard, that people will be willing to listen to it, and that they will indeed correctly apprehend what is being said.

The first of these characteristics is an orientation to the visual. Many younger persons in American society are members of the television generation. They have been exposed to the television set for several hours per day, on the average, whereas earlier generations may have listened to the radio or read. This is seen in the disinclination of younger persons to read the newspaper, preferring instead to get their news from television networks and local stations. Further, many of the young people have spent a considerable amount of time playing video games. These are both very visual and very interactive; players can see immediately the results of their action. This has again contributed to a generation of students who do not do a great deal of reading. At one college, a student explained to the professor who had just assigned a considerable amount of reading that he did not read books; he only watched videos. This video-orientation affects the learning styles of students, who tend to learn more by doing than by listening or even by observing.

In our crafting of doctrinal expressions and our formation and delivery of sermons we need not and should not concede to this tendency. Persons will need to broaden their perspective or become more versatile in order to survive in our society. Some information is only available in printed form. Simply acquiescing to these tendencies will not help persons. Having said that, however, we can utilize and build on this tendency. The presentation of doctrine will need to appeal to the visual, whether actually or by provoking the imagination. Beyond that, drama and dramatic elements in preaching may prove fruitful in light of this phenomenon.

A second listener characteristic is a relatively brief attention span. This, again, in many cases, is related to the television culture. Long, abstract, complex arguments may not be followed, so that the conclusion is not accepted. In the realm of politics, the use of "soundbites"—short, slogan-like statements lasting just a few seconds—has become widespread. This does not mean that doctrine must be reduced to mottoes, but it does suggest frequent use of illustrative material in the construction of doctrinal expressions. It also means that doctrine may have to be presented in somewhat self-contained units, which can be absorbed at a single sitting, whether by listening or reading. Organization is also very important. The content of the statement must be coherent, and the various elements should bear an obvious organic relationship to each other. We will need to think through our statement very carefully from our own perspective, because material that could be perceived as digressive or extraneous will be lost. Only if it is apparent how each part relates to the whole or to the central theme or motif will persons be able to grasp and retain what is being affirmed.

There is also the factor of subjectivity and relativity—the tendency to view things from one's own perspective and in terms of how it affects one individually. This leads, in an extreme form, not simply to subjectivity, but to subjectivism, that is, the idea that this is true, not simply as it is in itself, but that this is true for me, but may not be true for you or others. In its more extreme form, it is unacceptable and will have to be contended with. In the more moderate degree, however, this says that doctrine will need to be stated in such a way that persons can see how this relates to them personally.

Inappropriate Concepts

We must ask, however, about the appropriateness of the concepts we utilize. For if we successfully teach denotatively what we wish to communicate, but convey a connotation that is opposed to or at least detracts from the basic Christian message, then we will be undoing what we positively accomplish. There are several ways in which a concept may prove unusable. It may be that it is inevitably attached to, or implies, another concept that conflicts with some other area of Christian doctrine or practice. It may be that the concept or terminology is associated in the public mind with a person whom we would not want to appear to endorse or whose views or actions we would not want to condone. It may be that the idea is acceptable to the general public, and so might be effective, but is strongly disputed on some more technical or scholarly level and thus is questionable for our purposes.

Let us note, then, a number of factors in our culture which, by their very nature, are so opposed to the fundamental conceptions and ethos of the Christian faith that they must be rejected and resisted. They must be taken account of, but must not be encouraged. It *may* be that initially they have to be appealed to, but this must be only as a means of leading persons to a different outlook.

One of these characteristics is egocentricity and anthropocentricity. In this scheme of things, the human is at the center of reality and of thinking. The human is the important factor, the value that all things must serve and the measure of all things, the one who judges the truth or pertinence of everything. God must conform, both to the human's standards of truth and justice, and to the wants and needs of the person. Philosophically, this is humanism, in which the goal of life is the realization and maximization of human desires. The human being is the highest object of value. This is widely seen in the criticism frequently leveled at God for not simply sending only good or enjoyable experiences into the lives of his children, or for not assuring that every person is saved, or for allowing something as unpleasant as future punishment to come to anyone. It is even seen in the nature of the ministry of some churches, which urge persons to come to God, who will meet all their needs and satisfy their wants, but do not mention commitment or sacrifice.

This is opposed, however, to the biblical emphases on the supremacy and lordship of God. So, for example, Moses is told to take off his shoes, because the place where he is standing is holy ground (Exod. 3:5). Samuel is told to reply to the Lord's call by saying, "Speak, Lord, for your servant hears." The psalmist tells us, "Know that the Lord is God! It is he that made us, and we are his; we are his people, and the sheep of his pasture" (100:3). Throughout Scripture, the Lord is to be obeyed, because he is the Lord.

Further, this egocentric approach is the very antithesis of Jesus' teachings. He said, for example, "For whoever would save his life will lose it; and whoever loses his life for my sake, he will save it" (Luke 9:24). The way to satisfaction and joy in life is not through seeking it directly. Real self-fulfillment is only found in serving God. Jesus himself exemplified such an orientation to life with his prayer in the Garden of Gethsemane, in which he said to the Father, "Abba, Father, all things are possible to thee; remove this cup from me; yet not what I will, but what thou wilt" (Mark 14:36).

A second characteristic of our culture is the desire for immediate satisfaction. Persons today want gratification of their wants here and now.

Waiting for years for something is unreal, and suggesting motivation on the basis of something not only far in the future but in eternity is ineffective. Something immediately present is believed to be of far greater value than something in the future. It is this application of the principle that is especially important. The prime biblical example of this tendency is found in the story of Esau, who traded his birthright for a bowl of vegetable stew.

This, while it might seem like a rather theologically neutral factor, is in reality very significant. There are consistent biblical warnings against this sort of short-sightedness. Jesus, for example, said, "For what shall it profit a man, if he shall gain the whole world, and lose his own soul? Or what shall a man give in exchange for his soul?" (Mark 8:36–37). The same thought was present in his words, "Do not lay up for yourselves treasures on earth, where moth and rust consume and where thieves break in and steal" (Matt. 6:19–20). Paul also added his testimony to the values of the eternal when he said, "I consider that the sufferings of this present time are not worth comparing with the glory that is to be revealed to us" (Rom. 8:18). Similar is his statement in 2 Corinthians 4:17–18: "For this slight momentary affliction is preparing for us an eternal weight of glory beyond all comparison, because we look not to the things that are seen but to the things that are unseen; for the things that are seen are transient, but the things that are unseen are eternal." Finally, the writer to the Hebrews speaks of the motivation that enabled Jesus to do what he did: "who for the joy that was set before him endured the cross, despising the shame, and is seated at the right hand of the throne of God" (Heb. 12:2). In light of these biblical testimonies, the desire for immediate gratification, which would preclude a person forgoing present pleasure or enduring present pain for the sake of an eternal value, must be resisted, and our choice of contemporary experience or categories to use in contemporizing the eternal message must carefully avoid this.

A third characteristic of our culture is egotism and egoism. This is concern for one's own satisfaction, welfare, and pleasure, together with disregard for that of others. This view is very widely found in our society. One can verify this simply by observing the books that are being written, bought, and read by people today. A few years ago, a Catholic order ran a full-page ad in a popular magazine. The ad showed the covers or dust jackets of the most popular books of the day. Among those titles were *Looking Out for Number One*, *I've Got to Be Me*, and *Winning through Intimidation*. Across the bottom of the page appeared just two words: "Jesus wept." Unfortunately, not only general books or secular books enunciate these themes. A study of popular Christian books reveals that it is books that purport to solve human problems and to bring happiness and other satisfactions to the person, that are the big sellers. Devotional books, which emphasize commitment to God or attempt to help the believer understand God better or assist a person in becoming holier, are relatively slow sellers. Indeed, because of these sales statistics, relatively few books on such subjects get published. Most of the sales of books in these categories are reprints of old classics.

A fourth principle of our contemporary world that must be resisted is the idea of mastery of others. This is the desire to have primacy over other persons, to subjugate them, to have them serve us in some sense, or at least not to serve them. In this model, any sort of submissiveness is seen as weakness. This is evident in prisons, where prisoners tend to view any compassion as a sign of weakness to be exploited. Jesus, however, contradicted this with his statement, "but whoever would be great among you must be your servant" (Mark 10:43). Paul also appealed to his hearers to think not only of their own concerns and needs, but also those of others, supporting this appeal with the example of Jesus, who, being in the very form of God, emptied himself of the prerogatives of deity and took on the form of a servant (Phil. 2:1–11).

Finally, materialism—attachment to and pursuit of the material possessions of this world—is an element in the life-view of many persons today. The accumulation of possessions is the all-compelling goal of many. Beyond the accumulation, however, is the display of that ownership. "Conspicuous consumption" is frequently a way of showing one's dominance over others. This is the driving force in the lives of many persons. Interestingly, it occurs on all economic levels. What a person at the subsistence level may think to be enough proves still to be insufficient when the person has gained more. There seems to be an insatiable desire for material possessions. For some, their whole sense of self-worth and self-esteem seems to depend on what they own.

This orientation is, however, contradicted by several biblical testimonies. Jesus, for instance, in addition to saying that one cannot serve two masters, God and money, also said that "a man's life does not consist in the abundance of things." Paul wrote that "the love of money is the root of all evil" (1 Tim. 6:10). Thus, certainly the Christian must resist and reject the desire for money and all that it can buy. It is a motif that cannot be utilized in the contemporary expression of the Christian message.

Selection of Positive Concepts

Having observed these guidelines regarding the appropriateness of images to use in attempting to convey the message in our time, we must now go on to the actual choice and utilization of such images. Our task is to find images, concepts, and terms from our time that are equivalent to those timeless truths as expressed in the specifics of another time. We will want to ask, in effect, "If Paul (or Jesus, or Peter, etc.) were saying this here and now, or writing this to us, how would he say it?" We will look for parallel expressions of the same matter, trying to avoid getting too general too quickly.

The Development of Creativity

There are some exercises that can help us develop the creativity and imagination needed to do this sort of restatement. One way to do so is to read the writings or translations of people who have tried to do this with the Bible. J. B. Phillips, in his translations of the New Testament and in his little book *Your God Is Too Small*, has given us a good example. Kenneth Taylor, in his *Living Bible*, and Charles Williams, in the *Cotton Patch Version*, have done much the same thing. Some of these, especially the *Living Bible*, have received a considerable amount of criticism from persons who believe translations should be a more literal, but these volumes are not simply translations in the sense of Scripture, but also a translation of thoughts and forms as well as an interpretation of sorts.

There are other things that we can do to stimulate our ability to move from one medium or one period to another. Reading the comic strips will often stimulate creativity. Comics frequently play to the imagination or utilize incongruous situations for their humor. Gary Larson's "Far Side," perhaps the best of these, is no longer being drawn but collections of the cartoons are still available in book form. Among currently running comics, John McPherson's "Close to Home," and the sports-oriented "In the Bleachers" by Steve Moore do the same thing.

I sometimes urge my students simply to brainstorm, to try to let their minds run wild, so that the unusual enters them. They may have a large number of ideas, most of which are unusable. If out of a hundred ideas, however, they have five that are genuinely creative and fruitful, they may have accomplished something very helpful in the task. In all of these endeavors, it is imperative that we continue to ask ourselves what would be equivalents of these concepts in the present time. In particular, in evaluating the ideas that we come up with, we will want to weigh carefully whether this is a fresh statement of the old concept or a revision.

It is also helpful to be dialogical in our attempt to shape and express these truths. We must ask, either literally or figuratively, what people are saying, and more than that, what they are hearing, in our expression of the message. It would be an excellent thing for the pastor-theologian to form a team of church members to meet with on a regular basis. He would then share with them the various conceptions he is formulating and ask for some feedback. This could also be done as a sort of debriefing after the actual sermon has been preached, but I would recommend that this be a supplement to the prior feedback, rather than a substitute for it.

Perhaps the use of a variety of concepts may be one of the most important dimensions of the process. The full truth of the doctrine probably exceeds anything that we can literally express. Using several concepts or images instead of merely one may provide a larger glimpse, and may collectively help evoke greater understanding.

In addition to making the concepts intelligible, it is important as well to make them relevant, or to show persons how these doctrines apply to them. There are persons for whom the question is neither "What does it mean?" nor "Is it true?" but rather, "Does it matter?" Their problem is lack of interest, with lack of understanding or of belief possibly following and resulting from that. It may be that they have difficulty seeing how these rather abstract, transcendent ideas relate to their lives here and now. With such persons, it is important that we find some point of beginning, or "point of contact," within their experience, for what we are endeavoring to do. They need to see how this doctrine can make some difference in their lives.

The Method of Correlation

There are a number of ways that this can be done. One, which has been adapted from the thought of Paul Tillich, is the method of correlation.[11] This is his apologetic or answering theology. For our purposes, this method can be understood as involving two poles, the questioning pole and the answering pole. We first examine the culture into which we are attempting to state the message, and ask what questions are being asked within that culture. It is important not to collapse either of these into the other, deriving the answer from the question itself, or dictating the question with the answer. In the former case, we are really restating modernity to itself, rather than giving it an answer. In the latter case, we may be giving people answers to questions they are not asking, and may not even care about. While they may not be asking the right question, later we can move them to do so. This will involve exposing oneself to the popular culture of which average persons and secular persons are part and by which they are influenced. If one is attempting

---

11. Paul Tillich, *Systematic Theology* (Chicago: University of Chicago Press, 1951), vol. 1, pp. 59–66.

to express a doctrine to a particular ethnic or age group, then it is important to focus on the culture of that group. This will require reading what these people are reading or what reflects their reading, and sampling the music, movies, radio programs, and television programs they are listening to and watching. While this may be a difficult discipline at times, it is important.

Dimensions of Ultimacy

Several years ago, Langdon Gilkey argued for what he termed "dimensions of ultimacy" within the experience of even the most secular persons.[12] He readily acknowledges the secular orientation of much of modern human's mentality. Yet even within this experience, he contends, there are dimensions of the experience that go beyond secular experience. Persons cannot and in effect, do not, if they really think seriously about it, live by their own rules or on their own terms. For example, even the most secular, humanistic, scientist, when his child is born, does not look down and say, "A new baby *Homo sapiens* has been born." It is a matter of finding these transcendent dimensions of life, and relating the message, the doctrine, to them.

There are a number of these dimensions that can be identified in contemporary American culture. One is the sense of depersonalization. We live in a world in which we are just numbers or statistics, cogs in the great machine of business or government. We may sometimes wonder whether anyone knows who we are, or whether that really matters. Yet to this question, the Christian faith proposes the answer of the all-powerful, all-knowing God, who knows even the number of the hairs on our head, who knows when anything happens even to the sparrow, one of the smallest, least valuable, and least important creatures. Another question is the issue of relativity of truth and ethics. We live in a world of relativism, in which there is a tendency to regard everything in terms of "that all depends"; nothing is right or wrong per se, but right or wrong for you, but perhaps not for me. Yet in this sort of world, we still have to choose, and society has to make judgments that go beyond relative circumstances. When we think about it, if right and wrong are relative, then when two or more standards collide, the answer as to which is correct is the view held by the stronger person. Might quite literally makes right in such a situation. If there is no objective standard, nothing that is right or wrong independently of who holds it, then there is no hope for the minority or the weaker to make claim for their rights and their convictions.

---

12. Langdon Gilkey, *Naming the Whirlwind: The Renewal of God-Language* (Indianapolis: Bobbs-Merrill, 1969), part 2, chapters 2–4.

Examples of Some Usable Concepts

Let us now note two sample areas in which we may be able to utilize more contemporary ways of thinking to give form and expression to the timeless doctrine.

Divine Transcendence

One crucial aspect of the biblical teaching regarding God is his transcendence, that is, his otherness or superiority to humans and to the creation. This, of course, is paired with the complementary concept of divine immanence, God's presence and activity within nature and the human race. The customary way of thinking of this transcendence has been spatial, the idea that God is high above us or far off, removed from the creation. This was a natural one to use, for it is part of the imagery of biblical passages such as Isaiah 55: "For my thoughts are not your thoughts, neither are your ways my ways, says the LORD. For as the heavens are higher than the earth, so are my ways higher than your ways and my thoughts than your thoughts" (vv. 8–9). Note that the statement is put in the form of a simile. There is no reason that the height in the latter part of the comparison must be spatial, just because it is in the former part. Spatial otherness is not necessarily part of the essence of the doctrine. Simply otherness and superiority are involved. We have now come to see that the spatial elevation concept is not really usable. Nor it is fully appropriate biblically and theologically. Since God is spirit, and does not dwell in temples made with human hands, he is really not in a location that we could reach by traveling long enough and far enough in a spaceship.

Two concepts, drawn from the insights of Søren Kierkegaard, are both helpful and appropriate here.[13] One is the idea of qualitative difference. God is not simply the same kind of being as we are, but is quantitatively greater. We are created, dependent, and limited. He is uncreated, self-sufficient, and unlimited, in knowledge, power, goodness, and so on. We have power, but he is omnipotent. We have had a point of beginning, but he is not simply much older than we are; being truly eternal, he is infinitely older than us. In fact, he is ageless. This is a significant point that the doctrine of divine transcendence is making: that he is a different kind of being than we are. This qualitative/quantitative distinction is not always readily understood today. Modern science has tended to reduce qualities to quantitative differences. Thus the difference between colors, like red and green, can be reduced to differences

---

13. A helpful exposition of these concepts in Kierkegaard's thought is found in Martin Heinecken, *The Moment before God* (Philadelphia: Muhlenberg, 1956), pp. 81–83, 90–93.

of wavelength of the light waves. I have sometimes had students who were doing "B" work come to me and ask to raise their grade by doing additional work. My answer, put as tactfully as I could, has always been that, if it is merely additional work of the same quality, perhaps we could look into the possibility of granting the student additional course credit, but that a higher grade required not more work, but better work. There is, in my judgment a difference between "B" and "A" work that involves not merely greater quantity, but a higher quality, which can often be related to the higher realms of Bloom's taxonomy of the cognitive domain. (Note the two metaphorical uses of "higher" here, as in speaking of transcendence.)

The other helpful idea here is that of dimensional beyondness. This is the conception that God is not simply somewhere in the three (or four) dimensions of our universe, but is in a totally different dimension of reality. Thus, no amount of travel within our dimensions can get from us to him. What is needed is a transition from one set of dimensions, one form of reality, to another. That transition is death.

Human Nature

We have seen that the data of Scripture seem to require the idea of existence in our current, bodily form, but also the concept of an intermediate state, in which the earthly body lies dead in the grave and the resurrection has not yet taken place, but there is still conscious, personal existence. How is this to be understood, or what categories are to be used to grasp this? As we observed, for much of its history the church handled this by the use of a body–soul dualism scheme, which fit well with a kind of metaphysic that was popular, but that both the metaphysic and the current understanding of the biblical material now seem to render such an approach unusable. Consequently, in the twentieth century, several models have been proposed.

One of these was the liberal theology of the immortality of the soul. Rejecting the biblical idea of bodily resurrection as untenable, Harry Emerson Fosdick adopted instead a conception of the human in which the person dies and that is the end of the body, which decays. The soul, however, is immortal, and survives the death of the body.[14] The difficulty of this approach was that it failed to do justice to another set of biblical data, those pertaining to the resurrection, a concept found throughout the biblical revelation and consequently an essential factor in Christian theology.

14. Harry Emerson Fosdick, *The Modern Use of the Bible* (New York: Macmillan, 1933), pp. 97–104.

A very different approach was that of neoorthodoxy and the biblical theology movement. They found the idea of immortality of the soul to be nonbiblical, deriving instead from Greek philosophy. They restored the idea of resurrection, even resurrection of the flesh. Given the absolute unity of the person held by these theologians, however, there was no place for the idea of the intermediate state in the traditional sense.[15] Two attempts were made to deal with the problem. One was the idea of instantaneous resurrection, a conception that immediately upon death one receives the new resurrection body.[16] This, however, left the problem of the body, which still remains decaying in the grave. The other approach was something akin to the old idea of "soul sleep." On this view, there is no conscious existence between death and resurrection, so that the next experience one has after death is that of resurrection. Because there is no intervening experience, the resurrection is experienced as if it were immediate. Yet this also failed really to account for the passages of the type we have examined above.

We must ask whether some concept within contemporary experience will retain this full meaning and in an intelligible fashion. Here again, while recognizing that contemporary science is not the final word but only the most adequate current understanding, we find help in the concepts of physics. One useful concept is the idea of different states of being. In an Einsteinian universe, we now understand that matter is not quite the solid phenomenon that it appears to be. What seem to be solids may actually be simply charges of electricity. Matter and energy are convertible into each other. Thus, thinking of the theological problem at hand, we may utilize what I choose to call "contingent monism." On this view, humans may exist in a materialized state, their usual condition. They may also, however, exist in an immaterialized state. These two would correspond respectively to the ordinary life and the existence between death and resurrection. Then at the resurrection, they are rematerialized again, although apparently in a somewhat different material state (a "spiritual body," 1 Cor. 15:44).[17] Popular illustrations or parallels to this metamorphosis could be drawn from the ability of given molecules, for example, of H_2O, to exist in solid, liquid, or vaporous form.[18]

15. Emil Brunner, *The Christian Doctrine of the Church, Faith, and the Consummation* (Philadelphia: Westminster, 1962), pp. 383–85, 408–14.

16. W. D. Davies, *Paul and Rabbinic Judaism* (London: SPCK, 1955), pp. 317–18.

17. Philosophical interpretations of this problem can be found in Paul Helm, "A Theory of Disembodied Survival and Re-embodied Existence," *Religious Studies* 14, no. 1 (March 1978): 19; and Bruce Reichenbach, "Life after Death: Possible or Impossible?" *Christian Scholar's Review* 3, no. 3 (1973): 240.

18. For a more complete development of this concept, see *Christian Theology*, pp. 536–39.

We have seen that after obtaining the doctrinal teaching of a portion of Scripture, it is necessary first to universalize it and then to recontextualize it. This is difficult but important work, which will provide rich rewards in helping us make the doctrine both authoritative, or biblical, and relevant, or contemporary. Having done this important work, it is now time to give the doctrinal teachings sermonic expression.

Part 3

Delivering Doctrine in Sermonic Form

10

Expository Doctrinal Preaching

Believing and preaching the Bible are top priorities for a Bible-based ministry. Nothing is more important for the church than the explanation of God's Word. Among the ways in which she meets that responsibility, preaching is the most important. Preaching that explains the Bible is often called expository preaching.

How are we to understand the term "expository preaching"? The term may refer to what we do in preaching (we explain the Bible), or how we do a sermon (the method we employ in the explanation).

The term "expository" means to explain or make plain. Thus, when a minister explains a text of Scripture, that minister is doing expository preaching. Another preacher, however, may employ the method of continuous explanation of successive Bible verses from the beginning through the end of a book and classify that, alone, as expository preaching.

This is the complicating factor in a discussion of expository preaching. What, exactly, is it? Authors of books on the subject do not always agree on the definition. Furthermore, they do not always clarify whether it is a sermon form or a type of sermon development.

For more than a century, expository preaching was classified as a sermon form and distinguished from textual and topical preaching.[1] Such classification and distinction have caused confusion about the exact nature of expository preaching, which continues in current discussions of the subject.[2] According to this long-standing system of classification, the textual sermon takes as a text one, two, or three verses of

1. Andrew Watterson Blackwood, *The Preparation of Sermons* (Nashville: Abingdon-Cokesbury, 1948).
2. Sidney Greidanus in *The Modern Preacher and the Ancient Text* (Grand Rapids: Eerdmans, 1988), p. 10.

Scripture and derives its point structure directly from the text. An expository sermon takes as a text more than two or three verses of Scripture.[3] The sermon presentation, or structure, usually is a discussion of the words, phrases, and sentences of the text in the order of their appearance. The topical sermon, contrariwise, claims a general biblical truth as its basis, but derives its structure from the nature of the topic rather than a biblical text. A topical sermon, thus, does not explain the exact content of a text. A text may suggest a topic, but the idea for the topical sermon more often originates outside Scripture.

Andrew W. Blackwood Sr., with his numerous volumes on preaching, popularized this traditional method of sermon classification. His definitions have not been accepted and employed by all authors. Much discussion continues about the exact nature of expository preaching. One of the most instructive came fifty years ago.[4] Donald Miller, after a review of several of the more popular definitions, including those of John A. Broadus, Henry Burgess, F. B. Meyer, and Andrew W. Blackwood Sr., summarized the characteristics of expository preaching found in the definitions: First, there is almost universal agreement that the length of the passage handled is involved, that is, the number of verses in the text determines the definition. Second, this type of preaching is characterized by detailed analysis, implying that if such detail is left out of a sermon, it is not expository. Third, the method of preaching is highly explanatory in nature. Fourth, according to Miller, each of the definitions insists on "the idea of consecutive handling of an extended portion of scripture."[5]

In their preaching, some ministers reveal a commitment to all four characteristics, plus they extend the "consecutive handling of an extended portion of scripture" through one book of the Bible at a time until completing each book. For them, this serial preaching through Bible books is expository preaching.[6] This method is gaining popularity in contemporary pulpits.[7] Bible book preaching requires time, especially if the minister decides on a longer book, such as Isaiah or Acts. A

3. Blackwood, *The Preparation of Sermons*, p. 64. Cf. *Expository Preaching for Today* (Nashville: Abingdon-Cokesbury, 1953), p. 13, and *The Fine Art of Preaching* (Grand Rapids: Baker, 1976), p. 34.

4. A recent example is the discussion by Greidanus in *The Modern Preacher and the Ancient Text*, p. 20.

5. Donald G. Miller, *The Way to Biblical Preaching* (Nashville: Abingdon, 1957), p. 20.

6. John MacArthur Jr., in *Rediscovering Expository Preaching* (Dallas, Tex.: Word, 1992), is a contemporary exponent of this method.

7. R. T. Kendall, pastor of the Westminster Chapel in London, reported that he spent almost three years preaching through the Book of 1 John. "What Kind of Preaching?" lectures delivered at Southwestern Baptist Theological Seminary, Fort Worth, Tex., February 9–12, 1988.

commitment to begin, nevertheless, is a commitment to finish, no matter how long the series may take. Or is it? A famous preacher of another era, Bernard of Clairvaux, preached for eighteen years on the Song of Solomon and only reached chapter 3, verse 1.[8] We may yet ask whether one may preach verse by verse without going all the way through a book, and still be doing expository preaching. The traditional definition appears to leave open two possibilities for expository preaching: (1) It may be accomplished by preaching on lengthy passages without proceeding through an entire book; (2) it means preaching through the whole book.

No universal agreement exists, though, that expository preaching is a method of sermonizing. Haddon Robinson contends that expository preaching is a philosophy rather than a method.[9] He asserts that it is "an attitude toward Scripture."[10] If a preacher bends his thought to Scripture, that preacher is doing expository preaching.

John R. W. Stott suggests that the practice of explaining the meaning of a given text, whether done in a serial fashion or not, is expository preaching.[11] Even if the preacher provides an outline arrangement of the teachings of the text, the sermon still qualifies as an expository sermon—provided the preacher explains the Bible. In fact, more than a century ago, Broadus offered explanation as a functional element of the sermon, and stated that outline subpoints are explanation by means of subdivision. In this case the sermon may be thought of as an expository-biblical sermon. The outline, according to Broadus, serves only to make the sermon an advanced homily.[12] E. C. Dargan explains that the converts to Christianity who brought training in rhetoric with them to the Christian faith are responsible for the rhetorical outline form of the sermon. He implies that such a pattern of development would not disqualify a sermon as "expository."[13] For the first three centuries of Christian preaching, sermons were simple expositions of Scripture (homilies without formal structure).

8. Clyde E. Fant Jr. and William M. Pinson Jr., *20 Centuries of Great Preaching*, vol. 1, *Biblical Sermons to Savonarola A.D. 27–1498* (Waco, Tex.: Word, 1971), p. 146. His performance raises one of the serious questions related to doctrine. How long would a minister preach in Song of Solomon before getting to a doctrine? To ask it another way: Would a pastor wish to preach for eighteen years and discuss only the doctrines found in Song of Solomon?

9. See *Biblical Preaching* (Grand Rapids: Baker, 1989), 19ff.

10. Ibid.

11. John R. W. Stott, *Between Two Worlds* (Grand Rapids: Eerdmans, 1982), is among them. See pp. 135–37.

12. See John A. Broadus, *A Treatise on the Preparation and Delivery of Sermons*, 5th ed. (Philadelphia: Smith, English, 1874), pp. 155, 262–74.

13. Charles Dargan, *A History of Preaching* (New York: Hodder and Stoughton, 1905), vol. 1, p. 65.

Donald Miller, after reviewing the traditional method of sermon classification, concluded that all biblical preaching is expository preaching, since all biblical preaching is an explanation of the Scriptures.[14] This view makes the terms "biblical preaching" and "expository preaching" synonymous.

Considering the definition of the word "expository," one may insist that expository preaching is simply explanation of Scripture. Such insistence means that the textual sermon, as defined by Blackwood and others, may also be expository, a possibility that the traditional system seems to exclude. Thus, some confusion about the term "expository preaching" remains. We may understand it in one of several ways: (1) as the treatment of a text that is longer than three verses; (2) as the consecutive treatment of a passage of Scripture; (3) as serial preaching through a book of the Bible; or (4) as all explanation of Scripture. Questions about sermon structure, such as whether one has an outline, confuses the issue even further.

All these definitions hold in suspension the issue of the topical sermon. In the traditional scheme, the doctrinal sermon may be considered topical, even incidental. In textual and expository preaching, doctrinal preaching is done only on those occasions when the preacher happens to encounter doctrine while preaching through a passage or a Bible book. Is the preacher to present doctrine only incidentally to a continuing explanation of Scripture? All books of the Bible contain some doctrine, to be sure, but we should preach doctrine because of the nature of the doctrine itself. Those who employ the method of continuous explanation may choose passages and books because of their doctrinal content, but they also may circumvent some points of theology by avoiding certain books. The minister should preach doctrinal sermons by design and not leave the impression that doctrine is incidental.

Thus we define expository preaching as preaching that explains and clarifies a portion of Scripture (the sermon text), the truth of which has been discovered through careful study, with a view to making appropriate application of the truth to those who listen. It is done with an acknowledgment that the Holy Spirit guides the entire process. The length of the Scripture portion claimed as a text does not determine whether a sermon is biblical. Too many preachers employ a text only as a point of departure for the "sermon," but do not really preach the contents of the text. The substance of the sermon must come from the Bible, a la Miller, in order to have an expository sermon. The sermon needs more than explanation, which is largely oriented in the past. The preacher should tell the listeners how the hearing of the sermon will

14. Donald G. Miller, *The Way to Biblical Preaching* (New York: Abingdon, 1957).

make a difference in their lives. This is application, a requirement for good expository preaching.

Expository preaching, thus defined, allows the preacher to take as a text (then explain and apply) any portion of Scripture, whether a word, phrase, verse, two verses, or extended portion exceeding two or three verses. Indeed, the preacher may draw passages from one book or from more than one book of the Bible in one sermon. The texts are no less biblical because they do not all come contiguously, or for that matter, from chapters in the same book of the Bible.[15] This practice actually may be desirable with some doctrines in order to guarantee more complete witness of Scripture to a doctrine and to make it more understandable.[16]

For example, in the Book of Galatians, Paul employs the word "grace" and emphasizes throughout the book that salvation comes by grace through faith alone. A minister, in one sermon, could read and explain the various verses (1:3, 6, 15; 2:21; 5:18) in which Paul mentions the word and echoes the message throughout the entire book.

Our understanding of expository preaching should not be restricted to one sermon form or method. All sermons ought to have biblical content, but all do not of necessity have to follow the pattern of consecutive exposition throughout a passage and book. Expository-textual, expository-passage, and expository-thematic sermons are all possibilities for biblical preaching. The biblical portion for the expository-textual sermon may be a phrase, a verse, or several verses; the amount of material chosen should contain a complete thought. An expository-passage sermon is one that has as its text a longer portion of Scripture from one chapter of a Bible book. For example, John 3:1–21 tells the complete story of the encounter between Jesus and Nicodemus. In the case of a doctrine, or theme, often suggested by a word in a verse, the theme or doctrine could more properly be explained by the analogy of faith principle, bringing other passages of Scripture into the sermon text. This sermon, then, becomes an expository-thematic sermon.[17]

---

15. In fact, some preachers who declare themselves to be "expository preachers" and insist on serial preaching follow this exact practice in their sermons. They do as Donald Grey Barnhouse did—bring the entire weight of Scripture to bear on one particular verse of Scripture. Barnhouse used the imagery of an inverted pyramid to illustrate his method.

16. This tends to be a thematic sermon. For more detailed information on this practice, see the chapter in this volume on topical doctrinal preaching.

17. The authors employ the term "thematic" instead of "topical" to distinguish biblical topics, or themes, from nonbiblical topics. This is not to express disapproval for topical sermons, which should be labeled "topical." The topical sermon is one in which the preacher brings a topic under the careful scrutiny of Scripture. Another way of saying this is that the preacher brings the topic to the Bible and shines the light of biblical truth on the topic to make it more understandable. See the chapter in this volume on topical preaching.

Reconciliation, as mentioned in 2 Corinthians 5:20, provides one illustration. Each of these three major categories allows for a variety of sermon forms.

We have attempted to define an expository sermon as one that has biblical substance rather than designate it as a special form of preaching.[18] For too long, expository preaching has been treated as a special form.[19]

Preaching Different Types of Expository Sermons

Expository-Textual Sermons

Brief passages, only one or two verses in length, may contain complete messages. Psalm 27:1, John 3:16, Galatians 2:20, and Philippians 4:13 are among those passages. Whether the verse speaks of courage, or salvation, the life Christ brings by faith, or strength for daily living, it stands as an entity. Other verses that accomplish the same purpose include Romans 3:23, 5:8, 6:23, Luke 13:3, James 2:23, and Hebrews 13:5. Jesus taught many good lessons with pointed remarks, parables, and proverbial statements. For example, each of the Beatitudes has a message all its own. Eight of them are stated each in single verses. Likewise, Matthew 13 contains two one-verse parables (vv. 33 and 44). Both parables teach something about the kingdom of God. Paul also chose few words, on occasion, to express profound truth. The benedictions with which he closed some of his letters are masterpieces of expression, such as those in 2 Corinthians 13:14, Galatians 6:18, and Philippians 4:20.

A two- or three-verse passage may express much doctrine. Some of the more familiar short texts come from the didactic books of the New Testament—such as Romans 1:16–17, Galatians 2:19–21, Mark 1:14–15, and Matthew 28:19–20. Ephesians 2:8–10 is one of the great texts on salvation. The passage is a complete unit of thought. It has a definite beginning, progression, and ending. It offers an understandable pattern of organization of its own. A sermon on salvation by grace may take each point directly from the text, in the order found in the text, and remain within the limits of the passage. "By grace, to salvation, through faith" is a workable outline. For the minister whose habit is to preach the three-point sermon, the phrases fit quite naturally into the pattern. Thorough reading of the Book of Ephesians reveals Paul's penchant for the comparison-contrast method of writing. These verses develop a

18. See Miller, *The Way*, 15–16.
19. Ibid., 18.

contrast between "the result of works" and the "gift of God" and suggest a two-point form of sermon development. Here is a clear illustration of how the form of the text becomes the form of the sermon.

One requirement for a sermon text is that it contain a complete thought. As each citation in the preceding paragraph demonstrates, a single verse may teach a vital doctrine. The preacher, then, may prepare expository-textual sermons on these smaller units of Scripture.

The passages of this kind, admittedly, are parts of larger contexts and they require great care on the part of the minister during sermon preparation. A preacher must constantly be on guard not to lift passages out of context and force meaning into them.

Preaching from these expository-textual passages has numerous advantages. For one thing, their brevity means they become more comprehensible for the listener who may not be familiar with the Bible. For another, their use permits the preacher to concentrate the hours spent in preparation. They come from books with which the minister already is familiar, thus shortening the study time in a legitimate manner.[20] This practical consideration may be vital to a preacher's good spiritual health. In the fast-paced life of the pastor of a local church, time for sermon preparation seems harder and harder to find. We have a difficult time trying to sound profound without having paid the price of proper study and preparation. Six to ten hours spent on three verses will provide time for deeper comprehension.

A second advantage relates to form and content. Since these texts with fewer verses often provide their own structure, the preacher becomes increasingly familiar with the thought patterns of biblical writers and their material. The shorter, more pointed statement is a salient feature of some Bible authors. Structure has so much to do with the communication of a message. The advantage of getting to the point and making the point is most significant for today's preacher.

Another advantage that accrues to minister and congregation is in the realm of Bible knowledge. The members of the congregation will learn more doctrine from more passages of Scripture. In five Sundays a pastor may cover the same doctrine from five different biblical authors or five passages from the same author. Those who listen will receive the benefit of consistency in Bible teaching on the essentials of the faith.

---

20. This provides the preacher with a valid shortcut in sermon preparation. This is not "cheating" on preparation, but building on the backlog of accumulated knowledge about the Bible. At the same time, however, the minister should not assume that he knows the meaning of a passage and thus can skip serious investigation. We learn from a text every time we read and study it. This axiom holds for the minister as well as the member of the congregation.

The expository-textual sermon is not without some disadvantages. One is the very "favorite verses" approach cited earlier in this chapter. A person may think of the Bible as a collection of verses and passages with special meaning and never learn the complete story of which those verses are a part. The expository book advocate may insist that in-depth knowledge of a few books of the Bible may be preferred to limited awareness of some verses in several books. A steady diet of expository-textual sermons would contribute to that exact problem.

Another disadvantage is the loss of context. The Bible is more than a collection of snippets of truth, as valuable as those snippets are. Context is vital to understanding the message of Scripture. A preacher can summarize only so much of the context of a passage, as one must do in a text of shorter length. In every expository-textual sermon the challenge is balancing explanation, illustration, and application of the biblical text. With too much explanation the sermon tends to be a lesson in history. With too little the listener may fail to understand the contemporary application. Illustration, furthermore, is necessary to facilitate comprehension, especially with the more complex subject matter, such as doctrine. Doctrinal texts also necessitate specific statements of application since they may be highly cognitive and their application less obvious.[21]

Expository-Passage Sermons

Sometimes a sermon text requires a longer passage. An example is found in Exodus 3. The account of God's call to Moses begins with the first verse and continues into chapter 4. Verses 1–9 form a complete textual unit, establishing that God spoke to Moses through the burning bush.

The big idea of the text seems to be captured in the affirmation "God speaks." Thus, the doctrine would be revelation, that is, God reveals himself through speech. The purpose of the revelation was to send Moses to Pharaoh with the message that God intended to deliver his people from Egypt.

On the basis of the immediate context of the passage, one could preach a sermon on God's providence. He informed Moses that he had heard the prayers of his people and intended to respond. That was his plan all along, even when they despaired and remained in slavery. In the call God invited Moses to get in step with his purpose for Israel. He had heard their prayers.

This sermon may be presented in a continuous commentary fashion, in which the dramatic moment is portrayed through taking the steps

---

21. For that reason the authors include a chapter on the narrative doctrinal sermon, in which we seek to demonstrate that doctrine may be found in a story.

with Moses that led him to the bush. The movement may be inductive, leading the listeners to the point of discovery of the mission of Moses. That mission becomes clear by the completion of verse 9.

Conversely, the preacher may wish to fashion a standard rhetorical outline for the sermon. The points also could follow the development of the story of the text itself. First, Moses catches sight of the bush while going about the duties associated with tending the sheep. Second, he turns aside to see the strange sight in order to determine exactly what is taking place. Third, he hears the unmistakable voice of God. Fourth, he confronts a decision about responding to the call and getting involved again in God's plans for Israel. God makes clear that he hears the cries of his people and declares his intent to respond in keeping with his purpose. Moses could be certain that he had a call from the living God.

A text including the remainder of the third chapter, through verse 22, could stress the doctrine of God. The statement in verse 14, "I AM who I AM," speaks of the nature of God. Various translations include "I will be what I will be" and "I am," in the sense that "I exist." The Hebrew root word is from the verb "to be." The words establish the existence of the God of the Israelites.

To be sure, this text, 3:1–9, is a part of a larger scenario that includes the first nineteen chapters of Exodus. The text illustrates how a preacher may take a part of the whole and employ it as a text, proclaiming a doctrine within one segment of a larger passage. The passage also demonstrates that more than one kind of sermon development may be possible with the same text.[22]

A second illustration comes from Romans 1:13–17. This text, unlike the one from Exodus, is not part of a larger narrative. The limits of this text, verses 13–17, are not easy to establish. We may choose such a division because it is a complete sentence and contains a complete thought.[23]

The text speaks of Paul's desire to go to Rome to preach the gospel. He declares his sense of spiritual obligation to the Romans with the words: "I am obligated" (v. 14). Moreover, he affirms his readiness for the mission when he declares: "I am so eager to preach the gospel" (v. 15). His purpose is further revealed with the proud affirmation: "I am not ashamed of the gospel, because it is the power of God for the salvation of

---

22. See more on this in the chapter on dramatic preaching. The preacher may present Exodus 3:1–9 in an expository-passage format, as a narrative, or as a dramatic monologue sermon. This is only one of a number of passages with such potential for a rich variety of sermon forms.

23. A preacher may choose a text that is a sentence fragment suggesting a great biblical teaching and have a valid text. Such a choice usually leads to a thematic sermon. See the section on the thematic sermon in the chapter on topical preaching.

everyone who believes" (v. 16). Then he reaches the climax of the thought when he relates that belief in the gospel makes one right with God (v. 17). This being made right with God is the meaning of "righteousness."

The doctrine of justification by faith is the central idea of this text. The words of this Scripture arrested Martin Luther as he attempted to gain right standing with God through good works and self-denial. He confessed his sins, made a voyage to Rome, and denied himself adequate food and comfort—even to the point of sleeping on a bare floor—in order to gain the favor of God. None of it brought him satisfaction. Then he discovered this wondrous truth in Romans. Justification, rightness with God, comes only through faith. The term "justification" suggests that a person has been charged with a crime, has been found guilty, and is awaiting condemnation and execution. Instead, he receives a full pardon. That is what God does for the one who believes the gospel (v. 16). Paul could be proud of it; Luther could exult in it; we may proclaim it.

One possibility for preaching from Romans 1:13–17 is the inductive sermon. In this sermon the preacher explains the text by the method of continuous commentary, with a plan to reveal the big idea of the sermon only at the conclusion. By explaining the passage word by word, phrase by phrase, sentence by sentence, and verse by verse, one may recreate the mood of the text by plodding steadily toward the grand declaration of verse 17.

A second possibility is to take the "I am" declarations of the passage and form a natural division of the text into three parts. These, then, become the key phrases, points, through which a sermon may be developed. This development tends to stress evangelism or mission, as the congregation listens to the apostle's heartbeat for missions.

This passage also contains a text for the expository-textual sermon. Verse 16, "I am not ashamed of the Gospel, because it is the power of God for . . . salvation," may suffice, or it may be read together with verse 17, with which it forms a natural link.

The preacher should come to a passage and study it in detail in search of the doctrine(s) it contains. Without a willingness to do such an inductive study, the interpreter may miss the joy of discovery. No student of the Bible who has a familiarity with Scripture, though, can begin a study completely unaware of its content, whether it is doctrinal or some other teaching. One may even commence the hermeneutical process with a doctrine in mind, that is, go to a particular passage knowing it contains a specific doctrine. This would be the case, for example, with Romans 1:13–17. All students of the Bible, though, know the unusual excitement that comes from making a new discovery in a text. The practice of forcing one's presuppositions on the text, without testing them via the process of interpretation, erodes biblical authority in preaching.

Through the process of interpretation we often find more than one gem of truth in a portion of Scripture. In Exodus 3:1–22, we discover three doctrines—revelation, providence, and God. The more dominant one, to be decided by the interpreter, should become the basis of the first sermon one preaches from the passage. If the text continues through verse 9, the doctrine is revelation. If the text includes verses 13 through 15, the doctrine of God is dominant and should be the focus of the sermon. The inclusion of the entire chapter, twenty-two verses, means providence becomes central. The determination of the amount of Scripture to include as text helps establish the main idea of the sermon.

Isaiah 6:1–8, another passage of medium length, presents material for a strongly doctrinal sermon. Though it, too, relates to a call, the drama again points primarily to God and what he can do to accomplish his purpose. Such passages, known as "theophanies," place great emphasis on the God who calls. Other similar accounts in the Old Testament reveal something about the manner in which God reveals himself (cf. the call of Jeremiah in Jer. 1:1–10; of Amos in Amos 7:14–15).

The expository-textual method and the expository-passage methods of preaching both are particularly suited to preaching serially through a book of the Bible.

Exegetical Preaching

Pure exegesis, or verse-by-verse preaching, is the kind in which the preacher begins with chapter 1, verse 1, and preaches continuously through a book. The sermon done in this manner usually follows the pattern of organization found in the text. The method may be designated as "oral exegesis" since it follows the design of a commentary, consisting largely of sequential commentary on the text.

This running commentary sermon has the advantage of keeping the preacher in the text. "Eisegesis," or reading one's own ideas into the text, becomes much more difficult, since the preacher's guide is the text itself. The singular disadvantage appears to be the potential loss of contemporary application. Some themes in some books may require more than extensive explanation (i.e., include illustration and application) or may seem to be abstract and irrelevant to the lives of the listeners.

Some homileticians consider serial preaching alone to be expository preaching.[24] Continuous explanation is a proper method for sermoniz-

---

24. John MacArthur Jr., in *Rediscovering Expository Preaching*, p. 340, when asked about preaching through a book, says: "This is the purest form of expository preaching." He adds: "[P]reaching verse by verse through books of the Bible is the most reasonable way to teach the whole counsel of God" (p. 341). R. T. Kendall also is an advocate of book preaching.

ing, but expository preaching should not be limited to one pattern of sermon organization.

When done well, pure exegesis presents the Word of God as it is recorded and acquaints the listeners with the biblical material. The method, however, requires more than opening the Bible and beginning to speak. This kind of preaching demands steady, disciplined study for sermon preparation.

The first and often most difficult decision is to determine which book of the Bible from which to preach. A commitment to it, after all, is long-term. The young minister may prefer to begin with a shorter book. Once the preacher has decided which book of the Bible to present to the congregation, the next step is to become acquainted with the entire book before the first sermon. To become familiar with a book, one must read it through several times, perhaps as many as twenty-five. The first reading should be done in the original language, or with a copy of the original open beside one's favorite translation. The preacher's knowledge of the biblical languages should be complete enough to enable employment of them as useful tools of study.

Background information also is essential for book preaching. Authorship, purpose, date, audience, and place of writing, along with all other introductory facts, help prepare the preacher to speak with authority and confidence. The near and remote contexts of the book are necessary to show how it fits into the overall design of the Bible.

Preliminary work yields material to be used throughout the series. To be completely prepared, the preacher should sketch an outline of the entire book in order to have a grasp of the whole prior to speaking of the parts. Those parts should be defined carefully in order to fit together for the forming of the whole. This principle may be stated as an axiom: Know how to conclude before you begin.

Rather than beginning with the first verse and preaching until a certain amount of time has expired, the minister might prefer to determine the number of verses each sermon should cover during the preparation stage. Every sermon should leave the congregation with a big idea or theme to remember. Stated another way, the sermons in the series ought not to have a ragged edge; they ought to have smooth finishes and possess a certain wholeness. Otherwise, the individual listener may go away from the service confused or with a feeling of incompleteness.

Since some books of the Bible are known best for their doctrinal content, the pure exegesis method is helpful for the preaching of doctrine. The Minor Prophets have much doctrinal content. Amos, for example, speaks clearly and directly about the judgment of God. Micah repeats some of the great doctrines found in the larger book of Isaiah, such as teachings about the Messiah. Malachi is well known for its passages on stewardship. In another section of the Old Testament, the Book of Ruth speaks eloquently of the providence of God. The shorter New Testament Epistles with doctrinal themes include Galatians on salvation by grace and Colossians on the preeminence of Christ. Ezekiel, though not one of the shorter books, is a choice place to begin in the Old Testament. Romans is a good selection from the New Testament.

The preacher should commit to a series from a book specifically because he or she knows it contains doctrines about which he or she wishes to preach. When presented as part of a series on a book, the sermon on doctrine comes as no surprise to the congregation. This is a proper way to preach on doctrines that may be controversial or about which wide differences of opinion exist. A pattern of choosing books at random and beginning without thorough study may lead the preacher to a difficult doctrine that surprises and finds the preacher unwilling or unprepared to preach on that particular point of the faith.[25]

With the best of planning and preparation, some difficulties still may attend serial preaching. One is the maintaining of focus on the unity and purpose of the book. The minister will be required to restate both frequently, at least once in each sermon. Without some repetition, one may tend to fragment a book while preaching through it.

Another difficulty is the amount of time spent in one book of the Bible. Some of the longer books may require literally years for exposition. During that time, without the balance of different forms of sermons, the preacher may neglect other portions of the Bible. Conversely, the material presented, while good, may not correspond to the seasons of the Christian calendar or of the local church calendar. To break the sequence, of course, would be contrary to the conviction that led the minister to serial preaching in the beginning.

At the same time, listeners may struggle to maintain interest in the same book over an extended period of time. Even if their interest should not diminish, it would be possible for those who attend church regularly to go every Sunday for years and hear sermons from only a few books of the Bible. Without supplementary classes or home study, they would fail to learn the whole counsel of God.

Pure Exposition

Expository preaching may go beyond pure exegesis to pure exposition, which attempts to make clear the meaning of passages without word-by-word, phrase-by-phrase analysis. The amount of biblical material included as text is greater. In pure exposition, the preacher sum-

---

25. Planning for doctrinal sermons is the subject of a later chapter in this volume.

marizes subblocks of a passage during the course of the sermon. This kind of preaching usually follows the outline suggested by the biblical text itself—an exegetical outline, that is, an outline of the passage that grows out of the exegesis of the text. Organization conforms to the flow of the text, using the points and the order of the text.

Matthew's record of the founding of the church (16:13–20) serves as an example. In the first three verses Jesus inquires about the reports on his identity. The next verse, 16, resounds with the great confession of Simon Peter. Jesus replies, in verse 17, that Peter came to his knowledge through revelation from the Father. Then comes the great statement establishing the church: "On this rock I will build my church." The passage closes with Jesus giving the keys of the kingdom to Simon Peter.

The passage, taken as a whole, speaks of the church as the people of God, but it contains other doctrinal themes such as the various Old Testament images of Christ, especially the image of Christ as Messiah, and the mission of the church as it relates to the kingdom.

The report of Jesus' praying in the Garden of Gethsemane is a second example. Matthew 26:36–46 states that Jesus, upon leaving the scene of his last observance of the Passover with his disciples, went to the garden to pray again about the will of the Father and the cross. He asked his followers to accompany him and to pray with him, but he wished to be alone to settle the matter of his Father's will. According to Matthew, he walked away from them a short distance to finalize the issue of his death on the cross. Three times he returned to check on the disciples; three times he found them fading away into sleep. He expressed surprise that they could not maintain prayerful watch for one hour. At last he declared that his time had come and they should get on with the arrest. The soldiers already had come with Judas; they took him away.

The exegetical outline of this passage falls into segments that form a natural scheme for the development of a sermon. Each movement in the drama intensifies the issue of God's will for Jesus to go to the cross. The entire scene provides a view of the increasing agony of Christ as he struggled to confirm the Father's will. The controlling idea is that Jesus sought confirmation of God's will about the cross through prayer. The manner in which he conducted the prayer may become the outline of a sermon on the necessity of prayer to determine, or confirm, the will of God.

John 13:1–20, the story of Jesus' washing the disciples' feet, is a third example of this approach to the sermon. The setting is the upper room during the last Passover meal Jesus took with his followers. Before he began to wash their feet, John reports, Jesus recognized that his hour had arrived, that he had come from the Father and would go to the Father, and that all things were given to him. He also loved the Twelve until the very end, knowing that one of them would betray him. The doctrinal issues here are the preexistence of Jesus, the destiny of Jesus, and the servant role he assumed. Ultimately he was pointing toward his sacrifice on the cross.

Verses 1–4 form the first block of material for the sermon. Jesus, in a mood of somber reflection, arose from the table, laid aside his garments, and wrapped a towel around his waist. Verses 5–11 tell the story of the actual washing of the feet, the surprise of Peter, and the strange response of Jesus when Peter attempted to stop him. In the concluding verses (12–20), Jesus interprets his deed for the disciples.

Divine destiny, betrayal, identity with the mission of Jesus, the cleansing of salvation, and the lordship of Christ all are mentioned within twenty verses. Each is related to the death of Jesus on the cross. The reinterpretation of the Feast of the Passover, the context in which they all appear, provides the setting for the Master's teachings about himself and his earthly mission. His example of service, the washing of the disciples' feet, serves as a guideline for the development of the sermon on the servanthood of Jesus and, in addition, offers opportunity for a creative object lesson sermon. The preacher may have the courage to wash the feet of a member of the congregation during a worship service in order to demonstrate the spirit of Jesus!

This method of sermonizing carries with it the advantage that it enables the preacher to cover larger portions of Scripture by expressing blocks of thought with summary points. Word-by-word discussion of such passages would require more sermons or fewer verses for each text. By formulating a point for the expression of each division or portion of the sermon, the preacher can progress through an entire biblical event within the time limit of one worship service. In this era of continuous fragmentation of life, wholeness and completeness present worthy goals for preaching.

The practice of covering longer passages by summary points also has a disadvantage: The method may not allow sermon time for extensive exegetical treatment of significant individual words and phrases in one of the thought blocks. One way to offset this difficulty is to make subpoints of such words and phrases. Smooth progression through the sermon material is so vital, though, that the minister should seek to avoid more than two levels of subdivision within each sermon point.

The Thematic-Expository Approach

A doctrinal theme or topic found in a passage may help determine the sermon structure. In order to clarify or identify the doctrine, the preacher may present the contents of a single passage in order to focus on the doctrine. For example, the doctrine of the resurrection is prominent in Romans 6:1–11. Paul employs the death, burial, and resurrection of Jesus as an analogy for understanding the meaning of baptism. Both teach that the Christian is dead to sin and alive to God. A sermon from this text may conclude that the doctrine of the resurrection is central to our understanding of the act of baptism. Baptism, a dramatic portrayal of the resurrection, shows that the person baptized has died to sin and been made alive in Christ.

A sermon of this type takes the entire passage and explains its central teaching, organizing the sermon to reveal the doctrine with which it deals. Baptism followed by the living of a new life reemphasizes the sacrifice of Jesus followed by his post-resurrection glorification.

The opening remarks of Paul to the Philippian Christians in Philippians 1:1–11 represent an outpouring of love and joy based on the grace of God. Paul mentions the "good work" God has done (v. 6), "the day of Christ Jesus" (vv. 6, 10), the sharing of God's grace (v. 7), "the fruit of righteousness that comes through Jesus Christ" (v. 11), and "the glory and praise of God" (v. 11). In order to preach a doctrinal sermon from the passage, one would search for a unifying word or concept. The word appears in verse 6. It is the word "perfect" (as in the KJV), or "carry to completion" found in the declaration that "He who began a good work in you will carry it on to completion until the day of Christ Jesus." The Greek word in the verse derives from a word that means to accomplish a purpose. Paul was declaring that God would finish what he started with the Philippians when they believed the gospel. He based his confidence on what God could do. Related truths are that they are separated unto God ("saints," v. 1), they are recipients of grace as he had been (v. 7), and they would prove themselves until the day of Christ (v. 10). Implicit in the entire passage is Paul's belief that Jesus would return soon. That belief had a direct bearing on his present life and the lives of the Christians in Philippi, for whom he had great love and gratitude.

The first seven verses of chapter 1 of 1 John refer to the preexistent Christ, the fellowship of believers, confession of sin, and cleansing from sin. The latter emphasis, cleansing from sin by the blood of Jesus, is prominent. A sermon from this text could be inductive, building to verse 7. Indeed, 1 John is a good choice for book preaching. The first sermon suggested here would prepare the congregation for a continuing discussion of the reality of sin, which is John's concern in the early part of the Epistle.

Some doctrines require that the preacher go beyond the contents of one passage of Scripture in order to prepare sermons on them. Each sermon then has a multiple-passage text, with a common doctrine or theme. This topical sermon is the concern of the following chapter.

11

Topical Doctrinal Preaching

A number of difficulties attach to the discussion of topical preaching. One is that the word "topic," according to the traditional system of definition and sermon classification, is a rather broad, vague term. The categories expository, textual, and topical seem to suggest that the topical sermon cannot be either expository or textual, yet it can be preaching. The topical sermon, by definition, speaks to an issue, personal or social in nature, which comes from the context of economics, politics, sociology, law, or some other realm of human life.

Another difficulty is that the topical sermon relies on no specific biblical text for its structure. Thus the sermon has a limited biblical authority. The role of Scripture is secondary; it may, at best, speak of the topic in some indirect way. Given its breadth and its loose biblical connection, we may ask ourselves whether we still need the topical sermon. Perhaps we should admit that the topical sermon is invalid and abandon the category altogether. To do so, however, would be to ignore important facts.[1] One of them is historical: Topical preaching is an important part of the history of preaching. Indeed, numerous preachers have demonstrated its effectiveness.

One of the most influential preachers in American history, Harry Emerson Fosdick, was a topical preacher. His method was to raise some problem of life and then propose an answer based on a biblical truth. People stood in line outside Riverside Church in New York City

1. A recent handbook of homiletics lists them first among considerations of sermon form. Another contains essentially the same material. A volume dedicated to the issue of hermeneutics retains the system of classification. See Sidney Greidanus, *The Modern Preacher and the Ancient Text: Interpreting and Preaching Biblical Literature* (Grand Rapids: Eerdmans, 1988); Michael Duduit, ed., *Handbook of Contemporary Preaching* (Nashville: Broadman, 1992); Donald L. Hamilton, *Homiletical Handbook* (Nashville: Broadman, 1992).

to hear him. Others listened to him on network radio. Still others purchased his printed sermons. Because of Fosdick's particular style, the topical sermon has sometimes been called the life situation sermon.

Halford Luccock, professor of homiletics at Yale and author of numerous books on homiletics, was also a renowned topical preacher. Some of his more famous sermons include "On Catching the Wrong Bus" and "Keeping Life out of Stopping Places."

One of the factors accounting for the popularity of such preaching was the time in which Fosdick and Luccock lived. The world was passing through great crises—two World Wars with a global depression in between them. Poverty, worry, loneliness, sorrow, fear, and gloom seemed to envelop the entire human race. The Bible did not speak directly about such issues as dictatorships versus democracies or savings and investments versus stock market crashes. Preachers who would speak to those issues had to go topical. They did not abandon the Bible to do so, but the relation of their sermons to biblical texts could not be described as direct. They spoke of the issues and referred to the Bible for general principles or teachings that would relate as closely as possible.

As the twentieth century draws to a close, the appeal of topical preaching has not waned. Robert Schuller's popularity is documented by attendance at his church's worship services and the extent of his media ministries. Norman Vincent Peale, whose preaching ministry spanned most of the century, was one of the most popular persons in American public life. The sermons of both preachers majored on the topics of the power of optimism and a positive outlook on life.

To abandon the category of the topical sermon would fail to take into account a second important fact—the nature of human existence. Some issues of the post–Cold War era are different but social, moral, and personal crises are just as numerous as ever because of human nature, which remains the same in every generation. The church should not ignore them. We should speak to those issues that are the same in every generation, as well as to those that are distinctive to our own, such as abortion, euthanasia, capital punishment, and prayer in public schools. The Bible does not raise these issues by their modern names, but one part of the preacher's task is to tell how the Bible speaks, in principle, to human existence. Biblical-theological principles surface when we consider the witness of the whole of Scripture,[2] which may not be as obvious in the study of a single text or word. The discipline of systematic theology is predicated on this axiom. Fruit of the labor of theologians in the form of summary statements is found in the various confessions

---

2. See the earlier chapters on the value of theology for preaching and on extracting biblical truth from numerous passages.

and creeds of Christendom. These Christian principles, too, may serve as sermon texts.

Confronted with the proof of its effectiveness in the history of preaching and the stark reality that the issues that called it forth in other generations still plague humanity, the minister can include the topical sermon in the arsenal of sermon forms. Some issues may be handled from the pulpit better in this manner, such as personal freedom, choice, citizenship, voting, individual responsibility to governing authorities and rights, to name a few. At the same time, the qualities of the topical sermon require the minister to limit its use.

Because it has some association with biblical truth, the topical sermon qualifies as a sermon. Ronald J. Allen underscores this connection with Scripture and contends for the retention of the topical sermon.[3] He defines the topical sermon as one that "interprets a topic in light of the gospel but without originating or centering in the exposition of a biblical text or theme."[4] This definition is consonant with the traditional understanding of the topical sermon. Allen also offers a helpful definition of a topic. It is "a need, an issue, or a situation which is important to the congregation . . . which calls for interpretation from the perspective of the gospel, and which can be better addressed from the standpoint of the gospel itself than from the standpoint of the exposition of a particular passage (or passages) from the Bible."[5]

Having affirmed its value, he recommends that the preacher serve up a topical sermon for the congregation, but only for a healthy change of diet. Expository preaching, he insists, should be the staple in the diet. Furthermore, Allen states, interpretation of the topic in light of the gospel ought to be the center of the topical sermon. The sermon answers the question "How does the gospel lead us to understand the topic?"[6]

Scripture's Relation to the Topical Sermon

Two major qualities of the topical sermon have a direct bearing on the answer to this question. First, the topical sermon begins with consider-

---

3. Ronald J. Allen, *Preaching the Topical Sermon* (Louisville, Ky.: Westminster/John Knox, 1992). Allen reminds us that three other contemporary writers discuss the topical sermon and retain it as a valid option for preachers. See Fred B. Craddock, *Preaching* (Nashville: Abingdon, 1985), pp. 171–75; David G. Buttrick, *Homiletics: Moves and Structures* (Philadelphia: Fortress, 1987), pp. 333–448; and Thomas G. Long, *The Witness of Preaching* (Louisville, Ky.: Westminster/John Knox, 1989), pp. 80–84, 92–95. None of these authors discusses the topical sermon as a part of the former method of classification of sermons as expository, textual, and topical.

4. Ibid., p. 3.

5. Ibid.

6. Ibid., p. 5.

ation of the topic. A topic may originate from a wide variety of sources outside the Bible. With the topic in mind, the preacher begins to search for the text to help with the topic, instead of reading the text first in search of the topic.

Second, the structure of the topical sermon is determined by the nature of the topic itself instead of by the biblical text. The content of the biblical text, then, serves to illumine the topic, that is, enters the sermon through allusion, inference, or implication. Exposition of specific words, phrases, or sentences is not characteristic of the topical sermon.

The topical sermon may relegate the text to an indirect role, one of providing support for the controlling idea of the sermon instead of serving as the direct basis of that idea. The preacher is, in fact, taking the sermon idea to the text, then employing the teaching of the text to lend as much confirmation, validation, and authority as possible to the content of the sermon. In addition, the topic, which determines the structure of the sermon as well as choice of the sermon text, may in fact tend to dominate the text. This structural requirement weakens the biblical authority of the sermon.

Scripture's secondary role in the topical sermon creates distinct differences in sermon preparation. Because the topical sermon begins with a subject, not an idea, the minister must manage a larger amount of information. Also, due to the nonbiblical nature of the subject, the minister must conduct a different kind of research, looking into some realms far removed from lexicons and commentaries. The entire sermon preparation process becomes more demanding and laborious. Failure to do adequate preparation means the minister runs the risk of revealing an amateurish ignorance.

Another great difference arises at the point of crafting sermon structure, which derives from the topic instead of the text. In some cases the nature of a topic makes it possible for the preacher to take mental flights of fancy into previously unknown regions during the preparation of the sermon, as well as during the preaching of the sermon. Without the guidelines of the text, the topic's design may lead one farther and farther from the Bible and lessen to a greater degree the connection with the text, which is already loose. During the sermon, the preacher may lose sight of the text and never mention what Scripture says about the issue. This is especially likely to happen with moral-ethical issues. When a sermon fails to bring the teaching of a text to bear on the topic, it loses its relation to Scripture, which is already ill-defined, and risks venturing into the realm of opinion trafficking—a veritable minefield. Someone "out there" may have a better opinion. Someone surely is going to have a different one, and your listeners may prefer it to yours.

The preacher eventually loses the authority that comes from being a spokesperson for God.

Knowledge of the qualities of the topical sermon and the ways in which they affect preparation to preach, coupled with a determination not to forfeit all biblical authority, should prevent the minister from making fatal errors and enable him or her to preach the topical sermon with confidence. Besides, many of the vital issues confronting humanity raise, in one way or another, biblical-theological issues. Topics are not always clearly nonbiblical versus biblical, although some arise in culture while others are clearly derived from the Bible. The preacher's task is to clarify each issue, then present a word from God about it. We may shine the light of the gospel on some issues that otherwise would have no light shed on them from the church.

The Topical Sermon

For example, consider a topical sermon on happiness, an important personal issue. The desire for happiness is basic to humanity. Many people seem to want it, though few seem to find it. Surely there must be a way to be happy. The Bible has a word for "happy." The word is "blessed," found in numerous biblical passages, the best-known of which is the Beatitudes, which constitute the first part of the Sermon on the Mount (Matt. 5:1–12). A Bible teaching may help us understand this crucial topic. One may correctly assume that God wants his children to be happy. Further, one may surmise, on that basis, that there is a way to be happy. The Bible legitimizes the sermon subject. Therefore, a topical sermon on "How to Be Happy" is a valid one. The "how to" title, so popular in books, magazines, and manuals, suggests some means by which happiness may be achieved, that is, a sermon structure. Why not propose some ways (three, of course) to achieve happiness? First, know good. Knowledge of what is good will lead to the desire to practice goodness. Second, be good. After all, a person must be at peace with self, or that person will never be happy. Third, do good. Making others happy, especially family members, brings great joy.

Three ways to attain happiness are established. All are clear statements of truth associated with a general biblical teaching. Thus, the sermon appears to meet the test of a good topical sermon. The mere mention of something that is true generally and can be found in the Bible does not necessarily make for biblical preaching, however. References to words and ideas that appear in the Bible do not make a sermon biblical. The topical sermon, though, is a discussion of an issue in light of Scripture. Jesus' use of the word "happy" implies, at least, that he wishes his followers to be happy. He does not go so far as to say the threefold plan of our proposed sermon is how to achieve it.

As outlined here, the sermon is a development of an implication found in Scripture, which can be a valid pattern of organization for a sermon.[7] The sermon on "The Way to Happiness" takes us from a topic—happiness—the idea for which originated outside Scripture, to a Scripture passage that mentions happiness, to an implication found generally in the Beatitudes about happiness. These steps, to be sure, remove us a great distance from the textual sermon and from the exposition of scriptural teachings about happiness.[8]

Because of all the limitations of the topical sermon, the minister should preach it as an occasional sermon. The ease with which we may think of slogans, catchy phrases, and other witticisms that are so prevalent in our culture may tempt us to "go for it" too frequently. A series of three or four snappy words strung together to form an outline, along with some illustrations from the latest newspaper or television sitcom, make sermons interesting and appealing. The subject of happiness lends itself more easily to topical preaching because one may take it from the Bible as well as from culture. Besides, it is a popular subject. Three easy words or phrases, however, will not be adequate or come so quickly with other issues.

Hoping to attract more listeners, some ministers prepare next Sunday's sermon by picking a word out of their cultural, secular vocabulary, and then look for that word in the Bible. They then refer to its occurrence in the Bible and classify the sermon as a biblical sermon, instead of recognizing it for what it is—a topical sermon. Such preaching shows a great disregard for the use of the word by the biblical writer and the thought pattern of the language that caused the writer to incorporate it in the exact spot and manner in which he did. Correct interpretation of Scripture always takes into account the way the biblical writers thought and used their words. The best topical preaching also gives due regard to the relation of that interpretation to the sermon topic.

The phrase "Just do it," popularized by a brand of sports shoes, is a cultural buzzword. When the company employed a famous basketball player to promote its shoes, the slogan caught fire. In a society so enamored with superstar athletes, the phrase quickly became a neologism. "Just do it" is a synonym for action. Eager pastors seized on the

7. See discussion in H. C. Brown Jr., *A Quest for Reformation in Preaching* (Waco, Tex.: Word, 1960), pp. 88–89.
8. A verse-by-verse exposition of the Beatitudes reveals that happiness comes as a result of proper ethical behavior by kingdom citizens.

phrase as an equivalent of living the Christian life. If you are hesitant about living for Christ, "Just do it," they intoned. Did James not say: "Anyone, then, who knows the good he ought to do and doesn't do it, sins" (4:17)? The simple solution, then, is to "Just do it." If only the matter of living for Christ should be so easy. Of course, James said to do good. His instruction becomes quite specific. In its context (4:13–17), his exhortation to do good relates to proper consideration of the will of God and knowing what is right. Without due regard for the message of James, as it relates to doing, the minister risks preaching a sermon that will have the ring of a television commercial. Members of the congregation may retain an image of a skilled professional basketball player gracefully dunking a basketball and fail to remember the biblical injunction. James spoke of knowing what is right to do and failing to do it. Know the topic. Know the Bible. Know how the latter relates to the former. Adherence to these guidelines will make for a stronger topical sermon.

The topical sermon may reveal the church's acquaintance with her world, her ability to communicate, and her determination to speak a word from God about the issues inherent in life. Also, it can perform a more vital function: making the congregation aware that the great issues of life are theological in nature. How persons relate to each other, to societal issues, to institutions—all these are significant. More vital than all these, though, is humanity's relation to God. Preaching is unique because it pinpoints this relation. We may accomplish this pinpointing through the topical doctrinal sermon.

The Doctrinal Topical Sermon

We define the topical sermon as one which interprets a topic, with reference to a biblical text or theme which illumines, or informs, the topic.[9] A topic usually originates in culture. Aware of its importance, the minister decides to preach on it. With a topic in mind, such as abortion, capital punishment, or the teaching of religion in public schools, the minister turns to the Bible for support in the sermon.

The definition of text is vital to the ultimate form of the sermon. "Text" may mean a specific passage, or it may mean something broader, including a number of passages from different locations in the Bible. The former would lead to a textual sermon; the latter would lead to a multiple-passage text sermon.

First, the minister may employ one passage of Scripture and tell how it speaks to a specific need, issue, or life situation. This methodology re-

9. Cf. Allen's definition, *Preaching the Topical Sermon*, p. 3.

sembles that of the expository-textual sermon, but differs in that the subject itself directs the interpreter to the text. The preacher does not happen upon a topic while reading or preaching serially, but decides on the basis of a desire to preach on a specific topic. Driven by the topic itself, the preacher is looking for a text which contains information about the topic. Second, the preacher may combine multiple passages and use them as a sermon text. In the sermon the minister will declare the particular common truth which they teach, as one would do a topic of systematic theology.

In either case, at the conclusion of the process of interpretation, the preacher should allow the text to determine the content of the sermon, thus preventing discussion of the topic per se, with no scriptural monitoring of contents. The sermon speaks what the text says about the topic. At the center of the doctrinal topical sermon lies explanation of Scripture. This, in turn, establishes some limits for the discussion of the topic, but assures biblical authority for the sermon.

A variation of the proposed sermon on happiness illustrates the first of these forms. Point of origin: The desire to be happy is a part of being human. What does the Bible tell us about happiness? A word search on "happy" or "happiness" leads to Psalm 1, the first part of which states "Blessed (happy) is the man who. . . ." Our topic raises two questions: (1) What is happiness? (2) How may a person have it? Psalm 1 responds by declaring that a happy person is one who walks on one of two pathways through life. One is the way of godliness; the other, the way of ungodliness. The text, then, speaks of happiness, but limits the discussion of the subject. In the first line it states that the happy person is one who leads a godly life. We may affirm, on the basis of this psalm, that a person will find happiness through godly conduct. The psalmist describes the way of the godly in both negative and positive terms, then contrasts it with the way of the ungodly. With beautiful imagery he portrays the prosperity and stability of the godly person. A listener should find this life so appealing as to want it. These six verses suggest a sermon on "The Way to Happiness," complete with its own structure for the discussion of the topic. Psalm 1 exceeds the "know good," "be good," "do good" approach to happiness.

The textual approach to the preaching of a topical sermon may seem too restrictive for some topics, such as happiness. Sometimes one wants to draw on the teachings of several biblical passages. Thus a multiple-passage text provides a helpful way in which to accomplish the topical sermon. For example, a word study of the term "blessed," employed by the King James translators in Psalm 1 and Matthew 5:1–12, confirms that "happy" is a good translation and lends credence to the idea that happiness is a quality of character to be desired. The passages state explicitly that the happy person is one who is godly, and describe the kind of behavior associated with happiness. The remark by James that "we consider blessed those who have persevered" (5:11), along with Nehemiah's words that "the joy of the Lord is your strength" (8:10), substantiates the truth that happiness is attainable and durable.

In both forms of the topical doctrinal sermon the preacher starts with the topic in mind and then consults Scripture for the sermon text. The text, in turn, becomes the primary factor in the development of the sermon. That is, the preacher attempts to say what the text says about the topic, instead of straining to find a place to tie a topic into Scripture.

Topics may be social, ethical, or personal, as well as doctrinal in nature. Principles for the treatment of doctrinal subjects here apply to the treatment of these other issues as well. The Bible is a book about life. Thus it will have something to say about any issue related to life, whether directly or indirectly. Indeed, some topics that appear in the Bible also are public issues as well. Instead of proceeding from general life topic to Bible topic, the minister may prefer to reverse the procedure.

Doctrinal preaching provides us a way to address some of the volatile issues of the day without going entirely topical. We can give theological orientation and practical wisdom to the discussion. The church, after all, is supposed to offer a Christian message. If we are content to echo the culture, we blur or forfeit the distinctiveness of our identity and our message ceases to be unique. Other voices are crying in the wilderness.

For example, one of the most hotly debated topics for the past quarter century has been abortion. A sermon on this issue is certain of a hearing (as well as some kind of response). The Bible does not address the issue directly, by name. Is the preacher then limited to the strictly topical sermon?

The central issue in the abortion debate is the sanctity of life. Life is a subject about which Scripture says much. The Bible places a high premium on human life; it is a gift from God. A sermon on the biblical account of God's creation of humans in his own image will speak to the matter of abortion. Life is important because we humans are made in the image of God. To take a life is to violate that image. This is a doctrinal issue; it deals with the very nature of humankind.

Another subject that has generated extensive controversy is creationism. From the schoolroom to the courtroom to state legislatures, this issue has taken center stage. Some states of the United States have passed laws related to the teaching of creationism in public schools. Churches and pastors have not failed to raise their voices in this discussion. Topical sermons dedicated to presenting the "Christian" position, however, generally have revolved around the issue of whether the government ought to prevent the teaching of the biblical account of creation in public school classrooms. Ministers have said more about government limitation than about the biblical account of creation, which is the theological subject. The public issue has become the pulpit issue. Without a biblical message to clarify the subject, ministers have not advanced the discussion beyond the social level.

Attempts to speak a relevant word on these vital issues should not be limited to the topical sermon in which the minister begins with a topic. Perhaps a more fruitful approach would be to begin with the biblical teaching, i.e. preach doctrine to enable a better understanding of the topic.

Doctrine for Doctrine's Sake

Doctrines are also topics, albeit Christian topics. As much as people need to hear a doctrine associated with an issue, they need to hear doctrine much more. Then they know better how to understand and face a life issue. Too often, in our sermons we are attempting to equip our hearers to handle issues without a firm doctrinal underpinning. We have contended in earlier chapters that those local churches are stronger and more stable whose members know what they believe. Likewise, we have appealed to local churches to build and maintain their ministries on a solid doctrinal base. One way to build that foundation is for the minister to preach on the great doctrines of the faith. Both forms of the doctrinal topical sermon, the textual and the multiple-text sermon, serve well for such preaching.

For instance, the minister may begin by teaching the congregation about God, humanity, sin, and creation, then apply those teachings to worship, respect for life, and the ownership of property, as is the pattern of the Ten Commandments. Also, if the congregation is acquainted with the life, ministry, and teachings of Jesus, they will comprehend more easily ethics and the treatment of their fellow humans. Pulpit discussion which draws initially from the Scripture, with emphasis on the divine dimension, avoids the dilution or diminution of biblical authority which attends a strictly topical discussion, with emphasis on the human.

Preaching stresses the human encounter with the divine, thus the importance of a textual sermon on God. One distinguishing characteristic of the topical doctrinal sermon is that it is more subject oriented than idea oriented. Thus the immediate difficulty in such a sermon is determining how to preach on a subject so broad as God (or any of the other categories of systematic theology such as the Bible, the church, the Christian life, the person of Jesus Christ, the atonement, the resurrection, the second coming, or the Holy Spirit).

One way to narrow a subject is to find a limiting word or phrase. Theology professors often suggest that we do this with the doctrine of God by thinking of some great biblical statements about God: "God is spirit" (John 4:24); "God is light" (1 John 1:5); "God is love" (1 John 4:16). A sermon on the God whose essence is love will offer help for a world that knows so much hatred, violence, and abuse. To make love more specific, John declares, in the context of his remarkable truth about God, that God has given proof of his love (1 John 4:7–21, note vv. 7–10; cf. Rom. 5:8). Thus, we may narrow the topic to the demonstration of God's love through the death of Jesus on the cross. Given that 1 John 4:7–10 becomes the text, the passage then does its work of making a broad subject more manageable.

A textual sermon from 1 John 4:7–10 raises a doctrinal issue that is vital to daily life. This text does not exhaust the doctrine of God or tell all that the Bible says about the love of God, but it does say something important about it. The biblical-textual sermon model provides a structure that can make clear what it does teach, while giving the sermon unity and focus.

The second option for the sermon on God is to employ the multiple-passage text, which requires reading a number of passages that refer to God in order to discover the common teaching among all the passages. The Book of Hosea, for example, tells a story of love. It all begins well, with a happy home, with children. Then the story takes a tragic turn. The wife abandons her family and returns to a life of prostitution. The husband buys her back at a public auction. In the same story, the prophet declares that God cares for his people as a father pities his children. God searches for his people in the wilderness. These images communicate the story of God's love for his people. This remarkable Old Testament book provides a basis on which to relate divine love, redemption, and restoration to the issues of family trouble, infidelity, and brokenness, which are so prevalent in today's society. Likewise, the Book of Amos offers a biblical base for speaking on maltreatment of the poor and neglect of justice. Doctrine makes good topical preaching. Instead of looking for the doctrine in the topic, look for the topic in the doctrine.

The multiple-passage text doctrinal sermon requires diligent preparation. The preacher who plans to refer to several passages in one sermon will need to study all those passages to determine what they say. Otherwise, mere mention of them during the course of a sermon will only establish that the Bible mentions the subject numerous times— God's love, for example—but the preacher never gets around to saying exactly what the Bible says about it. This we might call "concordance preaching." Computer software makes this listing of all Scriptures on one word or subject quite simple. The Bible mentions love hundreds of times. With a click or two, a minister soon can know the precise number and announce it in the sermon with confidence without ever clarifying anything about love.

Passages that come from a single book make the entire book, in effect, the text and the result is a Bible book sermon. The multiple-passage text may also come from several passages in different books. Matthew 1:18–25 and Luke 2:1–20 both give accounts of the birth of Jesus. Though each has a distinctive emphasis, both identify Jesus by his names. All names they give capture the meaning of Old Testament prophecies about the one who would come from God.

Exodus 19:1–9, Joshua 24:14–24, and Nehemiah 8:1–10:39 share a common lesson on the solemnity of the covenant made with God. God initiated the covenant, which he made with Israel at the time he delivered them from Egyptian bondage. In all three passages the people declare their acceptance of the covenant and their intent to abide by its terms. Joshua and Nehemiah were reminding them of their agreement and calling them to renew it. Covenant in Old Testament bound both parties. Although Israel continuously broke its part of the agreement, God remained faithful to the terms of the covenant. His people's failure never caused God to alter his commitment to his people.

In a similar manner one may preach on the doctrine of the Holy Spirit. The fascination with glossolalia prompts one to think initially of the events of Pentecost and the gifts of the Holy Spirit. Gifts of the Spirit are prominent in Romans 12 and 1 Corinthians 12–14. These passages help limit the doctrine to a manageable textual unit. Romans 12:3–8 or 1 Corinthians 12:1–11 would serve well for a textual sermon on the gifts of the Spirit. For a sermon on the person of the Spirit, the Gospel of John is a good beginning point, relating words of Jesus found nowhere else in the Gospels. In John 14–16 Jesus himself identifies the Spirit several times. These references suggest a sermon pattern in which multiple passages are linked to serve as a text. In 14:16 Jesus speaks of the Spirit as "another Counselor" ("comforter" in the KJV). The Greek term for "another" means another of the same kind. Thus the Spirit is one of the same kind as Jesus. In 14:25–26 and 15:26–27 Jesus refers to the Spirit as the "Counselor" and as "the Spirit of truth." Then, in 16:7–16 he repeats the term "Spirit of truth" and outlines the work of the Spirit. The Spirit is to be to the believer what Jesus was when he was present on the earth.

Preparation of the doctrinal sermon requires honesty about presuppositions. The minister is not searching for a proof text to bolster a position already decided; that is, he has already made up his mind what he is going to say and is trying to find something that proves he is right.

To the contrary, he is looking for a text that will illumine the topic and must be willing to test all presuppositions against the truth of Scripture. The proof text method sometimes requires one to disregard all texts except those that affirm the interpretation already decided. An area in which we ministers are especially vulnerable is eschatology. With a scheme for the endtimes already in hand, the preacher needs only to align Scripture to prove the correctness of the scheme.

The doctrinal topical method seeks understanding of the text, which it in turn applies to the topic. No text is ignored a priori. The interpreter locates a specific text that contains teachings about the topic, then appropriates the truths related to the topic and incorporates them into the sermon. What the text says about the issue is the primary consideration. Scripture may validate, confirm, clarify, alter, or correct preconceived notions.

Conclusion

The biblical text is important to the topical sermon. "Without the built-in reminder of the text, the topical preacher may be tempted to regard critical theological analysis as only an option."[10] This is especially true in our generation when so many preachers are venturing into the political realm. Sermons on topics discovered in that faraway land tend never to get around to the biblical text. Instead, they tend to gravitate toward sensationalism.

Thus we see that topical preaching, with its beginning point outside the biblical material, poses numerous threats to good biblical preaching. On the other hand, with proper followthrough and regard for orienting the sermon theologically, topical preaching becomes a valid option for the preacher who seeks to achieve variety in preaching without sacrificing content or playing to the gallery of the current generation.

In some ways, topical preaching reflects positively on the church. The minister demonstrates that the church is willing to confront life instead of retreating into platitudes. In addition, the topical sermon brings a Christian perspective on social issues. Also, by insisting on a biblical perspective the minister helps the church retain the distinctiveness of the Christian message. Topical preaching, done well, helps the church answer the charge of some critics that the Bible is an antiquated book, a mere relic of the past to be viewed in a museum. The message of the Bible becomes a present-tense reality.

The doctrinal sermon is also a topical sermon—on a Christian topic. Starting with theological issues seems a wise course of action for a pas-

10. Ibid., p. 7.

tor and church who are convicted about the issues that confront us all in our human existence. The church specializes in the theological, the relation of the divine to the human. If we begin with doctrine, we have begun with the Christian answer to life itself.

Representative Topical Sermons and Preachers

For analysis, we choose sermons from the two topical preachers mentioned earlier in the chapter. One of the more famous sermons of Harry Emerson Fosdick is "The Power to See It Through." The issue of the sermon is "staying power." Fosdick's thesis is that "starting power and staying power are not the same thing in any realm."[11] He draws the idea from Demas, the one-time companion of the apostle Paul, and "familiar experience of a fine beginning and a poor ending." His purpose apparently is to encourage his listeners to cultivate those personal qualities that will see life through to the end.

The sermon begins with reference to Demas, who is mentioned briefly three times in the New Testament—in Philemon, Colossians, and 2 Timothy. Fosdick took the last statement about Demas to be an indication that Demas failed to see his commitment through to the end of his life. Paul stated that "Demas forsook me, having loved this present age." From the brief references made to Demas, Fosdick drew the conclusion that Demas had no staying power. He then surmised that our experience has taught us that too many persons have the same problem. The sermon, then, follows a structure suggested from consideration of the topic. His points, of which there are three, are implications drawn from the life of Demas.

Another sermon that grew out of an idea from the life of Paul is probably Fosdick's most famous. The title is "Handling Life's Second Bests."[12] Fosdick begins the sermon with a reference to a personal problem: "[N]amely, that very few persons have a chance to live their lives on the basis of their first choice."[13] In the introduction he mentions that Whistler, the artist, had to settle for second choice in his life. In the third paragraph, within two minutes of the spoken sermon, he clearly poses the problem addressed in the sermon: the "inescapable human problem of handling life's second bests."[14] He then proposes

11. Harry Emerson Fosdick, "The Power to See It Through," in *Riverside Sermons* by Harry Emerson Fosdick with an introduction by Henry Pitney Van Dusen (New York: Harper and Brothers, 1958), p. 29.

12. Harry Emerson Fosdick, "Handling Life's Second Bests," in *Riverside Sermons*, pp. 54–62.

13. Ibid., p. 54.

14. Ibid.

that one of the most impressive exhibitions of handling the problem in human history is Paul. His basis is Acts 16:6–10, especially verse 7, which states that Paul desired to go to Bithynia but the Spirit told him "No," and that Paul went to Troas instead. At Troas he heard the Macedonian call. He responded and went to Europe instead of Asia.

Fosdick surmises that because Paul wanted very much to go to Bithynia, Macedonia was second choice for him. By use of historical imagination, he draws a word picture of a missionary who is disappointed because of a change in plans. Paul, however, followed through and "rendered his most significant service with the left-overs of a broken plan."[15]

His contact with common human experience, so typical of Fosdick, is made when he declares that wanting Bithynia and getting Troas is a familiar experience. We often have to take second-best in our lives and make the most of it. To do that successfully is not so familiar an experience.

The sermon unfolds along the lines of making the most of second best, lessons drawn from Paul's response to his Macedonian call that enabled him to succeed. Paul had two elements in his life that enabled him to be victorious: his religion and his concern about people.

This sermon is not an exposition of biblical passages relating that Paul accepted Macedonia as a second choice. It is the development of an implication contained in the declaration that Paul intended to carry the gospel into Asia. The sermon does contain numerous references to Paul and some explanation of the biblical story of his call to a mission in Europe. The genius of the sermon, as of Fosdick's preaching in general, is its appeal to a common personal problem. As Fosdick states in the first sentence, the difficulty of having to live on the basis of second choice is almost universal.

In each of these sermons, Fosdick speaks to personal issues in light of the gospel. He bases each on a biblical text and explains some biblical material. Sermon structure, however, derives more from the nature of the topic suggested by the text than from the text itself. Staying power, for example, is associated with a certain integrity of conscience, with being captured by a cause, and with resources of interior strength renewed by great faiths (sic). These are not expositions of particular Scripture verses, but certainly are not inconsistent with the biblical teachings about the living of the Christian life.

In the chapter on dramatic preaching, the authors suggest a way to preach a sermon on Paul's staying power by means of an imaginary conversation with the great missionary about his refusal to give up,

---

15. Ibid., p. 55.

even in the middle of a terrible storm at sea. The secret: The providence of God controlled his life.

Other possibilities exist for preaching on the topic of living life on the basis of second choice, a vital issue for the Christian. A biblical thematic sermon on the will of God, based on passages about Paul, is one way to approach the matter. Another is to propose the teachings of Jesus about doing the will of the Father as a guide for accepting God's will as our choice, no matter our personal desires to do otherwise.[16]

Halford Luccock, who distinguished himself as preacher and professor of preaching, also preached the topical sermon effectively. On the subject of living through change, he proposed that one of the great liabilities of life is "sleeping through a time of great change, and failing to achieve the new mental attitudes which the new situations and conditions demand."[17] The idea came from his reading of Washington Irving's story of Rip Van Winkle, who slept through the American Revolution. That, followed by a conversation with a man who was giving uninformed opinions on "nearly everything in the world" caused Luccock to think about the number of people who were sleeping through the revolutions of their own generation. By revolution he did not mean political or military revolutions, but "the broader sense of real changes in the conditions of life which call for changes in thinking and attitudes and actions to fit them."[18]

Luccock then crafted the sermon to speak of changes that require new thoughts and attitudes. The biblical passages he cited as a basis for the discussion were Matthew 4:17 and Revelation 21:4, which declare that Jesus came preaching repentance and that God will make all things new. Luccock equated repentance with a call to change to fit new conditions. The sermon, then, is a brief look at three changed situations in which "former things are passed away."

The changes cited were: (1) changes in thinking about the necessity of a religious foundation for life; (2) the new fact that, potentially, there are enough natural products to suffice for the whole human race; and (3) the splitting of the atom made old words sparkle with new meaning. The conclusion of the whole matter is that Christians cannot ignore their responsibility to bring the Good News to a changing world. To fail to do so would be tantamount to sleeping through a revolution.

---

16. None of these suggestions is intended to detract from the genius of Fosdick for appealing to human experience in his sermons. His contribution to twentieth-century preaching is at the very point of relevance; he had the gift of making each person who listened to him feel as though the preacher was speaking directly to him or her.

17. Halford E. Luccock, "Sleeping through a Revolution," in Halford E. Luccock, *Marching Off The Map* (New York: Harper and Brothers, 1952), p. 120.

18. Ibid., p. 131.

The topic of change dominates the sermon. It is timely (still) and one about which the Bible speaks. Accurate biblical exegesis, however, reveals that the word for repentance has a broader meaning than change, though it does include that meaning. Luccock developed his sermon along the other lines suggested by the word "change." His sermon properly called for Christians to have new attitudes and actions in light of the changes discussed in the body of the sermon.

These two representatives of topical preaching illustrate that preachers may speak on the basis of broad biblical teachings as well as from specific chapters and verses. Their sermons can be relevant and interesting even when not done in the traditional sermon style. One factor that motivated Fosdick was the desire to demonstrate that the Bible had not been lost to modern humans.[19]

These representative topical sermons remind us of the importance of considering the position of the listeners with reference to the sermon topic.[20] Fosdick, Luccock, and others of their generation accomplished such consideration to a remarkable degree. We should remember, at the same time, that consideration of what the listener wants may lead to the sensational. Topical sermons already have an indirect connection with the biblical text. Once that connection is broken, the sermons easily may drift so far away from Scripture as not to have a connection at all.

Thus the preacher should be alert to the dangers of topical preaching. One of the most obvious is that the preacher will never bring the text to bear on a topic. Having begun with a topic that originated outside the text, we never get it into the text. We do not talk about the text, but merely refer to it. This is especially easy to do when discussing social, personal, or political issues. The danger is not present in expository preaching, in which "the biblical text tends to remind the preacher to ground the sermon in a theological point of view. If the hermeneutical movement leads biblical preachers from the text to local political issues, the text tends to remind the preachers to interpret the issues in light of theological conviction and not simply to air their own beliefs."[21]

19. That was the thrust of his Yale Lectures, *The Modern Use of the Bible* (New York: Macmillan, 1961).
20. Allen, *Preaching the Topical Sermon*, pp. 9–11.
21. Ibid., p. 7.

12

Narrative Doctrinal Preaching

Much of the Bible is narrative. Thus narrative preaching should be a more natural way to preach the contents of the Bible, and one would expect it to be very common. Yet narrative preaching is not commonplace. We may account for this lack by recalling the methodology so many contemporary pastors and teachers of homiletics learned during their seminary days. Our professors taught us that stories are important, but are to be used primarily as illustrations in sermons. The value of story used for illustration increases when it comes from the Bible. A subtle difference is evident: *Stories* are important. We did not learn as much about *story*. During the past twenty years, however, we have discovered that story has power as a sermon within its own right, not merely as support for sermon points in rhetorical outlines. The members of our congregations had been telling us all along that they remembered our stories, which we used to help make points, better than they remembered anything else. If that is true, why not make the sermon a story?

History of Narrative Preaching

About forty years ago a theologian, H. Grady Davis, wrote a book on preaching in which he suggested that a sermon idea can take the form of a narrative.[1] He observed that "too little use is made of narrative in contemporary preaching."[2] Davis obviously meant "story" when he spoke of narrative. That he meant for us to preach story sermons appar-

1. Henry Grady Davis, *Design for Preaching* (Philadelphia: Muhlenburg, 1958).
2. Ibid., p. 162. Davis first argued, on behalf of homiletics, that a thought, or idea, is inseparable from the form in which it is expressed. The form is the shape of the thought (p. 9). "The only way to extend or limit a thought . . . is by the words used to express it" (p. 4). He argued that "there is a right form for each sermon" (p. 9). Davis also noted that the ideas of the gospel "are mainly in the form of a story told" (p. 57).

ently was not so obvious at the time he wrote. Sermon as story only became a part of homiletical method more than a quarter of a century later.

With the publication of *Preaching the Story* in 1980[3] came a clarion call for the use of narrative in preaching. Soon followed Richard Jansen's *Telling the Story*, which echoed the emphasis of Steimle et al.[4] The publication of these two volumes achieved for the story sermons what Davis failed to do earlier. In the decade of the 1980s, a number of complete volumes were dedicated to the subject of story preaching, and some general homiletics texts included chapters on the story sermon. Meanwhile, a few ministers had begun preaching narratives. Story preaching, in both theory and practice, has become more common.

We may attribute this interest in story to several recent developments. First, homiletics has made more extensive application of the research within other academic fields, especially biblical studies and hermeneutics, to its own discipline. Recent findings related to narrative as a form in Old and New Testaments, and the significance of narrative for understanding Scripture could not escape the notice of homiletics, to be sure. The appropriation of some of the fruits of that research by homiletics, however, is a relatively new development.[5] The practice of taking the various forms of biblical material into account in the preparation of sermons has come about as a result of the new awareness of the work of biblical scholars. This practice, in turn, has led preaching to a greater consciousness of its dependence on biblical studies, hermeneutics, and the other disciplines. Subsequently, preaching has recognized that an interrelatedness exists among the various departments of theological education. Such awareness has led to a new appreciation of the contributions each department makes to all others and to the whole of which each is a part.

For much of the twentieth century, the divisions of seminary, or Bible school, comprised departments with different assignments. Each of the departments tended to view its task in isolation from the others, with no specific responsibility to discuss the relationship its subjects bore to those in the other departments. Cross-area classes with teams of teachers from various disciplines were rare, if not nonexistent. The biblical studies area taught the contents of the Bible. Hermeneutics classes explicated the history and methodology of interpretation. The

---

3. Edmund A. Steimle, Morris J. Niedenthal, and Charles L. Rice, *Preaching the Story* (Philadelphia: Fortress, 1980).

4. Richard A. Jensen, *Telling the Story: Variety and Imagination in Preaching* (Minneapolis: Augsburg, 1980).

5. For example, Tom Long in *Preaching and the Literary Forms of the Bible* (Atlanta: John Knox/Westminster, 1992).

homiletics department taught rhetoric, that is, how to take the facts gained from Bible study and construct intelligible sermons from them. In other days, one of the great difficulties of sermon preparation was that of "getting up an outline." Preaching classes were placed in the curriculum to ease the difficulty. The homiletics department, perhaps more than any other, bore the responsibility of demonstrating how to integrate all the disciplines of theological education for communication to congregations.[6] Each professor accomplished the task by showing how, in the process of sermon preparation, the minister draws material from all other areas of the seminary curriculum.[7]

Thus homiletics has gained a more comprehensive view of its role and has become a more willing conversation partner with biblical studies and hermeneutics, as well as with the other disciplines in the theological curriculum.[8] Its responsibility is no longer that of merely teaching methods of crafting sermon outlines. Preaching professors have a larger assignment than to tell their students to bring the "cargo" from all other classes and to promise that the homiletics class will provide a vehicle for delivering the cargo. Content and form, we know now, are not always separable. The form of the content may be the exact form of the sermon. This is especially true with narrative. The result: story sermons.

Second, we may attribute the interest in story to its success among oral cultures. In parts of Asia and Africa, chronological storytelling has become the primary means of communicating the gospel.[9] The reason, according to missionaries and missions strategists, is that people who are part of an oral culture understand a story sermon when they cannot understand a sermon developed in outline form. They may listen, and listen attentively, to a three-point sermon. When asked to tell what the sermon was about, they may remember points in a different order than they were spoken, or they may recall only one of the points. Rarely do they see the connection of the points or understand their meaning as a whole.

6. See the analogy of the "homiletical car" assembly line in chapter 7.

7. This includes Christian education and music.

8. This may mean that in the past homiletics has viewed its task differently, or that homiletics was not taken seriously as a partner in an academic discussion. Such an attitude as "We teach form while others teach content" perhaps has been a hindrance to the joining of the conversation by homileticians. On the other hand, the view that "Preaching is a practical, not a theological, discipline" has kept homiletics out of the discussion! The motivation for the writing of this volume came through a team-teaching assignment, combining systematic theology and homiletics.

9. New Tribes Mission experiments began on the island of New Guinea circa 1983. Their successes have been phenomenal and have been copied by missionaries throughout Asia. On a recent trip to the Philippines, one of these authors discovered the practice of storytelling is widespread and growing in popularity as an evangelistic method.

When the same people hear a story, on the other hand, they not only remember the story, but often can recite all or part of it after hearing it only once. They understand because they comprehend plot, character, and other components of story. Their education came through story. This discovery has profound implications for story sermons.

The communicative power of story is not restricted to illiterate peoples. A missionary in the Philippines has begun a Bible class among professional persons in the inner city where he lives, employing story as the means of teaching. He holds the class in a large bank conference room during the lunch hour once a week. Interest has remained high from the beginning, and the attendance increased for several weeks in a row. The missionary now has plans for expanding into other areas of the city.

Third, story has received more interest from preaching due to the success of drama. Drama's appeal is so widespread that ministers all over the world are incorporating it into worship services. Churches and church groups in various parts of the world, Europe in particular, invite pastors who employ drama in worship to speak at pastors' conferences. Taking their cue from the nature and impact of drama, increasing numbers of preachers are doing the sermon as story.

Definition of Narrative Preaching

Preach the story. Employ the narrative. That sounds simple enough. In practice, the decision to preach in story is only the beginning point. The first step in the implementation of the decision is to recall or to review the exact nature of a story sermon.

The story sermon may be defined in a manner consistent with the traditional form of story, a "Once upon a time" beginning, followed by an unfolding story line (plot) featuring characters, places, and events, then a conclusion that completes the story. This traditional structure is the one followed in this chapter.

Some authors, though, make a distinction between story and narrative. Eugene Lowry, for example, proposes a sermon scheme for narrative that differs from story understood in the traditional sense.[10] Lowry's method progresses through five stages. The first stage is to upset the equilibrium, or set a tension. The second is to analyze the discrepancy created in stage 1. In the third stage the preacher proposes clues to the resolution of the discrepancy. Fourth, the preacher helps the congregation experience the gospel or find the answer. The fifth and

10. Eugene L. Lowry, *The Homiletical Plot* (Atlanta: John Knox, 1980). Cf. *Doing Time in the Pulpit* (Nashville: Abingdon, 1985).

final stage is to anticipate the consequences that may come as a result of resolving the entire process begun with upsetting the equilibrium.[11] This plan, Lowry states, applies to both narrative (story) texts and non-narrative (didactic) passages. It provides a method for interjecting drama into the sermon, thus enhancing its appeal and avoiding the authoritarianism often associated with propositional preaching.[12] In this volume the authors employ the term "narrative" first in its broader meaning of "story."[13] Thus story holds much value for preaching and the story sermon may assume any one of a number of forms, depending on the kind of story in the text.

Types of Narrative Sermons

Possibilities for narrative sermons are numerous.

1. Story may be a recital of history, such as the Book of Exodus. At the end of Genesis Joseph's family is relocated in Egypt, due to the severe famine in Palestine. There they languish while hundreds of years pass. After several generations the Hebrews number in the thousands and remain in Egypt. As Exodus begins, the Hebrew population numbers in the hundreds of thousands and the burden of their bondage has increased to the point that it is unbearable; they cry out to God for help. The entire Book of Exodus is the telling of the story of their deliverance; it is a story of redemption.

Within the larger story a number of related subplots unfold. For example, the story of Moses the servant of God teaches much about God's ways of relating to human leaders, even when they fail.

2. Story may be a sketch of the life of a person. In the lives of Bible characters we often learn great truths about God. Some of the more prominent include Abraham, Sarah, Jacob, Rebekah, Moses, Miriam, Deborah, Gideon, Ruth, Esther, David, Daniel, John the Baptist, Mary the mother of Jesus, Simon Peter, Paul, and John the brother of James. Abraham's life reveals that Jehovah is a covenant-making God. Sarah's life is a testimony to the wonder-working power of God. Rebekah played a key role in the struggle between her two sons Esau and Jacob. Jacob's name was changed to Israel, meaning "one who perseveres with God." Jacob personified the identity of God's people. Moses and David both committed serious crimes and experienced the forgiveness of God. Ruth's story illustrates the beauty of loyalty. Daniel's life testifies to

---

11. In *The Homiletical Plot.*

12. It also allows for the moment of discovery, as does the inductive method of Fred Craddock.

13. We also include a chapter on dramatic preaching, in which we discuss the use of elements of drama in the sermon. See chapter 13.

faith. The birth of Jesus unfolds through the narratives about Mary and Joseph. John the Baptist's identity is that of one who speaks for God. His message was a thunderous cry for repentance. Every mention of the name of Simon Peter recalls the great confession: "You are the Christ, the Son of the living God" (Matt. 16:16) and the founding of the church (Matt. 16:13–20). Paul gave us in life and in word the term "grace" (1 Cor. 15:10). John's name is synonymous with the love of God, expressed best in the Gospel of John (3:16).

3. Story may be shorter narrative passages. Brief narratives in both Old and New Testament are rich in doctrinal content. Amos' encounter with Amaziah (Amos 7:10–17) is brief, but makes the point about judgment quite clear. Ezekiel's vision of the wheel within the wheel (Ezek. 1:10) dramatizes that the presence of God is a fiery presence and that God may go wherever he wishes. Doctrine is self-evident in the accounts of the birth of Jesus (Luke 2:1–20), the epiphany (Luke 2:22–39), the coming of the Holy Spirit in the story of Pentecost (Acts 2:1–13), and the mission of the church in the report of Peter's visit to the home of Cornelius the centurion (Acts 10:1–48). One also finds stories within stories in both Old and New Testaments. These shorter narratives underscore again that stories communicate, *as stories*.

4. Story may be presumed story, that is, story behind the text. Numerous didactic passages have underlying stories that are found elsewhere in Scripture. This provides another alternative (in addition to Lowry's) for handling the non-narrative text. For example, each of the Epistles of Paul grows out of the story of his missionary journeys in Acts. When the apostle says to the Philippians that God will bring to completion the work which he began in them (1:4–6), one immediately remembers the Macedonian call and Paul's subsequent trip to Philippi, reported in Acts 16:6–40. Jesus referred to the story of Jonah when he said, in reference to his own death and resurrection, "For as Jonah was three days and three nights in the belly of a huge fish, so the Son of Man will be three days and three nights in the heart of the earth" (Matt. 12:40). Paul's discussion of sin via comparison of Adam and Jesus in Romans 5:12–21 presumes the stories of creation and redemption.

5. Story may be implied. A number of the short, pithy remarks of James bring to mind stories with doctrinal-ethical lessons. For example, the rebuke of the church for treating the rich and the poor with a double standard (2:1–12) sparks the imagination and pricks the conscience. James surely had in mind one or more specific instances of maltreatment of some poor persons who had come into the assembly. Each person has worth and dignity in God's sight, whether or not that person has wealth. Perhaps James knew someone in the congregation who had judged another because of economic standing. In our own

world of the haves and the have-nots, the issues of preferential treatment of the rich and the rush to judgment are quite real.

These references indicate the vast amount of biblical material available for the minister who is trying to decide about story preaching.

Decisions Involved in Narrative Preaching

All the possibilities make the decision to preach in story easier. Once the minister decides to do one of the narrative forms in a sermon, other decisions follow in rapid succession. The first is to determine the limits of the unit of Scripture, pericope, which is the text. Classic stories, such as the call of Abram in Genesis 12:1, have clear beginning points. The end of Abraham's personal pilgrimage comes with the record of his death in Genesis 25:8. Matthew 1:18 declares that the birth of Jesus happened in a certain way. Matthew 2:12 completes the story of the child's birth with the visit of the Magi.

The definition of a story text can be more difficult than in a didactic passage. When a story is embedded within a long narrative, the interpreter must grasp the flow of the larger passage and determine the beginning and ending points of a smaller portion of the story. For example, Saul's visit to the witch of Endor (1 Sam. 28:7–25) is part of a narrative detailing Saul's pursuit of David. His insistence on calling up Samuel from the dead so he could confer with him raises interesting questions about the afterlife, not to mention that Saul went against a specific prohibition of God about conferring with one who had a familiar spirit.

The second decision is to decide the level from which to tell the story—social, personal, political, emotional, or spiritual.[14] At the social level the minister tells how a biblical person functioned within the community. Jeremiah's speeches at the temple entrance reveal an essential part of his ministry (Jer. 7:1–8:22; cf. the story of Amos): to warn of God's judgment. The personal level may be done in the form of character analysis. Samson, great hero of the Old Testament, was quite clever in word and deed (Judg. 13:24–16:31). His penchant for riddles and practical jokes makes an interesting study of personality. The chronicles of the kings are filled with political intrigue on the part of the var-

---

14. The authors are indebted to Professor Dan Kent for this idea. He refers to the surface level, at which one scans the whole landscape and points to the landmarks. Next is the emotional level, the one in which the preacher seeks to identify with the feelings of the biblical persons. Then there is the spiritual level, at which the preacher assesses the motives of certain characters. He warns, quite properly, that one must guard against reverting to allegory! (Dan Gentry Kent, unpublished Ph.D. colloquium paper, Southwestern Baptist Theological Seminary.)

ious monarchs of ancient Judah and Israel. Why, when they represented God, would they seek military and economic ties with neighboring states? Their failures speak vividly to God's people about the object of our trust. Simon Peter makes an interesting study in emotion. His moods ran the gamut from a declared willingness to die for his master (Matt. 26:35) to a denial that he ever knew him (Matt. 26:74). Spiritual qualities of biblical persons provide the minister with specific and helpful suggestions for members of the congregation to emulate. Mary's desire to listen to Jesus revealed a quality of character Jesus himself noted (Luke 10:42). Her compassion and devotion that led her to anoint the Lord's feet with costly perfume, which brought scorn from Judas, resulted in a statement by Jesus about his coming death (John 12:1–8).

The third decision about preaching a narrative is to select a perspective from which to relate the story. Possibilities include the following: (1) tell the story in connection with the continuing story; (2) tell the story as a free-standing entity; (3) tell the story as an interruption or parenthesis within the larger story; (4) tell the story from within the story—as seen through the eyes of one of the characters. Positioning oneself with reference to the story is a major decision in the preparation to preach.[15] The minister also (5) may take a position on the outside and repeat the narrative as an observer, such as a news reporter would do. One may (6) retell the biblical story in the present tense. The story of the prodigal son, for example, has been repeated in many families. In this case, the contemporary story becomes the biblical story. The identification must be unmistakable.

The fourth matter to be decided is the language of the sermon. Craft the language of the sermon to communicate the story best. Tense is an important consideration. The narrative tense may be the simple past or the imperfect. Some stories, such as the historical events, seem naturally to require some form of past tense. Descriptions of qualities of character, on the other hand, may have strong appeal when done in the present tense, as though the minister had transported his congregation into the past and is describing what they actually "see."[16]

This process of creating the language of the sermon, encoding the sermon, is a major task. One can scarcely overestimate the importance of writing manuscripts to improve the use of language. Encoding goes

---

15. This is also a feature of the dramatic monologue versus other dramatic sermon forms. The preacher may pose as a reporter looking in on the event, or as a participant, or as a reporter on the scene reporting to the outsiders, among other options. See the discussion in the chapter on "Dramatic Preaching," chapter 13.

16. The dramatic monologue done as role playing, treated in another chapter, is quite effective done in this manner.

beyond verb tense to include the choice of words, images, and ideas with which to tell the story. Good stories require active verbs and expanded descriptions of places, people, and events. They come to life in the imaginations of the listeners only if the preacher "sees" them and can tell what is seen. The storyteller should paint word pictures with color, should employ words that provide action and sound and infuse conversation with emotion.

Encoding also means telling the story in a precise sequence. Missionaries who employ chronological storytelling in oral cultures stress the significance of sequence. The storyteller is, in fact, giving an oral Bible to those who hear. The writing of manuscripts, in such cases, is not optional. With each repetition of a story the preacher must be careful to tell it exactly the same way. Stories abound concerning those who have not taken such care. Individual listeners have actually stopped the missionary and corrected him or her in those places where he or she said something in a different manner. In oral cultures missionaries find persons who can remember the stories word for word after hearing them only once.

The fifth decision is to find a way to clarify the doctrinal aim of the sermon in story. For a doctrinal sermon the preacher should have a specific doctrine in mind, in order to give direction to the sermon application. In the case of a doctrinal sermon, the specific objective is that the hearers understand some doctrine, something vital to their system of belief. This means the doctrinal sermon is highly cognitive in nature. To hear the sermon and to get the point is to learn the doctrine.

The sixth decision is to determine specific application. At some point the preacher should bring the story into the lives of the listeners; that is, should tell or show how "this means you." The minister may leave application to indirection and trust the individual to "find oneself in the story." The frequent employment of personal pronouns throughout the sermon may accomplish identification. A preacher may state the purpose for telling a story before beginning, the deductive approach that leaves no doubt about application. Also, one may step forward at the conclusion and clearly state that the story is complete and "we can see the point." The inductive method leaves the matter entirely to the listener, making numerous applications possible.

Constructing a Narrative Sermon

With all these preliminary matters decided, the minister is ready to write the sermon. Structure is significant in the story sermon. Though it has no outline as such, it has a distinct pattern. The pattern follows the structure of story: a beginning that sets the stage and suggests the plot, a middle portion that reveals the plot, and a concluding section that resolves issues related to the plot.[17]

Early in the formulation of the sermon one must decide how to introduce the theme (the beginning). The preacher has help from the text itself, which is a story. Narrative texts range from the introduction of timeframes—"In the year that King Uzziah died" (Isa. 6:1); to the introduction of places—"The angel of the Lord came and sat down under the oak in Ophrah" (Judg. 6:11, the beginning of the story of Gideon); to the telling of events—"When the people saw that Moses was so long in coming down from the mountain, they gathered around Aaron and said, 'Come, make us gods'" (Exod. 32:1); to the identity of persons—"Jesus continued: 'There was a man who had two sons'" (Luke 15:11); to references to geography—"Now an angel of the Lord said to Philip, 'Go south to the road—the desert road—that goes down from Jerusalem to Gaza'" (Acts 8:26). Each of these signals a story and the first words of the sermon may be the exact words of the text.

The use of language that will "invite" the listener into the story at the very beginning is critical. A common approach in literature is to say "Once upon a time. . . ." With the Bible story, the preacher needs to exercise caution with this kind of beginning. The listener's familiarity with fairy tales and fictional stories may trigger the mental response: "I am entering a fairy land." Yet, the preacher does wish to create that "Once upon a timeness" with the Bible story. To accomplish that feat, perhaps a formulistic beginning will suffice. "One day about two thousand years ago in the land of Palestine" signals that the event occurred in a real time in a specific place. Some Bible stories told as events that happened somewhere at some time seem real enough, but the listener has no knowledge of a specific location or date for them. We will also want to exercise the same caution with the "They lived happily ever after" kind of ending.

The next major consideration is the movement—progression, unfolding—into the middle portion of the story. This movement may be accomplished by means of a change of character. The account of the Lord's promise to Abraham that he and Sarah would have a son in their old age (Gen. 18:1–15) begins with the discussion of the three men with Abraham (vv. 1–3). When they asked about Sarah, Abraham replied that she was in the tent. Sarah was standing in the tent door behind him

17. These, we may note, conform to the rhetorical outline so long suggested as the proper method of sermon development—introduction, body, and conclusion—but do not result in a standard, that is, three-point, sermon. The story evolves (develops) along certain lines and will not be signaled by "first, second, and third" because its nature is different.

at that very moment, and overheard the conversation (v. 10). At that point in the narrative, she becomes the key figure.

Mark tells the story of Jesus' discussion with the Sadducees about the law of levirate marriage. In the middle of the discussion, "One of the teachers of the law came and heard them debating. Noticing that Jesus had given them a good answer, he asked him, 'Of all the commandments, which is the most important?'" (Mark 12:28).

Movement also may be achieved by a change of scenes. At the conclusion of his temptation in the wilderness, "Jesus returned to Galilee in the power of the Spirit" (Luke 4:14). Later, in Nazareth, he went to the synagogue where he read prophecies concerning himself from the Isaiah scroll.

Another way to make progress is to change the timeframe. The story of Jesus healing a blind man (John 9:1–41) apparently covers several hours. After he anointed the man's sightless eyes with clay, Jesus told the man to go and wash in the pool of Siloam. The man obeyed and returned with sight. Immediately his neighbors asked him how the miracle happened. When he told them about Jesus, they took him to the Pharisees, whose only concern was that Jesus had violated the Sabbath. An intense discussion followed, at the conclusion of which Pharisees threw him out of the temple. Jesus heard about their deed and found the man to speak with him about believing on the Son of God (v. 35).

The tragedy of Judah and Tamar in Genesis 38, a story within a story, changes in each of these ways: First characters dominate the story; then the scenes change; next, action moves very slowly; and suddenly jumps in time of several years take place. So it is with narrative structure.[18]

The revelation of plot is essential to narrative. This plot, or theme, equates with the central idea of the rhetorically developed sermon. The storyteller must know from the beginning the underlying theme, or themes, but does not reveal them in a deductive manner. He reveals them, instead, by filling in details of the story. The plot becomes evident through the words and actions of the persons, or in the changes of events that occur, or through the passing of time. The listener is involved and, ideally, will begin to see the plot developing along certain lines. These are suggested by certain words, phrases, or character traits. The listener begins to see the constants among the variables in the story. Sometimes the "point" becomes clear only at the end of the story.

Language, character portrayal, and plot presentation help make the story happen. History, geography, culture, and numerous other factors

18. This observation also came from Dan Kent in the colloquium paper referred to above.

must be interwoven into the story in order to retain the dynamics and keep it moving.

At the conclusion of the story, the plot becomes obvious and the whole of the story becomes clear. Resolution of all issues raised in the story must occur here. Questions are answered; open issues, addressed. At the end of his story, popularly known as "the story of the good Samaritan" (Luke 10:25–37), Jesus required the lawyer to answer for himself the question: "Who is my neighbor?" The listener should have a mental grasp of the whole, as one views the landscape from the perspective of the mountaintop. No part of the story is complete or understood completely apart from the whole. The story in Mark 12:28–34, for example, concludes with a discussion between Jesus and the scribe who asked him about the greatest commandment. Jesus replied that the commandment to love God with all one's heart is the first commandment, and the second greatest is to love one's neighbor as oneself (vv. 29–31). The story ends with Jesus' remark that the scribe was "not far from the kingdom of God" (v. 34).

Jesus appeared in the synagogue in Nazareth (Luke 4:14–30) to announce that the prophecy of Isaiah was fulfilled, in him, before the very eyes of those present. The conclusion of the story of the healing of the blind man is complete when he declares his belief on the Son of God (John 9:38).

Several facts become clear in this method. First, the story takes time.[19] A storyteller cannot rush; rushing will cause the storyteller to neglect essential elements of the story. Second, details are essential. Details create signposts along the pathway of the story journey. Third, description is vital and brings characters to life. People are interested in other people. Character qualities of persons in the story are indicators of lessons to be gained from the story. One must determine where in the narrative to point to these lessons. If they are not left until the end, then the preacher must determine how and when to step outside the narrative and state the lessons as they appear (as done in a verse-by-verse commentary method of preaching).

An Example of a Narrative Sermon

The story of Joseph (Gen. 37–50) serves as a good example for doctrinal narrative preaching. In this story, the reader, or the listener, sees the righteousness of Joseph contrasted to the wickedness of the brothers. Their bent toward evil dominates the early part of the narrative, but the

---

19. This is the thesis of Lowry's *Doing Time in the Pulpit*. In the sermon we are "doing" time instead of managing ideas.

goodness of Joseph becomes more and more obvious as the story continues. At the point of the famine in Canaan, the destiny of the evil brothers appears certain: They will starve to death and Joseph's revenge will be slow and painful. Genesis 50:19–20, though, reveals the underlying theme of thirteen chapters of the book: "God meant for good what the brothers intended for evil." A story sermon from Genesis 37:1–50:26 may follow this plan:

The Beginning

About fifteen hundred years before the birth of Christ, the second generation of Abraham's family was established in the land of Canaan, or Palestine. Isaac, the son of Abraham, had twin sons, Jacob and Esau. The Bible tells the story of Jacob. In his own family, Jacob had some problems. Favoritism by a parent will create problems. Jacob loved his son Joseph more than he loved all his other children, because Joseph was born when Jacob was an old man. To show his love, the elderly father made for his son an ornamented robe and presented it to him. No doubt the very sight of the conspicuous robe caused the anger of Joseph's brothers to seethe. They hated Joseph and could not speak to him without losing their tempers. The potential for an explosion within the family grew with each passing day. Soon some spark would ignite the fire of some brother's anger.

The ignition came as a result of a dream. Young Joseph dreamed, not once but twice, that his brothers would bow to him and serve him. In the dream he saw himself and his brothers tying bundles of grain in a field. His bundle of grain stood taller than the others and looked around. The other bundles bowed to his. In his second dream, the sun, moon, and stars paid homage to him. For some reason, he told his brothers the contents of his dreams and provided his own interpretation. He would rule them. They could stand it no longer. His words stirred their anger and hatred toward him. Even his father was disturbed by his favorite son's dream.

The flash point came when the brothers worked out a scheme to get rid of Joseph. One day, as they sat in a field near Dothan with their flocks, Joseph walked right into their plans. Jacob had sent him to check on his brothers. They must have been delighted to see him walking toward their camp. Their chance had come at last. All of them except one wanted to kill him. At Reuben's insistence, they compromised and decided to seize Joseph, strip him of the distinctive robe, and throw him into a pit. Nature would take its course and they would have no guilt. With one lie to their father, they would be free. Meanwhile, Reuben was secretly planning to sneak away and help Joseph out of the pit.

As they were eating their breakfast of bread and cheese, the brothers saw a company of traders passing nearby. They were on their way to Egypt with spices to sell. Why not sell Joseph to them as a slave, thus ridding themselves of their pesky brother without murdering him and making a little money on the side? The scheme worked out better than they had hoped. They agreed on the plan and, to cover their tracks, dipped Joseph's coat in animal blood and took it back to their father to substantiate their "theory" that wild animals had devoured his favorite son. How they kept Reuben quiet is still a mystery. Joseph was gone and life was going to be better for them. So it seemed.

The Middle

Down in Egypt, the merchants sold Joseph to an officer in the Pharaoh's army, who made him a slave.[20] More than once, hope for his life seemed to be lost. His owner's wife accused him of assaulting her. Though innocent, he was locked away in an Egyptian jail and forgotten. Throughout all his trials Joseph remained true to God and behaved wisely. His behavior eventually vindicated his good character, and he rose to the position of second in command in the Egyptian government.[21]

Then came another dream. The dreamer was not Joseph, but the Pharaoh. He, too, had two weird dreams. One was about skinny cows coming out of a river and eating fat cows. The other was about thin ears of corn on the stalk eating full ears of corn. Immediately upon awakening, the king sent for his magicians and demanded that they tell him the meaning of his dreams. No wise person in the entire kingdom could interpret them.

A butler in the court, who recently had served some time in prison, overheard the king telling his dreams and froze in his tracks. He had been in prison with a man who could interpret dreams. In fact, that prisoner had interpreted a dream or two for the cupbearer. He asked in return for the favor only that the cupbearer, whose dream he interpreted to mean release from prison, remember to give the king a message from Joseph. How could he forget? Upon hearing about the king's dreams, he remembered Joseph and told the Pharaoh his own story. Pharaoh quickly sent for Joseph and asked him the meaning of the two dreams. Joseph told him. It was the bad news, good news reply. The bad news was: A famine of seven years' duration was on the way. But there was good news, too. Seven years of plenty would precede the famine.

---

20. Note how the scene of the story changes in 39:1—after a story within a story in chapter 38. Joseph's life as a captive surfaces during the middle portion of the story.

21. This paragraph, a summary of part of the story, is done in this manner to make transition without losing continuity.

He suggested a plan for storing grain during the good years to sustain the nation during the famine. The king appointed Joseph to execute the plan, and gave him power to act on behalf of the government.

Everything happened exactly as Joseph predicted. The famine struck the land of Canaan as well as Egypt; Joseph's family there soon ran out of food and faced starvation. Jacob heard that the Egyptians had grain to spare and sent his sons to buy some. They were in for quite a surprise.[22] They had no idea with whom they would be doing business.

They did not recognize him. Besides, they figured he had been dead for a long time. Joseph recognized them, though, and his heart burned with compassion. He decided not to reveal his identity at the moment, choosing instead to wait until he could find out about his father back home.[23] At that point he held complete control over their lives. Something in his character, the same quality that helped him resist temptation and gave him patience to suffer during an unjust sentence in prison, prevented him from punishing his brothers. He had only to do nothing and they would die from starvation. He could murder them in a passive manner. He would be as free of guilt as they had assumed they would be when they planned to leave him in a pit to die. What's more, he could revel in his detachment and innocence; he could assure himself that they would die, and through no fault of his!

Joseph manipulated the brothers for a while, like a cat playing with a mouse. After discovering that his father was alive and well and that another son had been born to Jacob since the loss of Joseph, he accused them of being spies. He ordered that one of them be held in prison until the others could go and fetch the younger brother.

At that moment the burden of guilt fell on the brothers like the proverbial ton of bricks. Believing that Joseph could not understand them—he had been speaking to them through an interpreter—they discussed their deed of years ago. "We are receiving our just dues," they agreed. Reuben said, "I told you so. Remember, I tried to stop you from harming the child, but you wouldn't listen to me. Now look at what has happened." Joseph, who could understand them, turned away and wept. He held fast to his plan, though.

Back in Canaan, the brothers told their father about their unusual encounter. Jacob refused to send his young son, Benjamin. He now had suffered the loss of two sons, he declared, and that was enough.

22. Clues to the resolution of the story jump out at the listener, who knows something the brothers do not.

23. Here one begins to anticipate the moment when Joseph will reveal his identity. Suspense builds as he tricks and threatens the same men who attempted to kill him. Revenge is sweet.

But the famine continued and the family ran out of food a second time. Jacob relented, and even sent Benjamin with them. The second visit was no improvement on the first. Joseph tricked them again. He had a servant plant his personal silver cup in the sack of food given to Benjamin. Then, after the brothers had started on their return trip, he instructed his steward to go after them, accuse them of theft, and escort them back to Joseph's house. There Joseph spoke harshly to them about their treachery and said he would make Benjamin a slave for the crime. Judah began to plead for the life of the young Benjamin and told Joseph that if the boy did not return with them, their father would surely die.

Upon hearing these words about their father's loss of his youngest son two times, Joseph could not restrain himself. He sent everyone else out of the room. "Come close," he said. "I am Joseph your brother." Stunned by what they heard, they could not immediately believe their ears. He was alive! Their lives must have flashed before their eyes in that moment. Yet the earth's second most powerful man did nothing to them except embrace them and weep. He wept for joy; they perhaps wept out of anxiety or relief. Then they talked for a long time.

The Conclusion

The story ended when Joseph sent his brothers back to Canaan to bring their father and the entire family to Egypt. Then came another reunion and the joy of it exceeded that of the first. The old man Jacob died in peace, knowing the truth about Joseph. The brothers, meanwhile, figured among themselves that Joseph was waiting until Jacob died to exact his revenge. Were they right? After all, that is what any reasonable man would do. I suppose that is what any of us would at least want to do.

Joseph's brothers reported to him that Jacob's last request was that Joseph forgive the sins of his brothers. The only thing they could do was throw themselves on his mercy, bow before him, and wait for him to respond. Then Joseph said: "Don't be afraid. Am I in the place of God? You intended to harm me, but God intended it for good to accomplish what is now being done, the saving of many lives" (Gen. 50:19–20).

Something was going on behind the scenes all the time. God was at work bringing about his purpose for Jacob and his descendants. Joseph sensed that. Time revealed his spirit and the rightness of his actions. A man of integrity (a fact obvious through his behavior in Egypt), he behaved in keeping with his character; he waited to see the revelation of God's purpose. When he saw that he could be an instrument of keeping alive the promise extended to his father and his father's father, he willingly did so. Then he revealed his true identity, practiced forgiveness, and stated the purpose of God to his brothers and his father.

This story tells us that God is at work in the course of human history in ways we do not know and would not understand. Our responsibility is to remain faithful to God and leave the rest to him. Then we can be patient, remain strong, and forgive those who mistreat us. In the end, right and truth prevail.[24]

Cautions about Narrative Preaching

The minister should keep in mind several considerations about the narrative sermon, especially the "pure story" kind such as the sermon about Joseph.

1. The sermon tends to become a recitation of history, and may leave the impression that Christianity is a past-tense phenomenon. Skeptics and critics may actually see the benefits of studying the Bible, but view it from the same perspective as the study of any historical document, thus failing to find any application to persons or events of the present. The Bible, for them, may become the object of admiration, even scrutinous study, but of no personal religious value. Thus the sermon may make no particular difference to those who hear it. In fact, they do not truly hear. Faith, though, comes by hearing. The preacher proclaims the message of the Bible in order that those who hear will believe and live by faith in the God who speaks to us through his Word.

2. The sermon may become simply another story, such as found in any other great literature. The Bible is story and great literature, but it is a distinctive story. Preachers always should treat it as such and not leave the impression that the Bible is only literature. The doctrine that underlies Bible story sermons is the doctrine of revelation.

A corollary to this second caution is that the preacher is merely another storyteller. Connotations of this word could erode the image of the minister. He is more than a raconteur, peddling stories in the manner of the pied piper.

3. Storytelling may lead to a disregard for or neglect of the non-narrative sections of the Bible, especially if one is dedicated to the pure story and does not subscribe to Lowry's theory of narrative or find another way to do the other text forms. Lowry's scheme provides some avenues for preaching numerous portions of the Bible that preachers tend

24. This is a suggested sermon, giving the essentials of Joseph's story. The minister will need to make some decisions about whether to insert application statements at critical points in the story. These are only hinted at in this sermon. The movement here is more inductive, with the statement of meaning at the end. The reader should remember that this is a doctrinal sermon, intended more for understanding than for action.

to neglect.[25] Doctrine often is found in these areas, especially in the didactic passages; thus the storyteller could present doctrine in pure story sermons and treat some doctrines in other sermon forms.[26]

4. The minister may decide to begin preaching story sermons without proper regard for the amount of hard work required. Storytelling is an art; the story sermon becomes an art form. All works of art require time, work, and persistence.

5. The storyteller runs the risks associated with a method of communication that seems to have lost its appeal. News reporters, politicians, advertisers, and other experts in communication have made us the "sound-bite" generation. Story preaching seems to fly in the face of conventional wisdom about communication with the generation in a hurry.

On the other hand, story has a compelling quality. Recently a major television network aired a report about story writing as therapy for a group of persons who had tested HIV positive. The reporter told how the group meets regularly, sits around a table with lined paper notebooks in front of them, and writes. For many the telling of their stories is the therapy. After a designated amount of time for writing, individual group members read their material aloud. In that manner the others around the table identify emotionally and enter the stories of their friends. Those who spoke with the reporter emphasized the therapeutic value of expressing oneself and of telling one's story.

Rewards of Narrative Preaching

Great satisfaction comes, however, to the minister who completes the task and preaches in story. Rewards are numerous. First, the story sermon enables the preacher to retain a familiarity with the Bible. Instead of extracting "points" from the text, the preacher is telling the actual text, as in the story of Joseph. Telling the story means knowing the story. In the preparation of a story sermon the preacher enters the world of the text, as much as that is possible.

A second benefit is acquaintance with the characters. Every minister identifies with Isaiah, Amos, Peter, or Paul at the point of a call. Others have resisted the call and run away with Jonah, or sat with Elijah in the cave, or begged with Jeremiah for a place among wayfarers, out of the

---

25. Some of the forms proposed in the chapter on "Dramatic Preaching" are actually short stories, including the interview sermon from John 21; the famous encounter between Jesus and Peter following the resurrection; the diatribe featuring Jesus and Nicodemus in John 3; and the famous exchange in Matthew 16 when Jesus founded the church.

26. One may review the other sermon structures proposed in chapters of this book to find possibilities for doctrinal sermons with different forms.

traffic. Conversely, who has not wished for the certain revelation of God, such as Ezekiel's fiery wheel within the wheel? When a call to do the impossible comes, some perhaps have wished to put out Gideon's fleece to make certain God is speaking.

Third, knowledge of the setting of the Bible—place, time, event—comes with the in-depth study required for narrative preaching. The telling of a narrative gives the preacher opportunity to paint the big picture, complete with details. He or she takes time to give size, color, and flavor, in addition to character, at the end, standing back and inviting the congregation to view with him or her the complete picture. This benefit multiplies exponentially for the minister who has visited the land of the Bible. Description and explanation give the original story lasting impact.

Fourth, the minister may enable the listeners to find themselves in God's story. A good story identifies the listener in the story vicariously. Identification creates commonality; something mysterious happens and, though this community is in the realm of the spiritual and the mental, specific, concrete results occur. The resolution found in completion of a story may leave a feeling of spiritual satisfaction and create an understanding of meaning. That is precisely what the preacher wants to have happen in a doctrinal sermon! This "getting the point" is application. In story, much of this application is implicit and must be discovered by the listeners without any instruction or assistance from the preacher. They "see" the point on their own.[27] The sermon is more meaningful to the persons who see for themselves. This "seeing," of course, is accomplished by the work of the Holy Spirit, who is our constant companion in preaching and hearing sermons. Storytelling employs inductive movement; the preacher does not tell the point, then tell the story. He or she tells the story and, to a degree, leaves it with the listener to discover the point. The best application is that which the listener makes unassisted. Understanding of the story that teaches doctrine, then, is understanding of the doctrine.

Thus, listeners receive benefits from story sermons. They also learn the Bible. One hears much lament about the biblical illiteracy of the persons who fill church pews, both believers and nonbelievers. Story preaching helps solve this problem. Those who listen also become participants in the sermon. What's more, application is self-realized instead of imposed by external pressure. Discovery of oneself in the story is application of the best kind.

Perhaps best of all, benefits also come to the church, the community of believers. One is recognition. The church finds her identity in her

27. Lowry, *The Homiletical Plot*, pp. 51–52.

story. Another is mission. The drama of redemption becomes the message the church proclaims to the world.

The preacher has a number of options available for the shaping of the sermon. An exciting part of the weekly and daily task of preparation is deciding which one to employ in a given passage. The nature of the text itself, that is, its form, facilitates the decision. With so much narrative in the Bible, the story sermon is a good and viable option.

13

Dramatic Doctrinal Preaching

A hush fell over the audience as the members of the drama group took their places on the platform. The lights dimmed, a signal for the action to begin. A man lay sprawled on the floor, motionless and apparently lifeless.

As a man came walking onto the stage with his head held high and with his jaw firmly set, a narrator informs the audience that he was a certain Religion Professor from a prominent Christian college. As he passed by he saw the helpless man. He looked at him, discovered that he was seriously injured, and then remembered that he had errands to run. He left the scene wondering aloud whether others had been called to a ministry of helping such unfortunate people. Then, a young lady, whom the narrator identified as a medical student, stumbled across the injured man. She, too, stooped to look but did nothing but hurry away, mumbling something about an anatomy test.

By now the reader recognizes this scenario as a dramatic reenactment of the parable of the good Samaritan and can anticipate the remainder of the story. "Good Sam" is the retelling of the parable, with characters from contemporary life. The audience caught on quickly and got into the story, and the action held them captive throughout the entire drama.

This chapter addresses the question: Is drama compatible with doctrine? Perhaps it should be part of a larger question: Are drama and preaching compatible? The answer to the larger question, at one time, would have been a resounding "No!" Times are changing, however. The story of "Good Sam" is typical of dramas presented in worship services across America every Sunday. Congregations respond positively to them. Now the answer to the question of drama is "Yes." The pastor should consider doing the sermons in this format. Preaching should change.

The term "dramatic," however, conjures up the notion of the spectacular when associated with "sermon." We tend to associate drama with acting, performing, which employs histrionics, exaggeration, and affectation. The term, though, does have a broader and more positive meaning. Drama also applies to situations in life and literature that stir the imagination and emotions, according to the dictionary definition of "dramatic." The retelling of such real life situations or the reading of literature that recounts them also qualifies as dramatic. With specific reference to the Bible, much of it is dramatic. For example, the story of the exodus runs the gamut of human emotion and fires the imagination. Cecile B. DeMille's film *The Ten Commandments* has retained a popularity that all but defies explanation. Before the magic of special effects generated by computer and superimposing of images, the producers of *The Ten Commandments* portrayed the parting of the Red Sea with breathtaking realism. Some persons have seen the picture literally dozens of times. That speaks of its compelling power to attract and to retain interest.

Thus, the presentation of a message from God may be serious, indeed doctrinal, yet have in it elements of drama. We may look to the Bible for clear examples.

Biblical Precedents

One of the most dramatic moments in the Bible came when Nathan confronted King David with the story of a man who stole his neighbor's choice pet lamb to feed his company, when he himself had herds of animals from which to choose (2 Sam. 12:1–14). The prophet had one goal: to inform the king of his own sin through drawing a comparison.

Another famous confrontation in the Bible occurred when the eighth-century prophet Amos stood before Amaziah the priest of Bethel (Amos 7:10–17) and spoke bluntly about the judgment that was coming to Israel. Emotions ran high, doubtless, as Amaziah told Amos not to make such declarations and Amos retorted that he would speak because he had instructions to do so from God.

Stories and sermons often were accompanied by dramatic actions. Early in the Bible, in the case of Moses, one finds a striking example. When Moses appeared before Pharaoh, he punctuated his demands concerning the release of God's people in numerous ways. The first was the turning of Aaron's staff into a serpent (Exod. 7:8–10). When Pharaoh was unimpressed and had his own magicians perform similar feats (Exod. 7:11–12), Moses performed several other miracles to validate his speaking for God.

The prophet Ezekiel acted rather strangely, by human standards, to accentuate his sermons on God and judgment. For example, he drew an outline of Jerusalem on a clay tablet and then acted out the siege of the city. He then took an iron pan, placed it between himself and the city to represent an iron wall, and turned his face toward the pan (Ezek. 4:1–

3). Later, he dug a hole in a wall, strapped a pack onto his shoulders, and attempted to crawl through the hole. His action symbolized the exile of God's people in Babylon (12: 1–16). Other examples include cutting his hair and whiskers and burning them in a fire (5:1–17) to dramatize the burning of Jerusalem. In all these scenes Ezekiel acted alone.

Jeremiah, another Old Testament prophet, recounted his trip to the potter's house to teach Israel a lesson about the guiding providence of God (Jer. 18:1–17). He took a clay bottle, stood at the east entry into Jerusalem, and spoke to the people. As he presented his message he broke the pot, as God had instructed him to do, and declared that God would break the city and its people in a similar manner (19:1–15, especially vv. 10–15). Jeremiah also hid a leather belt in a hole and retrieved it after it began to decompose. He used it to teach the necessity for God's people to cling to him, as a belt clings to the waist (13:1–11).

The Old Testament contains numerous illustrations of appeals to the imagination and other dramatic actions. Isaiah told of a wood carver who made himself an idol and used the wood shavings to build a fire to keep warm. What kind of God is that? he asked (44:6–23). Micah and Hosea appealed to the courtroom image when bringing charges of infidelity against God's people (see especially Mic. 6:1–8). Elijah struck the waters with his mantle and parted them, so that he and his company of followers could cross the Jordan on dry ground (2 Kings 2:1–18, especially vv. 13–14). The Book of Hosea relates a real-life drama. Through the retelling of the prophet's marriage to Gomer, who becomes unfaithful to her husband and family, it tells the story of Israel's wandering from God. The story is filled with the agony of a broken home and a sad husband's reclaiming and reinstating an errant wife.

The prophets of Saul's era often acted in a rather strange manner when in fits of ecstasy. When Saul "prophesied" someone wondered aloud whether he was "one of the prophets" (1 Sam. 10:11). Some rather unusual actions sometimes accompanied pronouncements of Old Testament prophets.

In addition to these Old Testament instances we can also cite New Testament examples of drama. Jesus employed a number of elements of drama in his teaching and preaching. One was the object lesson. He took a coin and, while pointing to it, asked whose image was impressed on it. When told it was that of Caesar, he drove home his point: "Give to Caesar what is Caesar's and to God what is God's" (Matt. 22:21).

Matthew tells us that Jesus placed a child in the middle of the circle of disciples during a lesson on true greatness. "Therefore, whoever humbles himself like this child is the greatest in the kingdom of heaven," he said (Matt. 18: 1–9, especially v. 4).

One of the more dramatic moments in the life and ministry of Jesus occurred at the Last Supper. He took a piece of bread and a cup of wine, handed them to the disciples, and gave an entirely new meaning to the Feast of the Passover as he told them: "This is my body . . . This is my blood" (Luke 22:19).

Jesus' use of metaphor, simile, and similar stylistic devices provides illustration of the use of elements of drama in the language of the sermon. Drama may come through words alone, as they do their work in the imagination.[1]

All of this is to say that dramatic preaching does not always indicate the use of exaggeration, histrionics, and acting with the sermon. Oral style that employs elements of drama may enhance our sermons by appealing to the imagination and emotions.

Paul stood before Agrippa shackled with chains (Acts 25:23–26:32). Perhaps he lifted his hands, chains and all, and held them toward Agrippa when he said: "I pray God that not only you but all who are listening to me today may become what I am, except for these chains"(Acts 26:29). He was retelling the story of his conversion when on trial before the Roman governor. Of course, Paul did not choose his props! He only made use of the ones provided him.

Paul's use of imagistic language, especially metaphor, personification, and analogy, are particularly instructive in the matter of emotional appeals. He mixed athletic images in his remarks about the end of his life (2 Tim. 4:6–8).

The Book of James also is rich in imagery. His words about the tongue are unforgettable: "The tongue also is a fire, a world of evil" (3:6).

The entire Book of Revelation is a cosmic drama. John's use of language is effective and compares favorably with contemporary media. The reader can see the beasts, the angels, and Satan as they perform on the universal stage. Preachers may learn from the Revelation the value of vision and presentation, the power of words, and the retelling of the dramatic.

Types of Dramatic Preaching

These biblical illustrations demonstrate that drama and the presentation of a message from God, with doctrinal content, are compatible. We may draw other precedents from everyday life and from preaching itself to underscore the effect of drama and dramatic reinforcement of a message.

1. Elton Trueblood, in *The Humor of Christ,* gives a different slant on the language of Jesus, insisting that some of it was quite humorous (New York: Harper, 1964).

One of these authors remembers the lessons of a chemistry teacher from a long time ago because of dramatic actions used to punctuate lectures. For example, he presented a comparison between chemical change and physical change with great effect. He placed a vial of water on the Bunsen burner and brought the water to a boil. He pointed to the rising steam and noted that heat had changed the water to gas. "That," he said, "is a chemical change." Then he picked up a glass jar from the table, quickly turned and threw it against the wall, shattering it into a thousand pieces. To a startled class he reported: "That is a physical change." We laughed *and* we remembered the lesson.

An evangelist relied on the same principles during a sermon on backsliding. At the beginning of his sermon he placed a chair beside the pulpit. The sermon consisted of a list of sins Christians commit that separate them from God. He did not draw attention to it, but occasionally during the sermon he picked up the chair and put it back down. Each time he placed it in a different spot, a little farther from the pulpit. At the conclusion of the sermon he stood behind the desk and pointed to the chair, now several feet away, and declared: "You see. You did not pay much attention to my moving the chair a little at the time, but now it is a long way from where it originally sat. That is the way it is with backsliding. An almost imperceptible step once in a while and, before long, you are a long way from God." He made his point well, with a dramatic action, but without being spectacular.

Evangelist Billy Sunday was famous for his imaginary conversations with the devil, as well as his antics in the pulpit. This author once served as a pastor of a church in which Sunday had held revival services. As he stood by the pulpit with a senior minister who had heard Sunday, he asked: "You mean to tell me that Billy Sunday actually preached in this pulpit?" The older preacher replied: "Well, he preached all around it, but I would not say he preached *in* it."

These examples from Scripture, school, and church may provide guidance for the preacher who wishes to include elements of drama in sermons. What are the possibilities?

Dramatic Monologue

This is one of the most effective ways to communicate the contents of the Bible. The central events of the Christian story provide a natural starting place. Who does not associate character reenactment with the story of Christmas?

Christmas is a good time for the preacher to begin with this form of sermon. Consider telling the story from Joseph's viewpoint, or from that of the innkeeper, one of the shepherds, or one of the wise men.

Congregations expect and appreciate drama. This makes the task easier for the beginner. Also, the preacher is beginning with a cardinal doctrine—the birth of Jesus.

Presentation of a dramatic monologue as Joseph works well. After telling his story, Joseph could step forward into the congregation and relate the lessons he learned. First, he repeats that he refrained from sexual union with Mary, as required by the law and the practice of betrothal. At the same time he trusted Mary to do the same. Besides, both of them received personal messages from God declaring that the conception took place by the work of the Holy Spirit. This is the message of the virgin birth: God accomplished the conception of Jesus by working a miracle in Mary's body. She did not conceive in the normal manner. Joseph and Mary were both devout believers in God.

Second, Joseph could attest to the birth of the baby to a human mother. He was present at the time. Also, he was there when the shepherds came in from the fields and reported the message they had received, that is, the Savior had been born. Later, the wise men came in search of the newborn King of the Jews. Then, when Joseph and Mary took the child to the temple to dedicate him, Simeon and Anna had declared that, with the birth of Jesus, the promise of God finally had come true. How could Joseph forget the scene in the temple when Jesus was twelve years of age? "Yes," declares Joseph, "Jesus is God in the flesh. I know from my personal experience from before his birth."

The preacher could proclaim the same message by presenting the story as Joseph, then stepping out of character to provide explanation and application of the story. If he dresses as Joseph, he must physically move from the platform or from one location on the platform to another to signal that he has become the contemporary preacher and is no longer speaker in character. Another possibility is to announce the change of character. This is easier to accomplish if the preacher does not dress differently for the presentation. In that case, he must prepare to make appeal to the imagination as he asks the listeners to see and hear him as Joseph for the duration of the retelling of the text. These same principles apply to any character portrayed.

Easter also provides an occasion on which to do dramatic monologue sermons. The characters surrounding Jesus are familiar and their actions well known. Consider Simon Peter's declarations and subsequent denials, Pilate, Judas, the centurion at the cross, the thieves who were crucified alongside Jesus. Following the resurrection one may wish to plan portraying the two on the road to Emmaus, "doubting" Thomas, or Peter by the seashore.

The preacher may perform a dramatic monologue as Simon Peter, for example, recounting the story of his discovery of the empty tomb.

Then he could step out of character and explain that the point of the story is to establish eyewitness accounts of the resurrection of Jesus. The monologue captures the "you are there'" quality of the historical event and the explanation, coupled with application, brings the message of the Bible into the present. Such a presentation may carry much stronger appeal than the traditional approach, which is: "Let me tell you three things about the discovery of the empty tomb." Having Peter or Mary Magdalene tell what it was like to be there adds a dimension that is unavailable in the format of the rhetorical outline.

The Bible is a book about people. People who come to church are interested in other people. The dramatic monologue sermon appeals instantly to the imagination and provides a means by which listeners may identify with persons in the biblical story.

The Interview Sermon

Some incidents, such as the post-resurrection appearance of Jesus to Mary in the garden or the disciples by the sea (John 21:1–25) may be done as interview sermons. This is another example of form and content being equal.

The preacher may wish to tell the story from the different perspectives of the characters or may act it out. In either case, the form requires preparation. Fred Craddock speaks of this as "experiencing" the text.[2] During the process of interpretation the preacher enters into the text to identify with the biblical persons and dialogues with the text to determine its depth of meaning, thus developing a "feel" for the text. Craddock speaks of this as finding a place to stand in the text. Others, including Gardner Taylor, stress this identification with the text as a necessary part of understanding it.[3] This is one of the fruits of the continuing rapprochement of homiletics and hermeneutics. By living for a while in the world of the text, meeting its characters, sensing their moods, breathing the air of the world of the Bible, the preacher is prepared to speak the message of the text. The sermon becomes an act of reliving the text and recreating its experiences in the lives of the listeners. A sermon thus may do more than talk about a text; it may become a reenactment of the spirit of the text. The best preaching occurs when spirit (of the text) meets spirit (of the listener). This kind of preaching requires additional time for reflection on the meaning of the text; it includes more than word study and involves the preacher's emotions in

---

2. Fred B. Craddock, *Preaching* (Nashville: Abingdon, 1985), pp. 119–20.
3. Gardner Taylor, "Shaping Sermons by the Shape of Text and Preacher," in *Preaching Biblically: Creating Sermons in the Shape of Scripture,* ed. Don Wardlaw (Philadelphia: Westminster, 1983), pp. 137–42.

the making of the sermon. The preacher must take time to become acquainted with the persons and events of the text. More innovative approaches to sermons require more study, which is good for preaching and preachers. The preacher who studies more for creative sermons will improve the ability to preach the more traditional sermon forms, thus doubling the benefit of varying forms.

Other Scriptures that are stories of encounters between persons and naturally may become interview sermons include the encounter of Jesus with Nicodemus (John 3:1–21), Jesus and Simon Peter at Caesarea Philippi (Matt. 16:13–20), Jesus and the rich young ruler (Mark 10:17–31), Jesus and the Syro-Phoenician woman (Mark 7:24–30), Jesus and the disciples at the Last Supper (especially John 13:1–38), Jesus and Paul on the road to Damascus (Acts 9:1–19), Peter and John before the authorities (Acts 4:1–22), and Paul before his accusers (Acts 22:1–23:11; 24:1–26; 25:1–12; 25:23–26:32). The more familiar ones are those with which to begin. Paul on Mars Hill in Athens is a case in point (Acts 17:16–34). The word used for "reasoning" with the philosophers is the one from which we get the word "dialogue."

A number of possibilities exist for doing such interview sermons. For example, the preacher may act as both characters in a story, such as Jesus and Nicodemus. The interchange between those two followed the classic lines of diatribe: Two persons talked together in a common search for truth. As the conversation develops, the preacher may step from one side of the pulpit to the other, or may look from side to side as though looking at the other person involved in the conversation.

In a seminary sermon delivery class, a student presented a sermon on Micah 6:1–16 in the form of a courtroom drama. He acted as the attorney for God as he presented the charge against Israel. Then, with a change of voice, he spoke as the attorney for Israel and presented the response to the charge. The sermon followed the lines of argument between the attorneys for the prosecution and the defense. Of course, the world was looking in on the scene, as invited to do by God's attorney, and God himself was watching as well. For application, he took off his glasses, put the manuscript on the pulpit, looked at the congregation (class), and asked us to decide the case by our own vote. Was Israel guilty of unfaithfulness to God?

An interview sermon may take the form of a person from the present talking with some person from out of the past, the Bible. A member of the congregation may act as the biblical personality and the preacher may do an actual interview. The presence of a second person requires preparation by someone other than the preacher. Some complications may arise from such an arrangement, but it may be less a matter of preparation than of desire. Surely presentations involving two are less complicated than those by drama groups. Scripts, rehearsals, props, and stage management become large factors as well with the inclusion of a number of people in addition to the preacher.

A practical question arises from such considerations: When does the sermon cease to be the responsibility of the preacher? Another is: At what point does the act of proclamation become something other than a sermon? The traditional sermon is prepared and delivered by one person. In the preaching of the sermon, one person is the preacher. Those inclined to do some of the more creative kinds of proclamation ought to be prepared to answer such questions for themselves. A change in sermon form may have a ripple effect on one's understanding of the whole of the worship event. Taking the senior minister out of the role of preacher carries with it questions of identity as well. On the other hand, if the whole church proclaims the gospel, if the sermon is itself an act of worship, if the whole of the worship service is an act of proclamation, we may be prepared to think again about the preacher as the single leader of worship and the traditional sermon as the central event of worship.[4] The interviewer may conduct a "person on the street" kind of interview. This may be done with imaginary persons who pass by the pulpit and offer testimony or commentary on Bible events. Persons who witnessed the crucifixion could recount their exact feelings at the moment of Jesus' death. Mary Magdalene could tell of her elation upon discovering that the Lord had risen. Such an interview could have sense appeal, require proper use of the powers of imagination, and capture the attention of the listeners through personal involvement in the sermon.

A difficulty arises for the preacher who must act alone in a dramatic sermon (i.e., assume the identity of more than one person). The preacher must act as two different persons if this is to differ from the story sermon. A good storyteller may advance to this form quite easily. In many respects, the interview sermon resembles the dialogue sermon.

The Dialogue Sermon

This sermon form holds potential for great variety, as Harold Freeman suggests.[5]

---

4. This author prefers to think in more traditional terms. Preaching is not the only form of proclamation, but it is the highest form. Other acts of worship, indeed, proclaim the gospel. The sermon, however, as the preaching of God's Word, is the climactic event of worship. It is a part of the whole, granted, and not the whole itself. Nevertheless, the oral proclamation of the Word of God is the means God chose to bring the message of salvation (see 1 Cor. 1:17–21).

5. *Variety in Biblical Preaching: Innovative Techniques and Fresh Forms* (Waco, Tex.: Word, 1987).

Baptism appears to be a natural for the dialogue sermon. The pastor may wish to discuss with the candidate, perhaps in the baptistery, the decision to publicly profess faith in Christ, the commitment to baptism, and the importance of giving public witness of a changed life. The act of baptism is itself an act of proclamation. A dialogue based on Romans 6:1–14 is one way to declare one of the major passages on the doctrine of baptism found in the entire New Testament.

The Lord's Supper (communion), a regular feature of church life, presents the pastor with opportunities for innovation in sermon delivery. What pastor who serves in the free church (nonliturgical) tradition has not searched for another way to express the meaning of this valuable ceremony?

One possibility is to act out the Supper. In this presentation, the pastor could introduce the observance while standing behind the pulpit, then move to the table. At that point, the pastor could take each element of the Supper and comment on it just prior to inviting the congregation to partake. Those who assist in the service then would distribute the elements among the members of the congregation. In this manner, the worship leaders enable those in the pews to participate in the proclamation of the gospel. Indeed, the Lord's Supper is a visual representation of the entire gospel story. Participation, which is a renewed emphasis in worship among church growth advocates, may add depth of meaning for worshipers. The participatory sermon carries with it application for each individual who takes part.[6]

When Reuel Howe began the discussion of the dialogue sermon, he emphasized the nature of feedback during the presentation of the sermon.[7] Later authors such as Harold Freeman speak of dialogue as an act, that is, action instead of a communication phenomenon.[8] The dialogue sermon may take the form of an actual conversation between the preacher and persons sitting in the pews. It (the dialogue) may range from the completely spontaneous to the prepared script. This sermon form also may be presented as a panel discussion, with participants standing before the congregation or seated on the platform. One pastor invited the listeners who attended Sunday morning worship to return for the evening service, during which time he led a discussion of the morn-

---

6. David H. C. Read observes that proclamation is an act of the whole church. See his *Sent from God: The Enduring Power and Mystery of the Gospel* (Nashville: Abingdon, 1974), for this discussion and the presentation of an excellent theology of proclamation. The Bible does not belong to the preacher alone. When the preacher's voice is the only voice heard, that preacher still is giving voice to the church's message. This underscores the value of a participatory sermon (pp. 73–76).

7. *The Miracle of Dialogue* (New York: Seabury, 1963).

8. *Variety in Biblical Preaching*.

ing sermon. Another reviewed the morning sermon prior to the evening sermon and asked those present questions about the sermon idea and purpose, then invited comment on the sermon's application to life.[9]

The common thread running throughout all these approaches to dialogue is involvement. Listeners physically participate in the delivery of the sermon. Their participation excites interest within each one who hears the sermon. While it may have appeal, this method also carries with it numerous pitfalls.[10]

The Media-Augmented Sermon

The "Community Church" movement (Willow Creek primarily) has thrust media (and dramatic) sermons to center stage in all discussions of innovative worship methods. The "preaching service" has given way to the "worship service." The traditional sermon is no longer the centerpiece of such worship.

The media-augmented sermon is not an altogether new phenomenon. Ever since denominations and churches have been sending out missionaries, the same sending agencies have invited missionaries on furlough to report to churches. The report almost always included the showing of color slides and a table filled with items of interest from the country served. Although considered a "report" or a "testimony," this presentation usually came during a regular service of worship—at the time normally reserved for the "sermon." If one's theology of preaching includes preaching as bearing witness,[11] the missionary report surely qualifies as proclamation.

Slide presentations have given way to multimedia presentations, some of which would be the envy of major television producers. The single slide projector now has others stacked above it, all of them driven and synchronized by a computer and projected onto a giant screen. Pictures appear and disappear from all the machines. Sound and other forms of video now are fully integrated into the presentation. With the advent of multimedia computers, along with projection screen technology, text, graphics, and video may appear on the screen simultaneously. Often the person provides only the voice. Some presentations are professionally prepared, including narration. One risks the possibility that the media themselves eliminate the need for a real live person up front.

9. This is a variation of Freeman's "spontaneous congregational dialogue." See *Variety in Biblical Preaching*, pp. 113–14.

10. See a discussion of those pitfalls later in this chapter.

11. This is the metaphor Tom Long chooses for his understanding of preaching. See *The Witness of Preaching* (Atlanta: John Knox/Westminster, 1990), especially chapter 1.

Some churches feature a blend of two or more of these methods. Contemporary churchgoers may hear a preacher who is accompanied by a drama group, orchestra, rear screen projection, and sound effects. Multimedia sermons have progressed far beyond sounds on audiotapes, slides, and object lessons.

Others

Other choices for dramatic sermons include the following:

1. News reporter approach describing scenes and actions. This may include the "you are there" format so popular with satellite transmissions of live news coverage.

2. News reporter approach reporting, with edited video, after returning from the scene. This is kin to the multimedia sermon. Imagine the impact of a report from the day of Jesus' resurrection, complete with video of an empty tomb and quotes from the women who first discovered it.

3. Third-party observer, so popular in today's news reporting. For example, consider Peter's testimony in Acts 4:20 that he and John could not help speaking about the things they had seen and heard.

4. The hymn sermon. Lavonne Brown has written a helpful book in which he suggests ways to preach through hymn texts, many of which are based on Scripture texts.[12] An example is "A Mighty Fortress" by Luther, building on Psalm 46. Innovation may include singing the sermon, inviting the congregation to sing, or asking a musician to play the melody to ignite memory and prompt association of events with particular hymns (e.g., "They sang that hymn at my mother's funeral. Every time I hear it, I think of Mother.").

5. Question-and-answer format. This form is similar to the interview sermon. The minister may act alone or invite another person to assist.

6. Use of historical imagination. Some preachers do this frequently, and often incorrectly, with the story of David and Goliath. Background study may help with information the text alone does not provide and establish limits for the imagination. Done properly, this is quite effective.[13]

12. *Preaching the Great Hymns* (Nashville: Broadman and Holman, 1992).

13. Books proposing these kinds of innovative forms, appeals to the imagination, and the place of preaching in the life of the contemporary church include Elizabeth Achtemeier, *Creative Preaching: Finding the Words*, Abingdon Preacher's Library, ed. William D. Thompson (Nashville: Abingdon, 1980); Francis C. Rossow, *Preaching the Creative Gospel Creatively* (St. Louis: Concordia, 1983); Paul Scott Wilson, *Imaginations of the Heart: New Understandings in Preaching* (Nashville: Abingdon, 1988); Thomas H. Troeger, *Creating Fresh Images for Preaching: New Rungs for Jacob's Ladder* (Valley Forge, Pa.: Judson, 1982); *Imagining a Sermon* (Nashville: Abingdon: 1990); Webb B. Garrison, *Creative Imagination in Preaching* (Nashville: Abingdon, 1960); and Clyde Fant, *Preaching for Today*, rev. ed. (San Francisco: Harper and Row, 1987).

The Preparation of Dramatic Sermons

This kind of preaching does not just happen, any more so than does any other kind. Dramatic preaching, however, requires additional time for reflection on the meaning of the text; it includes more than word study and involves the preacher's emotions in the making of the sermon. The preacher must take time to become acquainted with the persons and events of the text. This requirement for more study, though, means the more innovative approaches to sermons are good for preaching and preachers.

Ordinarily, the minister sits in a study, surrounded by books, journals, papers, commentaries, tapes, and files to prepare the sermon. It is a solo performance from beginning to end. Innovations in preaching include all the usual steps in preparation and go beyond the ordinary.

First, the interpreter must linger over the text longer in order to identify with characters. Word study, sentence structure, paragraph formation, transition, and the usual components of exegesis must be more than facts to be grasped by the intellect; they must spring to life. The preacher must take time to interact with the text, to dialogue with the people there. He or she must investigate the historical, geographical setting of the text. The time of an event in Scripture assumes additional significance. In short, the preacher should remain with the text until he or she feels at home there.

Second, the interpreter must carefully craft the sermon in writing. Good drama requires good script. This will summon all the creativity learned in composition class and in sermon preparation class. Beginning with a summary of the meaning of the text, which in dramatic sermons often will include several chapters of the Bible, he or she will describe places, people, and events, adding color, flavor, sound, and motion.

Third, the preacher should practice the sermon by speaking it aloud, considering how the words will sound. Taping the sermon and playing it back is helpful for evaluating the quality of content and delivery.

Fourth, the preacher will give thought to the manner in which he or she will move from the world of the text to the world of the listener. This distance is not easy to traverse. With the traditional sermon, one may change verb tenses from the past to the present or say: "This means you." The dramatic sermon, however, requires some transition from a character who lived thousands of years ago to a preacher talking to the Sunday morning congregation, or movement from a scene far away to the local church. The very act of stepping forward or turning one's back and then turning around may suffice. The minister may say: "Now I wish to step out of character and speak to you as your pastor." To relo-

cate in time and space, one may suggest: "Now we will return to Specific City and ponder the lessons of the Bible message."

Fifth, the preacher should plan carefully the transition to time of appeal or public invitation. Possibilities include the invitation to respond
to God in faith as biblical personalities responded, or a forthright challenge to act out lessons learned or to go out from worship and live out
a biblical principle. In each sermon the preacher ought to answer the
question: "What do I want the hearer to do, be, or become as a result of
hearing this sermon?"

Cautions in Preparing Dramatic Sermons

While it may have appeal, this method also carries with it numerous pitfalls. Primary among those is one that is an outgrowth of the component of preparation. The study for a group drama includes other persons. Such study may prompt the need for a worship committee in the
church membership or a team of researchers and writers to assist with
sermon preparation. The preacher, then, becomes dependent on the results of the study and writing of others, while retaining personal responsibility for the outcome.

How far may a pastor go and still retain personal control of sermon
production? With conventional sermon preparation the minister is sole
owner of the sermon and sermon preparation. The preacher who senses
the need to prepare and deliver a sermon due to a divine call may request help from others who do not share a similar call. How thin can
one spread this without diluting the message?

On the other hand, if the gospel belongs to the church, and if proclamation is an act of the whole body, dramatic preaching may force more
persons in the congregation to take seriously the church's responsibility
to bear witness to the world.

A related issue, perhaps, is that of biblical authority. Is the preacher,
in fact, the custodian of the message by virtue of calling and office?

Second, in order to perform a dramatic sermon the preacher will
need items not found in a pastor's study, such as a shepherd's staff, a
robe, a pair of sandals. More advanced presentations will require stage
props, sound effects, different kinds of lighting, and other kinds of
equipment.

The pastor, already harried by a demanding schedule, bears responsibility for oversight of supplemental preparation. The involvement of
a number of additional persons in the process increases the likelihood
that some part of it will go undone and lessens the likelihood that the
minister can monitor all the preparation. Although the people who
would agree to assist usually are among the most reliable in the congre-

gation, the pastor should remember the extra time required and the additional tension created.

Preachers who become more dramatic run the risk of appearing as actors instead of proclaimers. This risk, a third pitfall, becomes greater for the pastor who preaches in a traditional manner. The congregation may think of the pastor as artificial, as a pretender, or as a different person (in the negative sense of hypocrite). A dramatic flair may put the listeners into communicative shock, thus disrupting all communication.

Thus the need for additional study and preparation assumes greater importance. The pastor should consider preparing the congregation for a departure from normal sermon delivery. Congregations are amazingly flexible when not surprised or shocked.

For all the challenges offered by dramatic preaching, the preacher who pays the price of preparation for creative sermons will become able to preach better the more traditional sermon forms, thus doubling the benefit of variety in preaching. Moreover, the benefits for the congregation are numerous. They will see the amazing variety in the contents of the Bible. They will "meet" biblical characters. They will "visit" biblical places. The Bible will become a book that pulsates with life, no longer a collection of words on pages.

A Sample Sermon

An interview with the Apostle Paul, based on Acts 21:27–28:16.

Moderator: Today I am talking with the church's first missionary about his trip from Jerusalem to Rome. This trip is well known because of the giant storm that blasted the ship on which Paul traveled. Paul, please tell us why you were on board the ship sailing to Rome in the first place.

Paul: The Romans themselves encouraged me to go to Rome because I appealed my trial case to Caesar. My dual citizenship entitled me to that when the Jews in Jerusalem accused me of defiling the temple and attempted to kill me. The commander of the Roman garrison in Jerusalem intervened when they created an uproar that disturbed the entire city. As the soldiers were about to wrench me away from the unruly mob, I asked permission to address them. The commander agreed. I then gave the testimony of my salvation to the crowd. When I mentioned that God sent me to the Gentiles, they screamed: "Kill him! He is not fit to live."

With that, the Romans took me away. The commander ordered his men to lash me until I confessed my crime. When I asked if it was proper to whip a Roman citizen without so much as a trial, that stopped them in their tracks. His soldiers melted into the crowd and the commander unshackled me. He turned me over to the Jewish council for trial.

The proceedings were a mockery, of course. When Ananias the High Priest ordered someone to slap my face, the whole thing took an ugly turn. I called him a whitewashed tomb and informed him that he was breaking the law in order to try me! I remembered that the Council was half Sadducees and half Pharisees, told them that I was a Pharisee, and watched as a great clamor arose. They got into a shouting match, began to pull me in different directions, and very nearly tore me apart. The Roman commander came to my rescue by ordering his soldiers to take me back to the armory.

The next morning more than forty Jews got together and took an oath to kill me. They even got the priests and elders to join the conspiracy. My nephew got wind of the plan and warned me. I sent him immediately to the commander with instruction to tell what he had heard.

The commander arranged to send me to Caesarea at nine o'clock that same night. He sent two hundred spearmen and seventy mounted cavalry to escort me. He prepared a letter to Governor Felix that put the entire case in his hands. You can imagine how relieved he was finally to place me under someone else's care.

The Jews discovered what had happened to me and, five days later, sent their best lawyer to press the charges against me in Caesarea. He misrepresented the case against me, naturally, but the governor allowed me to speak in my own defense. Again I recounted the story of my conversion and mission. You know, Felix himself almost became a believer when he heard my testimony. He put me in prison, saying that he would hear me again at a more convenient time. Some convenient time: Two years dragged by; then Festus succeeded Felix. There I was, still in chains when Festus came to power.

Three days after he arrived in Caesarea, Festus left for Jerusalem. That was just the chance for which my accusers had been waiting. Somehow they gained an audience with Festus and told him about me. They insisted that he return me to Jerusalem for trial, with another secret plan to waylay me and kill me. Festus replied that the proceedings would go better if they held the trial in Caesarea upon his return. About ten days later he returned and reopened my case.

The Jews came gladly and accused me falsely again. Festus was anxious to please them, so he asked me if I were willing to go with him and my accusers to Jerusalem for a trial. "No," I replied. "I demand the privilege of appearing before the emperor." A Roman citizen could do that in a capital case. Festus had no choice; he declared that I could go to Caesar.

A few days later King Agrippa arrived in Caesarea with Bernice for a visit with Festus. During their visit Festus told Agrippa about my case.

He informed Agrippa that I was a leftover from the days of Felix and repeated the story of the Romans' involvement with me. Agrippa decided that he would like to hear me.

The next day, then, they brought me before Agrippa. Bernice was there, too, along with Festus and military officers, prominent citizens, and conducted the whole matter with great pomp and ceremony. Festus moderated the meeting. He told the crowd that I had appealed to Caesar, but he had no case against me. He could not send me to the emperor without a case. He was really trying to get Agrippa to handle the problem and get it out of his own hands. Agrippa agreed to hear my story.

Again I told my story, with joy and enthusiasm. I gladly retold my conversion experience and my call to be a missionary to the Gentiles. The power came upon me, and, as I stressed to the king that my call came from heaven and I could only obey, he stopped me with a shout. "You are mad," he screamed. "Your study has broken your mind." Of course, I was not insane, and quickly told him so. I could see that he, like Felix, had come under conviction, so I told him I knew he wanted to believe. He reacted with shock. "You expect me to become a Christian on this kind of evidence?" he asked. "Yes," I told him. "Whether my evidence is weak or strong, I wish you were as I am, except for these chains."

That did it. Agrippa left with the others of the royal entourage. They talked among themselves and Agrippa declared that I had done nothing worthy of death. If I had not appealed to Caesar, he added, he could set me free. But I had appealed to Caesar, and to Caesar I would go. That all accounts for my voyage to Rome.

Moderator: You had a lot of courage to stand before your accusers and your judges and give your testimony. Just think, you could have been set free if you had not appealed to Caesar. Please tell us about the journey itself.

Paul: I only knew that the encounter with Jesus had changed my life. I was not guilty of the charges the Jews made against me, and I wanted to prove it.

Finally, the Roman authorities made arrangements for my transportation. Several other prisoners and I were placed in the custody of an officer named Julius, a member of the elite imperial guard. They informed us that the boat was to make several stops along the way; thus we knew we were in for a long, hard trip.

At least Julius allowed me to go ashore and visit with friends along the way. The second day, for example, when we docked at Sidon, I enjoyed the hospitality of friends.

Setting sail from Sidon, we ran into strong headwinds and the sailors had a difficult time holding course. So they sailed north of Cyprus and followed the coast by Cilicia and Pamphylia, then landing at Myra. There the officer in charge transferred us to a ship from Alexandria bound for Italy.

After several days of rough sailing, we drew near to Cnidus. The winds had become so strong, however, that we cut across to Crete. Overcoming great difficulty with the wind, we finally landed at Fair Havens, near the city of Lasea. The weather simply was too dangerous for us to continue, so I talked to the officers about continuing the trip. I told them we were headed straight toward disaster—shipwreck, loss of cargo, injuries, eventual death.

Although I was a veteran traveler, they ignored me, choosing instead to listen to the ship's captain and owner. Winter was coming and Fair Havens was not a safe harbor in which to spend the winter. The majority of the crew voted to sail up the coast to Phoenix and spend the winter there. At exactly the same time, the winds died down and began blowing lightly from the south. It was a perfect day for sailing, so they weighed anchor and set sail, as they had planned, close to the shoreline.

Soon my worst fears came true. A fierce wind began to blow us straight out to sea. It was a literal tornado on the water. They tried at first to fight it and turn the ship back toward land, but it was no use. They gave up and let the ship drift at the mercy of the violent storm. As we flew past a small island we hoisted the small lifeboat we were towing and lashed it down. All the possibilities we faced were bad ones. Some even talked of being hurled against the coast of North Africa.

The next day the storm grew more ferocious, so we began throwing cargo overboard. A day later we threw out everything we could lift. The storm continued to rage, for how long I do not know. We appeared to have no hope.

Moderator: You gave up hope?

Paul: At that point it looked hopeless. I guess I gave up hope for the ship.

I took over and called a meeting of the crew. I did not really want to say "I told you so," but I said it. "You should have listened to me at Fair Havens," I told them. "Then all of this would not have happened." Then I shocked them by adding: "But cheer up. Not one of us will lose his life, even though the ship will be destroyed. God will save all our lives," I continued, "so take courage. I believe God. We will be shipwrecked on an island, but we will be safe." Surely they thought I had lost my mind.

For two weeks we drifted on the sea, completely at the mercy of the wind. The fear of 275 people for their lives increased with every passing day until it held all in its grip. Finally, in the middle of the fourteenth night, the experienced sailors, with their ability to sense what is happening, decided among themselves that we were coming near some land. They sounded the depths repeatedly and, sure enough, each time the water grew more shallow. At first the water was 120 feet deep. Then, the next time, it was only ninety feet. Hallelujah! a sign that we were approaching land. Then we threw out four anchors to steady the vessel and waited for the day. Could we, after all, be saved?

Some of the sailors conspired to pretend they were letting down the emergency boat in order to put out more anchors and abandon the ship. I overheard them and cautioned them that they would all die unless everyone remained on board the ship. They gave up their plan and let the boat fall away into the night.

As night began to give way to day, I begged everyone to eat something. After all, I reminded them, no one was going to perish. We all ate a good meal and threw the remaining wheat overboard.

When daybreak came the sailors hoisted up the main sail so that we could drift to the shore. They aimed at a creek that ran inland. As we approached, though, and attempted to sail into an inlet, the bow of the ship stuck in the sand. We had run aground in sight of safety. The wind and water continued to batter the hindmost part of the ship and it began to break apart. Some of the soldiers on board cried: "Kill all the prisoners," but Julius, for my sake, prevailed on them to let everyone have an equal chance to make it to land alive.

Each one of us grabbed a piece of the timber from the broken ship and held on for dear life. The tide drove us right to the shore. Alive! Safe! Could anyone believe it? God had brought us safely through the worst storm and the sailor's worst nightmare. After two weeks in constant danger we stood, at last, on firm, dry ground.

Moderator: Paul, how can you explain that a man could stand on the deck of a sinking ship and say: "Cheer up, no one will die"?

Paul: The answer is quite simple: the promise of God. You see, the Lord had stood beside me one night after the second day of my ordeal in Jerusalem and told me not to worry. "Take courage! As you have testified about me in Jerusalem, so you must also testify in Rome." I believed God. I believed that, in his providence, I would go to Rome. Moreover, the angel of the Lord appeared to me at the height of the storm and told me not to be afraid, that I would stand trial before Caesar and that not a life would be lost. I believed him. Our God is mightier than a hurricane on sea. He is in control of nature and he is in control of me. I believed all the time the storm was raging that I would arrive in Rome.

This great story from Acts tells us how the doctrine of God, specifically God's sovereignty and providence, made an impact on the life of Paul. He never gave up, even in the worst storm of all his travels. He clung to the promise that he would someday arrive in Rome.

Do you believe God? If he assures you through his Word, through the inner voice of his Spirit, that a specific event will happen in your life will take place, you can live in confidence that he will keep his promise. You may have no other reason for your courage than his word. That is faith.

The purpose of this interview sermon is to reveal how a doctrine made a difference in life. Other possibilities for presenting this same sermon include a dramatic monologue or a simple retelling of the story in the third person in a narrative tense. The preacher may plan to make one point at the end of the story, as in the case here. This is the inductive method. You may prefer, instead, to do a dramatic monologue, then step out of character, and make the point followed by application to the listeners. The preacher could retell the story in segments, drawing a lesson, or point, from each segment in order to show application of the text.

For example, as Paul concludes his testimony in Jerusalem (23:23–35), the story reaches a turning point when the Roman commander decides to send Paul to Caesarea for his own safety. The next natural break in the sequence comes at Caesarea when Agrippa acknowledges that he has no choice but to send Paul to Caesar (26:30–32). If seeking to achieve the traditional three points, the preacher could do so by making a transition to conclusion at the end of the storm at sea (27:42–44).

Part 4

Getting It Done

14

Planning a Strategy and Program for Doctrinal Preaching

All preaching requires good planning and preparation. Doctrinal sermons will require additional effort due to their special nature. The busy pastor has difficulty finding enough time to prepare well, no matter what the subject matter of the sermon. Sermons with theological depth require even more time. This additional time is imperative, however, because this kind of preaching demands more reflection and awareness of the broader contents of Scripture. Planning ahead actually facilitates one's preparation, however, for when one knows that he will be preaching on a given subject (in this case, a given doctrine), material that he comes upon is recognized as usable for that message. There is also the benefit of having time to reflect on the topic, thus allowing ideas to mature. Good planning is a necessity for effectiveness in the ministries of the local church. This is particularly true for pulpit performance. The present chapter is devoted to the development of a strategy for preaching the doctrinal sermon.[1]

1. General works on planning a preaching program include Andrew W. Blackwood Sr., *Planning a Year's Pulpit Work* (Grand Rapids: Baker, 1975); J. Winston Pearce, *Planning Your Preaching* (Nashville: Broadman, 1967); Glenn Asquith, *Preaching According to Plan* (Valley Forge, Pa.: Judson, 1968); T. T. Crabtree, *The Zondervan Pastor's Annual* (Grand Rapids: Zondervan, 1968–); *Ministers Manual: A Study and Pulpit Guide* (early issues known as *Doran's Ministers Manual*), ed. G. B. F. Hallock, M. K. W. Heichner, and Charles L. Wallis (New York: Harper and Row, 1926–); *The Revised Common Lectionary: Includes Complete List of Lections for years A, B, and C / Consultation on Common Texts* (Nashville: Abingdon, 1992); Reginald H. Fuller, *Preaching the Lectionary: the Word of God for the Church Today* (Collegeville, Minn.: Liturgical, 1984); Hoyt L. Hickman et. al., *The New Handbook of the Christian Year: Based on the Revised Common Lectionary* (Nashville: Abingdon, 1992). Denominational publishing houses print planning manuals each year. They also publish planning calendars and notebooks for ministers.

Approaches to Planning Doctrinal Preaching

Assessing Congregational Needs

Since preaching does not take place in a vacuum, but in a concrete setting, the more one knows and understands that setting, the more one can plan intelligently the preaching to be done there. This assessment can be done in several ways.

1. One way in which this can be done is through the use of some sort of survey. This can be done either by asking people directly what doctrines or doctrinal problems they have questions about or want to know more about, or by asking people their understanding of certain doctrines and then inferring from their answers what areas need teaching. In either case, bear in mind that many lay people are not accustomed to being asked for their opinions and may misunderstand what is expected or feel threatened by the questions. One of the authors, as a young pastor, asked his congregation to fill out a questionnaire, indicating the subjects on which they felt they needed sermons. One person wrote on the back of the form, "I have heard of men-pleasers before, but I never heard of anyone who asked his people what to speak on so he could do what they wanted." Efforts will need to be made to prepare the congregation for such a questionnaire and ensure that anonynomy will be preserved. When this is done, quite reliable results can often be obtained. If the pastor has some skill in constructing and interpreting questions and answers, the indirect type of questioning is often the more effective variety.

2. Another way of assessing the needs of the congregation is by the use of focus groups. These groups are assembled by carefully selecting persons who reflect the makeup of the congregation. Group members can be trained in terms of the functioning of the group and the type of response the pastor desires, as well as the use to which their responses will be put. This type of approach also allows for explanation and interpretation, which is not possible with questionnaires.

3. Another useful method is to have people submit the questions they have. One pastor had a regular feature in his Sunday evening services called "The Question Box." People could place their written questions in a box in the sanctuary and each Sunday evening he would answer one of them. When several had accumulated, he would take an evening and instead of a message, would deal with all of the remaining questions. This also provided him with a clue to topics that needed fuller treatment than that provided by a sermon.

4. A pastor may do a sermon series giving a brief overview of Christian doctrine, perhaps devoting one message to each major doctrine. Verbal comments and questions will often supply clues as to which

areas need greater elaboration. This can be done by having an insert or a tear-off portion of the worship folder on which worshipers can register the questions that they think need to be answered. This can also be done with an adult study class covering the same subjects.[2]

5. The pastor will also want to take note of what other learning experiences of a doctrinal nature are taking place or have taken place within the congregation. For example, the Sunday school curriculum should be examined, to see whether there are areas that need to be supplemented, or even some less than fully adequate ideas that need correction or augmentation.

6. An analysis of the influences affecting one's congregation is also important and helpful. Some of this can be accomplished by a broad cultural analysis of the social and literary ethos. Reading and observing contemporary literature, music, television, and the daily newspaper are very helpful in identifying general cultural trends to which one's church members are also susceptible. Surveys of religious beliefs and opinions, such as those done by the Gallup and Barna organizations, are very helpful.

Beyond that, however, attempting to discern something of the church's history can be of great help. Sometimes a church arose out of a particular doctrinal dispute, or has come under a special influence, and the result is that certain topics need special attention, and care has to be taken to deal with these in a wise and tactful way. If relatively large numbers of members have been with the church for several years, then the history of the church going back some time may be significant. One of the authors served as interim pastor of a church that had carried on merger discussions for several months with another church, with the discussions finally breaking down. One factor in the discussions was the very strongly Calvinistic theology of the senior pastor of the other church. Because of the lingering questions in the minds of many people, the interim pastor decided to give a four-week series of Sunday evening messages on the issues of Calvinism and Arminianism. Normally, the evening service was held in the lower auditorium of this downtown congregation with an aging membership, and attendance averaged fifty to seventy. The first evening ushers were scurrying about getting more chairs to seat the two hundred people who came. The pastor had tapped a topic of great interest. An examination of the previous

2. A lay-level treatment of these topics, including study questions and teaching suggestions, is Millard J. Erickson, *Does It Matter What I Believe?* (Grand Rapids: Baker, 1992). Others in the same genre are Paul E. Little, *Know What You Believe* (Wheaton, Ill.: Victor, 1970); A. J. Conyers, *A Basic Christian Theology* (Nashville: Broadman and Holman, 1995); James Montgomery Boice, *Foundations of the Christian Faith: A Comprehensive and Readable Theology* (Downers Grove, Ill.: InterVarsity, 1986).

pastor's preaching plan will also be of help, even if it is merely reconstructed from the titles in the church bulletin file. Care must be used to ensure that one does not appear to be criticizing even implicitly one's predecessor, but areas of neglect or overemphasis may be evident from this endeavor. Consulting some of the longer-standing members of the congregation regarding the oral history of the church will often also be helpful.

We are not here minimizing the power of the Holy Spirit to guide the preacher in the selection of subjects. In one group that was less than a year old and still not officially organized as a congregation, one of the authors was brought in as interim pastor because the church planter had already left because of some problems that were present. At the interim pastor's farewell, one woman remarked to him, "You were like a man walking through a field filled with land mines. If you had made one wrong step and said something on the wrong issue in a sermon, the whole church could have blown up. You never stepped on a single land mine." Yet he did not know what those issues were. The Holy Spirit had guided him. We will certainly want to pray for that guidance, but we can also use the best of available information in the process.

Seizing Uniquely Timely Opportunities

Even when we have planned for some time in advance what we are going to speak on, it is still important to be sensitive to the Holy Spirit's leading. Even in the midst of a series one should pray, "What would you have me preach on this Sunday?" and be prepared to deviate from that series if necessary. This is especially appropriate when some event occurs that captures the attention of people. It may be a political, sports, or even weather event. When these things occur, one will want to ask whether there is something here that can become the basis for a sermon capitalizing on that attention. One will, of course, want to be sure to avoid exploiting a specific news event in such a way as to appear to be attacking an individual involved in that event, or even of passing judgment on the guilt or innocence of someone alleged to have committed a crime. Tastefully done, however, this can be quite effective.

One of the authors was serving an interim pastorate in a town of 20,000 persons some fifty miles from a major metropolitan area. The morning worship service was broadcast over the only radio station in that town. One Saturday a surprise major snowstorm hit that town, effectively closing it down. The chairman of the church called the interim pastor to tell him that the streets were unplowed and might not be open by Sunday morning, and that he should plan on not coming. When he verified that the interstate highway that passed through the edge of the town was open, the interim pastor assured the chairman that he would be there for the service, even if he had to walk in from the highway. He left early, allowing extra time for the walk which, it turned out, was not needed. On the drive to the church, he thought of the situation. He knew that the radio audience would be larger than usual, since there would be people from other congregations unable to reach their own church, and thought of the fact that this storm had caught everyone, including the highway authorities, by surprise. During the drive, he thought out a sermon on "The Surprises of Life," went to the pastor's study upon arrival, and roughed out an outline. He explained to the congregation before the broadcast began that the sermon they would hear would not be the one listed in the bulletin. He preached that message on the surprises of life, culminating with the biblical teaching that the Lord's second coming and judgment would catch people unprepared.

Analyzing One's Preaching Distribution

We will want to plan our doctrinal preaching with an overall strategy, not simply on an ad hoc basis. One way to ensure this is to keep a record of what we have preached on doctrinally. While this is a good idea with respect to various books of the Bible and issues of Christian living, it is especially important with respect to doctrine, where it will help preserve us from either fixating on one subject matter or neglecting certain doctrines and leaving holes in our doctrinal coverage. We will ask ourselves, for example, how long it has been since we preached on the doctrine of the Holy Spirit or the authority of Scripture. Keeping a chart with each doctrine and subdoctrine listed, and then marking the date we preach on it will help ensure this coverage. As we do so, we will want to note not only the sermons that were overtly and primarily doctrinal, but all the doctrinal dimensions of sermons that have had some other orientation as their major thrust.

This will of course involve some of the historical research we spoke about above. To make easier the task of a successor, who will inevitably come sooner or later, it is important to keep a good record of our preaching, preferably in some detail.

Expanding the Impact of Preaching

We will also look for ways to continue the thought about or discussion of the content of the doctrinal preaching beyond the actual preaching event itself. This may be done in several ways. One is to have some type of immediate feedback. In some churches, the worship service precedes the Sunday school, which includes at least one class at which the pastor is present and the group discusses the content of the message. At times it is possible to incorporate interaction time into the actual service itself. This works especially well when the group is a relatively small one. The evening service, being more informal, allows for this in a special way. In one church where one of the authors was interim pastor, he introduced a feedback session after the message in the evening service, something that had never been done in that congregation before. The church chairman told him, "We've never had this feedback feature before, and we don't know yet who the new pastor will be, but one thing we know: he is going to conduct these feedback sessions." Even where quite a large group is present in the service, feedback is possible. By placing microphones at appropriate places in the auditorium, or by having people write their questions on cards to be collected and given to the speaker, interaction can also take place in such a setting. Although this procedure is desirable for many kinds of sermons, it seems especially appropriate for doctrinal sermons, where there is often a need for additional clarification.

The pastor may also plan to correlate the sermons with the studies taking place in the adult Bible study class, without duplicating the lesson itself. This enables mutual reinforcement to take place between the two types of experience.

There are other ways to prolong the impact. One is by providing a place in the bulletin or insert for taking notes, and suggesting applications as well as urging worshipers to think of their own action applications of the doctrine. Then they are encouraged to keep track of these and see what sort of progress they are making. Checking periodically on these is especially helpful.

Reviewing the Calendar

Churches of all sizes plan calendars of activities. Each week newsletters from several churches come to this professor's desk. Each of them contains mostly promotional material related to a calendar. Is it too modest to propose a preaching calendar? For the preacher who needs help with planning, the calendar is a ready reference. What events on the schedule promote something for the congregation's instruction? For each of those plan a doctrinal sermon. In fact, newsletters usually follow a larger denominational calendar. On that calendar one will find such emphases as Religious Liberty Sunday, Christian Home Week, Missions Week (Home, State, and Foreign), Race Relations Sunday, and Stewardship Sunday. Some of them are distinctively doctrinal in nature, such as Christmas and Easter. The others, with some work, may imply some ways to preach doctrinal sermons.

The pastor may wish to review a full year's schedule, even if it is one from a past year, and circle all the occasions that lend themselves to doctrinal preaching. The events mentioned in the preceding paragraph recur annually, so he may project the same events year by year. Religious Liberty Sunday comes on the Sunday closest to Independence Day. It provides the pastor a wonderful opportunity to speak on the free moral agency of humans, an endowment from the Creator. Christian Home Week, usually Mother's Day, is a good time to speak of God as ideal parent. Various missions emphases are the best occasions on which to speak of the mission of God's people, given by Christ himself.

Christmas and Easter are the two best times to preach doctrine. These two cardinal events of Christianity, the birth of Jesus and the resurrection of Jesus, are by their very nature doctrinal. In all the preaching conferences this author leads, the preachers who attend speak of the difficulty of the special occasion sermon. They fear that they cannot say anything new; everyone has already heard, dozens of times, accounts of the birth of the Savior and his resurrection from the dead. This leads, naturally, to dread as one anticipates speaking of them yet another time. This fear can lead to intimidation. We soon feel overwhelmed by the need to speak on the most joyful occasions of the church year. Who of us has not revised Christmas sermons in the fond hope that we can say the same thing a little better this time? Each time, though, we walk away from the pulpit with the all but paralyzing fear that we have not yet said it the way we had hoped or planned.

Perhaps repetition and revision are not the best solutions. With proper long-range planning, the preacher can resolve to prepare new sermons for these red letter events. Newspapers, magazines, devotional guides, and denominational periodicals mailed during the last quarter of each year carry literally dozens of articles and stories about the upcoming celebrations of Thanksgiving, Christmas, and New Year. These articles, human interest stories, and statistics can become sermon starters or sermon illustrations. With these clipped and saved in files, the diligent pastor is getting ready for the sermons of the Christmas season.

The texts are decided by the events. The preacher with years of experience has studied the biblical material and has a backlog of notes ready for quick reference when the actual writing of each sermon begins. Each year's published material provides current and interesting illustrations and other support for the development of the sermon. Joy comes through the discovery of new ways to tell the old, old story. In addition, the people who gather in churches at the most special of times find excitement in hearing again what they already know. In the familiar they find assurance, comfort, and security. The story of the birth of Jesus, one we have heard repeatedly, never loses its fascination; it retains a compelling quality. The same is true about the story of the resurrection of Jesus.

Other events on the calendar may be more challenging for the preacher who wishes to plan doctrinal sermons. Some of them may call for more innovation and creativity proposed in the chapters of this text on dramatic doctrinal sermons. The preacher should remember, as well, that doctrine may not be the most appropriate content for sermons on all occasions. Some other pastoral emphasis may be more to the point, such as on Mother's Day.

Consider the Lectionary

An alternative to the local church calendar is the Christian Calendar, based on the Christian Year. This calendar also is constructed around the major events of Christmas and Easter. It differs in that it does not contain events that are not specifically or uniquely Christian in nature, events found on many local church calendars.

The Christian Calendar begins with preparation for the celebration of Christmas, Advent Season, four weeks prior to Christmas. It also suggests observation of several special events following Christmas, beginning with the dedication of Jesus in the temple (Epiphany). Other celebrations continue for the Sundays prior to preparation for Easter, Lenten Season. The Season of Lent culminates with Easter Sunday. Following Easter the calendar points toward Pentecost, then life in the kingdom of God, Kingdomtide.

Observance of the Christian Calendar is made easier by following the lectionary. This collection of Scripture readings is keyed to the major events of the Christian Year and its three-year cycle will take one through the major portions of the Bible. It takes all the work out of selection of the sermon texts. This decision about the text, as testimony from preachers verifies, is one of the most difficult in the entire sermon preparation process. In a recent volume on preaching from the lectionary, Eugene Lowry echoes this sentiment and recommends the lectionary preaching plan: "The most immediately obvious advantage of lectionary preaching is that it provides a thoughtful and well-established comprehensive plan for our preaching. Almost all the preachers with whom I have visited on this subject say there is nothing so chronically worrisome about the preaching office than to wonder 'well, what now?'"[3]

One of the lectionary readings for each week usually serves as the best one for the Sunday morning sermon text. With the text already de-

---

3. Eugene L. Lowry, *Living with the Lectionary: Preaching through the Revised Common Lectionary* (Nashville: Abingdon, 1992), pp. 26–27.

termined, the preacher may get to the task of exegesis early in the week. The other Scripture portions may be read at other times in the worship service.

Herein lies another of the advantages of the lectionary (beyond the provision of the sermon text): It is a valuable guide for worship planning. Indeed, the lectionary was designed to serve liturgical goals, rather than homiletical ones.[4] Numerous denominations, not in the liturgical tradition, now employ the *Revised Common Lectionary* in their worship. Pastors who use it speak of the joy of having the texts for their sermons for three years in advance.

Some pastors object to the lectionary on the basis that it is completely objective; it rules out their freedom to follow the Spirit's leadership in the choice of sermon texts.[5] One should note, however, that the decision to follow the lectionary for planning purposes does not rule out, a priori, the necessity to make changes occasionally. This holds true especially for those churches and pastors who are not in the liturgical tradition (as are Roman Catholics, Lutherans, and Presbyterians). It may serve as a guide, particularly for those occasions in the Christian Year observed by all churches of all traditions. The best calendar may be one that blends those of the denomination or local church and the Christian Year.

Certainly a partial use of the lectionary is a workable arrangement. It is possible to utilize certain important days of the year to call attention to crucial doctrines. This has the virtue of avoiding their slipping past without notice. Some of these and the appropriate doctrines are as follows:

Palm Sunday. The lordship of Christ.
Good Friday. Sin and atonement.
Easter Sunday. Christ's resurrection and the justification of humans.
Ascension Sunday. Christ's ascension and present mediatorial role.
Pentecost Sunday. The person and work of the Holy Spirit.

Use of Special Events

In addition to dates on the Church Calendar, there are special functions or rites that occur in the church. Some traditions call these sacra-

4. Ibid., p. 15. The opening statement in the introduction to *The Revised Common Lectionary:* "A lectionary is a collection of readings or selections from the Scriptures, arranged and intended for proclamation during the worship of the People of God." *The Revised Common Lectionary* (Nashville: Abingdon, 1992), p. 9.

5. Lowry presents the liabilities and assets of lectionary preaching in *Living with the Lectionary*, pp. 15–35.

ments; some, ordinances. They are special events of importance in the life of the church family. One of these obviously is baptism, and it provides occasion for doctrinal instruction regarding the new birth and about the doctrine of the church. The Lord's Supper is another of these, and it contains especially important teaching about the nature of atonement and salvation. Weddings hold many potentials; if, for example, the officiant traces the institution of marriage back to the creation by God, the doctrine of creation will be a logical emphasis to develop. Ordination, if administered by or in the local church, is an opportunity to discuss the doctrine of the church and of its officers and the nature of ministry.

Serial Preaching

Another strategy for the pastor who preaches through books of the Bible is suggested by the preaching method itself. Plan a certain number of sermons from the book chosen—perhaps one from each chapter. The Gospel of John, for example, would require twenty-one sermons. That, in turn, would mark out more than twenty-one weeks on the average calendar, in consideration of the other events to which worship services are dedicated (such as choir presentations). The pastor who plans such a series will discover that he has a six-month plan already in hand. Nothing remains for him to do except to place it on the calendar. For the pastor who prefers more than one sermon per chapter of the book, the plan extends. Remember the ancient divine who preached more than three hundred sermons from the Book of Ecclesiastes!

To plan for preaching doctrinal sermons would require the choice of a Bible book that contains much doctrine. The other, and obvious, choice would be to select only those passages from books such as John that contain specific doctrine. Beginning with the prologue to the book, John contains numerous exciting possibilities. Books that are noted primarily for their doctrinal content, on the other hand, include Romans and Galatians in the New Testament, and Genesis and Ezekiel in the Old Testament.

Serial preaching is regaining popularity in the contemporary church, and is an excellent methodological tool for didactic preaching. As verse-by-verse commentary, it requires much time. One may spend several years in one book of the Bible. While on study leave in England, one of these authors listened to a sermon by the late Martyn Lloyd-Jones which was just short of forty-five minutes in duration. It covered one phrase from one verse in one chapter of Romans. Projected over the entirety of the book this method would focus on Romans for a considerable length of time. In those denominations with average pastoral tenure of three years or less, this could present a formidable challenge: how to preach the whole counsel of God during one's stay as pastor.

The serial approach, then, may best be done in concert with another method of preaching. In those churches with two services per week, the pastors may plan for one sermon per week generated from the calendar planning method and one sermon per week from the book preaching method.

Preaching on Issues

Another approach to doctrinal preaching is to discuss current ethical issues and then relate them to doctrine. The debate on abortion is one such issue. Central to understanding of the Christian position is the doctrine of the sanctity of human life; life is valuable because humans are made in the image of God. Address the subject of abortion by preaching on the image God? That appears to be the answer. That is not to say that one should refrain from preaching an ethical sermon. There is a moral oughtness of the faith in the abortion issue. Moreover, there is a pastoral dimension. Some who have chosen abortion suffer great emotional distress and a deep sense of guilt. They need comfort and assurance such as a pastor would include in a supportive or therapeutic sermon. That will focus upon the nature of forgiveness, as one dimension of the doctrine of salvation.

Many of the contemporary social and personal crises stem from an incomplete or inadequate understanding of God and his ways of relating to humanity. A series of doctrinal sermons, followed by a series on these crises, would reveal that a church and a pastor understand what is at stake and have compassion for all who come short of the ideal human behavior. An example would be preaching on marriage in terms of the doctrine of creation, and then the problems of marriage and divorce today. By doing doctrine first, the pastor lays a foundation for ministry, his and the congregation's. A standard of reference is necessary for the construction of a system of values. For the Christian, that standard is found in the contents of the faith.

Indeed, the foundation in the building and operating of a local church is theological. Its existence is a result of a number of individuals who have been called out and shaped into a community of God. From the Old Testament story of Israel at Mount Sinai to the founding of the church by Jesus in the Gospel of Matthew, the Bible tells the story of God and his people. Essential to an understanding of the Church is an understanding of this ideal: "I will be their God and they will be my people" (Lev. 26:12). The Bible closes with the presentation of the ideal in a cosmic setting. The picture of the new heaven is a picture of God with his people with uninterrupted and unbroken community.

The church's mission comes from Christ himself: to penetrate the world and bring others into the community of faith. The Christian mission is grounded in the person and work of Jesus. He was God present with us (John 1:1–18). He preached the gospel of the kingdom of God (Mark 1:14ff.). He worked the works of the Father while he was here (John 9:1–4) and then entrusted that work to his followers (John 14:12ff.).

All this suggests that whether the pastor is talking about the nature of the church, its mission, its membership, or its future, the point of reference is doctrine. All forms of a church's ministries spring from theology. A generation in which our churches and leaders are preoccupied with demographics and utilitarianism needs this corrective word. Our being and doing cannot spring entirely from concerns for what people like, want, or will tolerate. Our ministries cannot be based completely on accommodation (catering). We who are God's people plan a strategy based on our knowledge of God and of humans. Needs differ from wants and provision differs from supplying.

Additional Strategies

1. Observe Denomination Days. Reformation Sunday will be a logical one, but there will be other days that are especially significant for various traditions.

2. Conduct Doctrine Weeks. These could be annual periods of special doctrinal studies, just as some denominations now have a week for study of a particular book of the Bible, or a special prayer week.

3. Sponsor Doctrine Conferences. Some churches have church growth conferences, evangelism conferences, or stewardship conferences. Why not have this as part of the life of the church, also, perhaps with a theology professor brought in as the visiting lecturer?

4. Promote Stewardship Sundays—held by many denominations. This gives the preacher the opportunity to emphasize doctrines such as creation, discipleship, and the final judgment and accounting.

5. Schedule Discipleship Emphases—comparable to catechism classes held by some denominations. These could include both doctrinal and practical dimensions of teaching.

6. Begin a new pastorate with doctrinal series. This is an excellent opportunity to familiarize the congregation with the doctrinal platform on which the pastor will conduct the ministry of the years to come.

7. Preach on Bible Distribution Days. This especially will expose people to the doctrine of Scripture.

8. Plan a series on favorite passages, both the preacher's and the congregation's.

9. Do a series on most familiar passages. This can be both review of beliefs long held and an opportunity to view them in a fresh way, as well as perhaps to see insights that have not been observed before.

10. Do a series on least familiar passages. This has the potential for broadening the textual basis for doctrines held.

11. Teach the doctrine in hymns (also good for dramatic sermons). Many traditional songs are rich in doctrine, especially those of composers such as the Wesleys, Luther, and other theologians. Much contemporary Christian music covers a somewhat narrower range of doctrines. The use of songs as sermon illustrations is a useful way of teaching that continues to bear fruit. Careful selection of songs sung, perhaps together with explanations of the doctrines, will enable much doctrinal instruction.

12. Sponsor "Answers to Contemporary Religions" series. There are many fruitful avenues of teaching here. At a conference he led on the New Age Movement in Interlaken, Switzerland, one of the authors found the interest level amazingly high. His belief that people in general are fascinated with, if not mesmerized by, numerous emphases of the movement was confirmed repeatedly during the three-session conference. Some expressed surprise, if not shock, to discover the affinity of much New Age thought with Christian beliefs. The emphasis on self-fulfillment, for example, is consistent with biblical teachings. The central feature of the Human Potential Movement, self-realization, is parallel and, in some respects, identical with the Christian doctrine of humanity.

The big question that followed, naturally, was: What can we do about these subtle and often indirect teachings? One part of the answer is to know what you believe about each of these. The Christian faith teaches, for instance, that each person has worth because each is made in the image of God. That image has been marred, however, by sin. To realize one's full potential, one must know God. The way to do that is to deal with sin and be remade in the image of Christ. God has provided a way in which to do that: through faith in Christ.

The all-pervasive influence of the New Age Movement is one incentive for doctrinal preaching. Persons who do not know what they believe are subject to this and other influences and may become easy prey for persuasive advocates of alternatives to the Christian faith. Thus we suggest that a place to begin with a doctrinal series is to preach on the doctrines of God and humanity. Who is God? Who am I? How does one know God? These may be the first three sermons in the series.

Guidelines to Bear in Mind in Doctrinal Preaching

1. Be aware that questions related to the doctrine in the sermon may arise. This reminder grew out of our classroom experience. The class talked about Saul's going to the witch of Endor and asking her to bring Samuel back from the dead so that Saul could communicate with him. This, in spite of the command of the Lord, underscored by Saul himself as king, that the Israelites should have no trafficking with witches, sorcerers, and the like. The discussion took place in the context of a discussion of a sermon on witches at Halloween.

The pastor who raises questions of a theological nature faces an obligation to be prepared to answer those same questions. In the case of the witch of Endor passage, for example, the issues are complex. Why would Saul defy a commandment of God, reaffirmed by his own mandate, not to consult with spirit agents? Why would the witch cooperate in an unlawful exercise? What about calling people back from the dead and conversing with them? This issue of communication with the spirit world is a very hot one in the New Age Movement agenda. Consorting with witches and communicating with departed spirits is common practice with some New Age followers. The Old Testament contains information about witchcraft that is intriguing. Listeners who are acquainted with that information may become interested in hearing further from the preacher, just as the curious on Mars Hill wished to hear more from Paul about the resurrection. For them his message stirred emotions very deeply.

Thus the preacher who started out to preach a dramatic sermon on a relevant biblical issue may arouse the imagination to a greater extent than intended and send the minds of listeners off into related areas that have no easy solutions. The discussion of these issues, as well as the central one originally addressed, should be a part of the preacher's agenda in the creative sermons.

The authoritarian stance in preaching is: I have the answers. In the sermon I will tell you the conclusion I have reached. Implied in this method is the assumption that those with any degree of intelligence will accept the answer given and agree with it (and with the preacher). Fred Craddock has objected to this stance on the basis that it allows the listener insufficient participation in the sermon.[6]

In this dialogical stance of the preacher, the listener is invited, indeed encouraged, to play an active role in the sermon. The best preaching

6. This statement is attributed to Fred Craddock. See Fred B. Craddock, "The Inductive Method in Preaching," in *A New Hearing: Living Options in Homiletic Method*, ed. Richard L. Eslinger (Nashville: Abingdon, 1987), p. 96.

will give those who hear something to think about, to act on, and something left over to take out of the worship service with them. The best preaching will bring people to the pastor's office in search of further answers, or in search of a way to converse further about the sermon's application. Good pastoral preaching will lead to opportunities for pastoral counseling or other forms of followup to the sermon. This is especially true of dialogical preaching.

2. Remember that thorough preparation is a necessity. Preparation for various kinds of creative doctrinal sermons may become a more complicated process than usual for the minister, and may involve more persons than just the preacher. For a dramatic monologue, for example, one must decide whether to dress for the part. Some parishioners joke about the "bathrobe dramas" presented at Easter and Christmas. Should the preacher defer to that mentality and present the sermon in the customary apparel, he or she faces the difficulty of employing language with sense appeal, that is, preparing to engage the imagination of the listeners by asking them to "see" what the preacher is saying.

Advance planning is necessary that has nothing to do with the actual content of the sermon. In addition to writing the manuscript, the pastor now must secure props to support the delivery. With other sermon forms, this process can become a time-consuming one that involves numerous persons. A doctor of ministry student at the seminary where the authors teach proposed a series of dramatic sermons for his final ministries project. His proposal included plans to make audio and video tapes, slides, photographs, charts, and backdrops, and to write scripts, hold practice sessions, and prepare handouts for some of the presentations to the members of the congregation. The idea received enthusiastic approval from the student's supervisor, church, and from the Doctor of Ministry Committee.

At the conclusion of the project, the student testified that the series demanded far more time and energy and involved more persons than he ever had imagined. A simple matter such as taking film to be developed can become a major factor, not to mention returning to pick up the photos when they are ready. Who can anticipate a problem with equipment at the processing lab? Ministers who may consider doing such a series should take note of the additional demands and make long-range plans before preaching the first sermon. When others become involved in the preparation of the sermon, their schedules, abilities, and commitments become factors with which the minister must reckon. As a rule, they bring enthusiasm and devotion to the task, yet they may lack the sense of call and urgency that are a part of the minister's life. At the same time, their participation is an occasional matter for them and is somewhat novel, while the pastor views the entire process from a quite different perspective; this is his or her call and vocation. Far from being occasional in nature, it is an integral part of life, if not every day, at least every week.

3. Anticipate the rewards of doctrinal preaching. Having said all this, we stress that knowledge of these facts should inspire the minister to greater effort to do doctrinal preaching. Surely each of us desires that our listeners become active participants in the preaching event. We pray for them to think about what we say; to let their minds dwell on the sermon so that they may discover further application of its truths to their lives. That each hearer would see how believing influences doing is our constant prayer. That we would be prepared to handle the response may be an altogether different matter.

As you think about how to prepare a plan for doctrinal preaching, weigh all the options and survey the scene presented in this book. Remember also to avoid too much experimentation. Your congregation, in all likelihood, is accustomed to listening to you in a certain way.[7] Confusion may arise from changing the structure of the sermon too frequently. Similarly, watch practicing creativity for creativity's sake. The best artistry does not call attention to itself.

4. Bear in mind the objectives of doctrinal preaching, and be alert to the presence of such factors. One should do so by keeping in mind the objective for such preaching, both generally and specifically. An overarching plan may be to edify the members of the congregation. Some of the more fruitful research in homiletics currently involves this very area: the way people listen to us. Recent texts, such as those of Fred B. Craddock[8] and David Buttrick,[9] have reminded us of the importance of the listener in the preaching event. These are good reminders, especially for some of the more creative sermon presentations discussed here.

First, to counter the widespread opposition to Christianity. A minister may preach on a doctrine with the specific objective of responding to threats and challenges to Christian doctrine that come from the world around us. Much popular culture has a different view of the origin, nature, and purpose of the human than that revealed in the Bible. Both criticism of the competitor and response to its charges is important.

Second, to present doctrine to refute error. That was the case, apparently, for Paul in writing of the Book of Galatians. Immediately after his

---

7. See David H. C. Read, *Sent from God: The Enduring Power and Mystery of the Gospel* (Nashville: Abingdon, 1974).

8. Fred B. Craddock, *Preaching* (Nashville: Abingdon, 1985), pp. 84–98.

9. David Buttrick, *Homiletic: Moves and Structures* (Philadelphia: Fortress, 1987).

greeting in the first six verses of the book, the apostle expresses surprise that the Galatians have gone astray so quickly after a false gospel. Then he speaks of the nature of the true gospel and declares anathema anyone who preaches any other. That purpose underlay the Book of 3 John as well.

Third, to present your own case in the sense of positive apologetics. Today persons may well accept the idea that Christianity is true, but so are several other religions or worldviews. What do we mean when we say something is true, and why do we claim a uniqueness about the truth of Christianity?

Fourth, to compare doctrines, with other denominations, or with parachurch movements. For example, some church groups understand speaking in tongues as a validation of the experience of salvation. If yours understands it differently, a comparison of the two interpretations makes for a good sermon. In many congregations today, the persons present have come from a variety of denominational backgrounds. Without seeming to demean the alternatives, the positive beliefs of one's church need to be presented cogently.

Fifth, to prepare your congregation to face the advances of some sect or cult. Such groups often target members of churches that have the reputation for not understanding the doctrines of their own churches.

Sixth, to prepare a home Bible study group or a cell group for the formation of a new church congregation. In the initial stages of church planting, the specifics of doctrinal belief are often not heavily emphasized. The closer the group comes to actually organizing into a congregation, the greater is the need for particularizing.

Seventh, to reaffirm beliefs already held. We sometimes forget that those who have held a set of beliefs, even for a long time, are also subject to questions about those beliefs, and need to have them reviewed and reaffirmed.

Eighth, to orient new members and to build up young Christians in the faith. Since, as we argued earlier, doctrines have very practical implications, this is of great importance.

Ninth, to acquaint seekers with your particular church. Community churches often follow the pattern of the "Community Institutes" practiced by Willow Creek Community Church in North Barrington, Illinois. These institutes introduce members and seekers to doctrine in a relaxed, informal class setting.

Tenth, to establish identity if you are new in an area. Residents may ask: "Who are you people?" A doctrinal series will answer for the community to which you belong. Doctrine is held by the body, not by the preacher alone. When the pastor speaks, he gives voice to the church's message.

The objective will influence the sermon form as well. A preacher is more likely to be didactic with orientation of new members, and to be more innovative with lifetime members. Conversely, age groups may require different forms. Narrative sermons appeal to children, more dramatic forms communicate with youth. Young adults may respond to propositional sermons, strangely enough, because of their "sound-bite" orientation. A pastor may wish to consider the age grouping of the church membership before deciding a strategy for presenting doctrine.

When Paul went to Athens he discovered a city consumed by idolatry. He entered the synagogue and reasoned with the Jews and visited the marketplace to talk with the philosophers. The term translated "reasoned" is the New Testament word that is the root word for "dialogue." Since he was in the company of philosophers, he employed a means of communication with which they were familiar. He even quoted from one of the Stoic philosophers in the middle of his sermon on the God of creation. His desire to communicate may have sprung from his conviction to "become all things to all men . . . in order to win some."

Scripture Index

Subject Index

Millard J. Erickson is distinguished professor of theology at Baylor University's Truett Seminary and at Western Seminary, Portland. He has written many books, including *Christian Theology, God in Three Persons,* and *The Word Became Flesh.* **James L. Heflin** taught homiletics at Southwestern Baptist Theological Seminary for many years before becoming general secretary for the European Baptist Convention. He is coauthor of *Proclaim the Word.*